MW01049956

Wellington's Command

A Reappraisal of his Generalship in the Peninsula and at Waterloo

G.E. Jaycock

Foreword by

Saul David

Pen & Sword
MILITARY

AN IMPRINT OF PEN & SWORD BOOKS LTD.
YORKSHIRE - PHILADELPHIA

First published in Great Britain in 2019 by
PEN & SWORD MILITARY
An imprint of
Pen & Sword Books Ltd
Yorkshire – Philadelphia

Copyright © G.E. Jaycock, 2019

ISBN 9781526733535

A CIP catalogue record for this book is
available from the British Library

Typeset in 10.5/13 Ehrhardt by Vman Infotech Pvt. Ltd.
Printed and bound in the UK by TJ International Ltd, Padstow, Cornwall.

Pen & Sword Books Ltd incorporates the imprints of Pen & Sword
Archaeology, Atlas, Aviation, Battleground, Discovery, Family History,
History, Maritime, Military, Naval, Politics, Social History, Transport,
True Crime, Claymore Press, Frontline Books, Praetorian Press,
Seaforth Publishing and White Owl
For a complete list of Pen & Sword titles please contact

PEN & SWORD BOOKS LTD
47 Church Street, Barnsley, South Yorkshire, S70 2AS, England
E-mail: enquiries@pen-and-sword.co.uk
Website: www.pen-and-sword.co.uk

Or

PEN AND SWORD BOOKS
1950 Lawrence Rd, Havertown, PA 19083, USA
E-mail: Uspen-and-sword@casematepublishers.com
Website: www.penandswordbooks.com

Contents

List of Illustrations

Foreword

The battlefield achievements of Arthur Wellesley, first Duke of Wellington, are impressive. He was never defeated in a major battle and his crowning victory, at Waterloo, was over the finest captain of the age, Napoleon Bonaparte. Yet I and other military historians have long felt that Wellington had certain weaknesses as a military commander, the chief of which was a tendency to micro-manage and an unwillingness to delegate authority to his subordinates.

Now, for the first time, G.E. Jaycock has produced a carefully argued and deeply researched study of Wellington's methods of Command and Control that confirms my suspicions and reveals, in clear and concise detail, his flaws as a leader of men. This is to take nothing away from Wellington's achievements, as is underlined within Jaycock's book. But rather to emphasize how much more effective Wellington could have been if his methods of Command and Control had been less autocratic and more collaborative. 'Wellington was a great commander,' concludes Jaycock, 'but he was not a great leader of men.'

At the same time, Jaycock rehabilitates the reputation of certain combat arms – such as the artillery and the cavalry – that were unfairly criticized by Wellington at the time, and emphasizes the talent and contribution made by a number of his subordinate commanders, including Generals Hope, Graham, Hill, Cole, Picton, Clinton, Erskine, Stewart (both Charles and William), Sherbrooke, Spencer, Hamilton, Long and Perponcher. 'The responsibility for his generals' shortcomings,' writes Jaycock, 'lay ultimately with him; his micro-management was inherently de-motivating.'

We are left with a more nuanced and rounded portrait of a Wellington as a brilliant, if flawed, commander whose generals and troops played a far more significant part in his many victories than history has hitherto recorded.

Professor Saul David

List of Abbreviations

AAG	Assistant Adjutant General
ADC	Aide-de-camp
AG	Adjutant General
AQMG	Assistant Quartermaster General
AW	Arthur Wellesley/Wellington
BL	British Library
C-in-C	Commander-in-Chief
CRA	Commander of the Royal Artillery
CRE	Commander of the Royal Engineers
CRHA	Commander of the Royal Horse Artillery
GA	Gwent Archives
GO	General Order
GOC	General Officer Commanding
HMS	Her/His Majesty's Ship
HRH	His Royal Highness
KGL	King's German Legion
LD	Light Dragoon
MGO	Master General of Ordnance
MS	Military Secretary
NLS	National Library of Scotland
QMG	Quartermaster General
RA	Royal Artillery
RAI	Royal Artillery Institution
RAM	Royal Artillery Museum
RE	Royal Engineers

RHA	Royal Horse Artillery
RMA	Royal Military Academy
RMC	Royal Military College
RN	Royal Navy
TNA	The National Archives
UDL	University of Durham Library
UNM	University of Nottingham Manuscripts and Special Collections
USL	University of Southampton Library
WD	*Wellington, Dispatches*
WND	*Wellington, New Dispatches*
WO	War Office
WSD	*Wellington, Supplementary Dispatches*

Maps

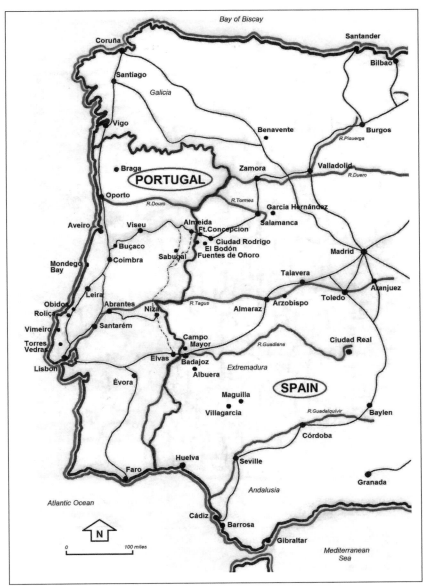

Map 1. Portugal and Western Spain Theatre of Operations, 1808–12.

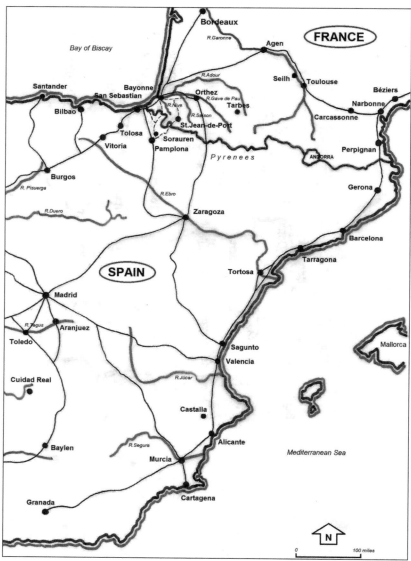

Map 2. Eastern Spain and France Theatre of Operations, 1812–14.

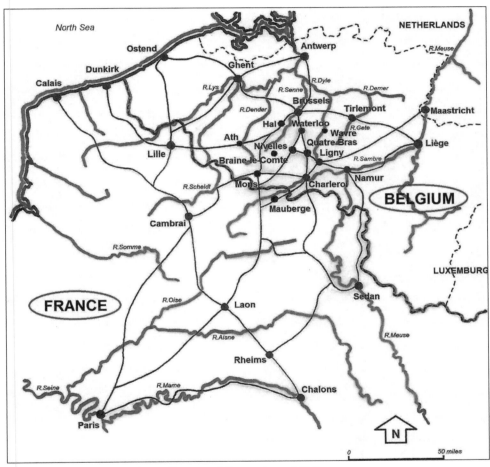

Map 3. France and Belgium Theatre of Operations, 1815.

Introduction

Wellington Triumphant

'The events may not change, but how we see them does.'[1]

In 2011 the National Army Museum voted the Duke of Wellington, jointly with Field Marshal William Slim, as Britain's greatest general; his record in battle speaks of an undeniable success. Yet, questions have always existed with regard to the army he led to ultimately overcome the French Emperor Napoleon. Over the intervening 200 years since the Battle of Waterloo, it has been regularly stated that Wellington's subordinate generals were unskilled and lacking in initiative; that they were merely inept, amateur soldiers. Similarly, the rank and file troops and notably the cavalry that Wellington sent into battle were often undisciplined and deficient; as Wellington famously referred to them, his soldiery was 'the scum of the earth'. From such a foundation that had its origin within Wellington's own professed estimation, his strength of personality and military genius are regularly recorded as *the* prodigious ingredients that generated success for otherwise unremarkable armies. Moreover, the ever assertive Wellington was certainly not averse to belittling or positively discounting the contributions of his Continental allies, and nationalistic English-speaking histories readily echo his snubs even to the present.

There is in consequence a perceived need to reconsider and reappraise the leadership that Wellington provided in light of the overbearing personality traits which he is recorded as having displayed, and the results that surely followed. This is in fact notwithstanding the copious volumes that describe the relevant campaigns; the attributes associated with Wellington's method of command still collectively require unambiguous description. Any other extraneous factor that had an impact or influence upon his military triumph should ideally also be recorded for the sake of equitability. Wellington likely relished the praise that success generated, but otherwise appears unequivocally to be an individual with an incongruous temperamental mix of harshness, imperturbability, but yet insecurity. Attempt is equally made here in parallel to see the relevant campaigns from the viewpoint of his woebegone subordinates; those individuals who were routinely blamed for any adverse situation. Indeed, to question overall whether the regularly offered explanation for Wellington's success, based overwhelmingly upon his individual pre-eminence, is satisfactory or sufficient. The central argument of this reassessment is that it is not.

Despite the bequeathed narrative surrounding the events of 1808–15, there has always appeared to be an equivocation or even an outright contradiction within the more astute voices that recorded the Duke of Wellington's exploits: 'Wellington's Peninsula army was never quite the equal of the legend that it has generated', and Wellington himself failed 'to influence masses, and his genius falls short [. . .]'.[2] Indeed, could an individual so obviously conservative and autocratic in outlook really be a pre-eminent leader of men, even within the timeframe of the early nineteenth century? Did the personality of Wellington alone really mould ineffectual infantry, cavalry and artillery troops, of whom he was repeatedly disdainful, into an indomitable force; or was not the reality more complex? This narrative therefore will re-examine Wellington's actions over the war years of 1808 to 1815, to specifically question his command effectiveness. The assertions made here aim not to undermine the stature of the achievements that resulted from his campaigns and battles, but rather to stimulate a reality check; too many persons have been traduced, both by Wellington himself and his biographers. The competence of Wellington's individual subordinate generals is indeed, if anything, once again insufficiently served here. It has been ironically noted some eighty years ago how little known and respected Wellington's generals are when compared with Napoleon's marshals, and this has not changed even to today.[3]

Certainly the sparser written record with regard to Wellington's subordinates shows disparate individuals whose temperaments ranged from the genteel to the bellicose, and indeed included more than one with reputed mental impairment. Some of Wellington's generals displayed marked administrative abilities, while for others their penchant was best seen in the heat of battle. Nonetheless, it was to be expected from all senior officers that uniform courage and commitment could be fully assured as integral to their chosen military life; these men would not have served without muscular patriotism. Yet, nevertheless, few armies have received comparable disapprobation for its members. Few generals have been as criticized as those serving under Wellington, notwithstanding the operational successes achieved. Napoleon Bonaparte may have come to symbolize those emerging and transformative ideas opposed to the continuance of outworn hierarchical aristocracies, but for Britain's armed forces the old ideas yet held sway and were indeed positively encouraged within Wellington's sphere of judgement. For Wellington, war was still very much about individual robust leadership.

This work will also proffer a generalized interpretation of the abilities of all the combat arms within Wellington's army, and clarification is particularly sought with regards to the impact of Wellington's leadership upon the combined arms effectiveness of these component elements of his army. The mark of a great general in battle of the time may be seen through the skill and degree of decisiveness with which he brought together the three principal army components: infantry, cavalry and artillery. Accordingly, by examining all aspects an enhanced and comprehensive perspective is sought upon the widely recorded views of Wellington's abilities, both to reinforce the reality of his strengths, but also to clarify and give substance to his weaknesses. Despite what has too often been a markedly nationalistic historiography, this reappraisal looks to provide a realistic and more rationally determinant view of Wellington's talents, and specifically his leadership command and control than has erstwhile been recorded.

I would acknowledge gratitude to longstanding friend Geoffrey Geddes for the conversations we have had with regard to Napoleonic battles and warfare. These have always fanned the lifelong flames of interest for the subject and led ultimately to the ideas contained within this volume. In turn, under the eye of Professor Saul David of the University of Buckingham, words were first put to paper and robust guidance and evaluation for this novice historian were received. Thanks are offered to Pen & Sword for readily agreeing, much to my surprise, to subsequently publish this volume; it felt a perfect fit. I need of course to thank also the trustees of the various institutions for their permission to review papers deposited in their individual collections. Lastly and certainly not in the least part I would thank all those friends and relatives who have had to specifically endure my exploration of Wellington's leadership. Foremost has been the support of my wife, Sue, but certainly not to forget the encouragement received from family friend Anne Sheasby, whose unforeseen death just prior to publication has been a blow. I hope that the representation of Wellington's command given here might spur others to delve more deeply into the careers of those many under-esteemed subordinates within the orbit of his omnipresent glory.

Chapter 1

The Wellington Narrative

'As no other person in your army is allowed to be possessed of a single idea, it would be ridiculous [. . .] to be guided by their opinion'.[1]

Arthur Wellesley, the 1st Duke of Wellington, is popularly credited with never having lost a battle, of extending British rule in India (1799–1805) and evicting Napoleon's French armies from Portugal and Spain (1808–14).* Thereafter in 1815 he climactically beat Napoleon Bonaparte himself at the Battle of Waterloo before becoming Prime Minister of Great Britain (1828–30). Yet, despite his triumphs, Wellington has been recorded as perennially critical of all elements of his own army, and certainly its generals: 'They are really heroes when I am on the spot to direct them, but when I am obliged to quit them they are children.'[2] His self-absorbed personal outlook: 'I have really no assistance; I am left to myself, to my own exertions, the mode of execution, and even the superintendence of that mode: but I still don't despair'.[3] Sir Brent Spencer, during his time as the Peninsular Army's second-in-command, was typically disparaged by Wellington for being 'exceedingly puzzle headed', and 'a very odd sort of man'. In like manner the subsequent second-in-command, Sir John Sherbrooke, was said by Wellington to have 'no bounds to his folly'.[4] Such belittling and recurrent criticism, to the very faces of his subordinates, was unexceptional. There is of course a large literature covering Wellington's campaigns, and the consensus today is that such quotes reflect a difficult and controlling man: 'habitually haughty and intolerant'.[5] Yet, only a tiny proportion of historians stray at all from a standard narrative, to consider events from other than the highly dominant viewpoint bequeathed by Wellington himself. His low opinion of subordinates is habitually accepted at face value: 'Wellington [. . .] was shamefully served by his subordinate generals', and, 'Few of his subordinates could be trusted to act independently'.[6] Such stock criticisms can be seen in the writing of his earliest chroniclers and collaborators, and they

---

* The Duke of Wellington (1769–1852) is referred to throughout simply as Wellington despite the birth name of Wesley, changed to Wellesley in 1798, becoming Viscount Wellington in 1809 and Duke in 1814.

have continued to the present day. The subsequent narrative will consider the evidence for an alternative interpretation, but will initially and doubtless all too briefly review the salient messages from the extensive historical literature that has covered Wellington's Peninsular War victories and Waterloo.

The military record of Wellington is undoubtedly that of a great commander, despite the occasionally recorded flippant, though credible pronouncement: 'Arthur Wellesley had that greatest of all military assets: luck.'[7] Those questions raised hereafter do not seek to refute Wellington's military status, but more specifically to ask whether his effectiveness could have been enhanced if he had been less aloof, autocratic and dogmatic in his approach to command. Wellington is the ultimate personification of a style of leadership in which the acutely authoritarian leader dictated every activity within his army. All policy would originate solely from him, strategic military goals were dictated by him, and all operational activities were directed and controlled by him; with no meaningful participation by any subordinate. Wellington indeed went even further to actually control tactical combat as far as he was able. All the evidence contained within 200 years of authorship concurs upon this scenario. It is certainly not unreasonable to conjecture whether the control exerted by such a commander typically expunged not only the effective autonomy, but also the confidence and judgement of others.

While he criticized the efficacy of all elements of his army, Wellington's infantry troops escaped with the lightest rebuke, despite such lofty assertions as, 'Do you see those fellows run [. . .] it is with those that I must win the battle': when spoken dismissively with regards to his (Nassauer) infantry at Waterloo.[8] Wellington's censure fell heaviest upon the cavalry: 'Our cavalry never gained a battle yet.'[9] Or worse, as written of the 13th Light Dragoons (LD) in 1811: 'Their conduct was that of a rabble.'[10] The artillery was less directly criticized, but was routinely disregarded, spurned or its contribution dismissed; a reader of Wellington's dispatch after the Battle of Fuentes de Oñoro in 1811 commented: 'you will be much surprised [. . .] not to find therein any mention of the artillery'.[11] A similar outcome occurred even after the Battle at Waterloo. Wellington's official dispatch immediately post-battle contains a mere half-sentence shared between the Royal Artillery (RA) and Royal Engineers (RE): 'The Artillery and Engineer departments were conducted much to my satisfaction [. . .].'[12] This was a very model of mean-spirited understatement. Criticism from Wellington extended to all facets of his command; even, 'the Chaplain's department did not shine'.[13] The assertive tone of Wellington's comments has given rise to three standard narrative threads within the histories of his life and career. Firstly, the contributions of the cavalry and artillery are largely taken as deficient; Wellington is routinely described as an 'infantry general' by necessity.[14] Secondly, that the generals who served under him were notably poor and made little contribution as Wellington alone fashioned a winning army. Hence the third most critical consequence is that Wellington's highly autocratic control must be adjudged an imperative that ensured the effectiveness of his army.

Reference is made hereafter to both key and representative samples of written works from the 200 years of Wellington historiography, and the perceived reasons why a standard narrative has been generated. Subsequent chapters will thereafter aim to reconsider the impact of the criticisms that Wellington made of his senior commanders and all combat arms; whether it was justified, and, more importantly, to examine the evidence of consequences that were counter-productive. It is certainly admissible to contemplate the possibility of speedier, less costly success for the Peninsular Army if a more gracious than grudging Wellington had fostered the initiative of subordinates and in parallel better enhanced the cohesiveness of the army's constituent parts. Wellington was manifestly one of Britain's great generals, but by showing more trust and being less dismissive of his subordinates it might rationally be suggested that his achievements could have been even more prodigious. It is reasonable to question whether Wellington's manner of command produced shortcomings that have hitherto largely gone unacknowledged. Wellington's personal character has been observed, but his victories have diverted questions about his methods.

In 1808 Wellington had the command of 10,000 men delegated to him by HRH the Duke of York, then Commander-in-Chief of the British Army. He would arrange these forces within six brigades for service in Portugal. Seven years later, at the start of the Waterloo campaign, Wellington's Anglo–Allied army stood at 112,000 men, within 4 corps. The structure of Wellington's army thus markedly evolved over the timescale 1808–15. As well as Wellington's own actions during the years of war, parallel consideration needs to be given to the generals of division as well as the officers commanding the important cavalry and artillery contingents and their troops, while also noting the relevant headquarters staff. Indeed, the bureaucratic structures of the army require reference to Wellington's command in order to explain the background to his leadership; both the changing extent of his control and how his effectiveness was impacted by extraneous administration. By 1814, Wellington described the battle-hardened army that he felt he had personally forged as 'probably the most complete machine for its numbers now existing in Europe'.[15] Previously, in 1810, he had commented: 'The army was and indeed still is, the worst British Army ever sent from England [. . .] The General Officers are generally very bad and indeed some of them a disgrace to the service.'[16] Consideration of the activities of all main parties, as well as the practicalities of their inter-communication during the war years of 1808–15, will ideally present a more truly objective view of Wellington the commander. The paucity of past objective scrutiny may be seen in the telling observation that: 'Too many lives of Wellington [. . .] regurgitate the more familiar tales, citing earlier biographies as their authority'.[17]

In 2006 historian Robert Burnham catalogued all the primary sources that relate to the Peninsular War, updating an original 1913 document produced by Sir Charles Oman.[18] The outstanding original source is naturally enough Wellington's own copious dispatches, collected initially within thirteen volumes by Colonel John Gurwood in 1834–9. Despite protestations to the contrary, in his lifetime Wellington certainly nurtured his own reputation and initially dispatches were doubtless determined for publication with due accord. Wellington had been pleased with Gurwood's original collation of his General Orders in 1832, such 'that he did nothing else all yesterday but read them aloud [to friends]'.[19] It has been recorded that Wellington specifically deleted reference in his dispatches to the hanging of twelve to fifteen men in India, in order to avoid controversy or recrimination.[20] Other dispatches, for example, those dated 5 September 1810 and 23 February 1811, have been found to have been doctored at a later date, and will be referenced as appropriate. In addition one historian certainly raises questions regarding the fortuitous disappearance of other dispatches from the 1815 campaign.[21] It may be considered that the unvarnished truth concerning particular events became something of a casualty in the process that Gurwood instigated, if only to a limited degree.

Beyond Wellington's personal written legacy, at the forefront of works by his contemporaries sits the six-volume *History of the War in the Peninsula* (1828–40) by Sir William Napier, a former regimental officer within the Peninsular Army and evident distinguished champion of Wellington's leadership: 'It is impossible to deny his sagacity in planning, his decision and celerity in execution.'[22] Napier nevertheless exhibits his own personal military experience when making some reasoned observations concerning operational effectiveness; such as the failure to pursue after Battle at Roliça, in 1808. He raises the possibility that Wellington's army could have also caught and surprised French General Loison, and thereby have, 'broken Junot's combinations and scattered his [entire] army in all directions'. He is also obviously cognizant with Wellington's character when noting some 'draw-backs' to his greatness.[23] Yet Wellington is fully the hero in the work and the subordinate generals are incidental; indeed Napier has been accused of having a 'malignant hostility for Marshal Beresford' and also of feuding with former Quartermaster General (QMG) George Murray.[24] Wellington himself was happy to personally assist with Napier's work, which was duly dedicated to him, but directly expressed no view upon it. He rather obliquely emphasized the need, 'to pay least attention to the statements of private individuals'; he wished his own pronouncements always to be the final and sacrosanct word.[25] He was happy to be perceived post-war as what has been described as the dispassionate 'paternalistic saviour' of Great Britain.[26]

Napier's account is a first major history of Wellington's Peninsular War; erudite, but plainly in thrall to the assertive self-regard of Wellington's ego. Other contemporaneous sources can be more than somewhat effusive: that of Lord Burghersh, a former aide-de-camp (ADC) to Wellington, for example fulsomely describes the 'transcendent services of Lord Wellington'.[27] Britain post-Waterloo was yet both triumphant and war-weary, though at first even the involvement of foreign arms in the long war years against France was too immediate to go unacknowledged. Wellington's supporters nonetheless had great scope to promote and embellish his contribution, both during and, more notably, after their hero's lifetime. Wellington epitomised British military prowess, and the perceived peerless position of Britain in the Victorian world. The continued popularity of the memoirs produced by the likes of Moyle Sherer in 1823 and George Gleig in 1825 only served to project a British pre-eminence that had prevailed both against and despite 'the reprehensible foreigner'. It was at this time that what would become the flattering sobriquet the 'Iron Duke' was first coined: by the *Freeman's Journal* of 14 June 1830. However, this may unfortunately have had more to do initially with the metal shutters that protected the windows of Wellington's home, Apsley House, from protesters rioting against his politics. In the latter nineteenth century the myth-making industry was sustained and greatly enhanced, as British society engendered a flag-waving and militaristic attitude of 'my country right or wrong' in response to various international crises. It may be noted that, likely for commercial reasons, the well-known work and collected Waterloo letters of Herbert Siborne published in 1891 certainly did much to dismiss the contribution of the Dutch-Belgians in 1815, while at the same time totally downgrading the efforts of the Prussian army. The German Kaiser, Wilhelm II, would duly create a veritable xenophobic nadir for Wellington's adherents, by stating in 1903 that 'the Germans had rescued the British army from destruction at Waterloo'.[28] The establishment of Wellington's dominance within British military history achieved full acceptance, and the result was an outpouring of Victorian historical works that repeated and embellished reference to his impeccable and matchless command of the army.

Indeed, the pre-eminent Peninsular War historian Sir Charles Oman noted that after Wellington's death in 1852: 'For two whole generations it seemed almost treasonable to breathe a word against his personal character – so great was the debt that Britain owed him.'[29] Oman's authoritative *History of the Peninsular War* was published in seven volumes (1902–30), and few subsequent students of the period have omitted to reference his work. Wellington's personality and leadership are recorded as being, 'autocratic to a fault', and prone to considering any question or criticism of his orders as insubordination.[30] Oman markedly gives full approval for the perceived necessity of Wellington's heavy-hand upon the generals. He records officers with 'down-hearted views', which angered Wellington and led to the oft-recounted accusation of subordinates 'croaking'; viz. defeatist grumbling. It is diverting, therefore, that Wellington would himself later in (political) life receive the same accusation: 'It is quite terrible how all our friends croak [. . .] no one is worse than the Duke'.[31] Yet, Oman emphatically concludes that, 'few commanders [. . .] saw more of their plans frustrated by a stupid subordinate'.[32] Oman offers mild plaudits solely for General Rowland Hill, as Wellington found him alone 'trustworthy'. Otherwise, in typical vein, Marshal William Beresford failed to control his subordinates at the Battle of Albuera in 1811, where General William Stewart combined 'over-zeal and want of discipline' to generate a crisis in battle.[33] Lack of co-operation between generals was seemingly endemic; General Thomas Picton at the River Coa in 1810, 'committed one of the greatest military sins, that of refusing to support a comrade in the moment of danger'.[34] As for Wellington's unappreciated Spanish allies, it is admitted by Oman that he was at fault when: 'A little more diplomatic language would have secured less friction, and probably better service.'[35] But, such insight is not applied by Oman to the generals. For them, absolute obedience to Wellington was the prime imperative. Any criticism of Wellington's command he states as stemming from the 'bitter hatred that was felt towards Wellesley by his political opponents during the second and third decades of the nineteenth century'.[36] This doubtless included criticism from former Lieutenant William Grattan in his long-frustrated lobbying for the distribution of a medal for Peninsular War veterans. Nevertheless, Oman does acknowledge, without subsequent clarification, that, 'His system of concentration of command is easily explicable, but its results were not altogether happy.'[37]

Oman indicates that Wellington's infantry focus was a necessity, since his cavalry forces never performed effectively, nor specifically pursued a beaten foe, and for which a basic lack of skill was to blame.[38] Oman's complementary volume, *Wellington's Army* (1913), lists several battles, including Orthez, as late in the war as 1814, where the cavalry is reported as having continued to perform poorly.[39] For the artillery there is surprisingly scant report, in fact just one page within *Wellington's Army*. With regards to army leadership, Oman names Wellington's favoured 'docile' generals as 'Hill, Beresford, Spencer and Cotton', with approving comparison to others more independent. He records Wellington raging at zealous subordinates who had done no more than think for themselves: 'Never do anything without my orders.'[40] Oman is thus dismissive of the performance of the generals; the narrative is one of Wellington being let down by inadequate subordinates, and by ineffectual cavalry and artillery contingents. This defining theme has been echoed to the present; the generals were deficient by not always following the ubiquitous leader's explicit orders. Wellington is credited for the successes, while any setback is rather a disobedient subordinate's error. The alternative viewpoint, that Wellington's overbearing command and control in fact generated a lack of initiative and ultimately less effective subordinates, is a theme unrecognized. Wellington ruled his army stringently, yet potentially he under-utilized his generals perhaps through arrogance and mistrust. Nonetheless, steadfast and influential devotees of Wellington have still found scope to find fault even with

Oman: accusing him of disliking Wellington personally, and allowing himself to be 'unduly influenced by occasional expressions of dissatisfaction in contemporary books, diaries or letters'.[41] These sources presumably again provide the reports from veterans of Wellington's army who had best knowledge of the realities of his command.

Following on the heels of Oman, Sir John Fortescue's *History of the British Army* (1910–20) duly incorporates the campaigns of 1808–15 within volumes six to ten. Fortescue confirms that, 'Wellington was in fact his own chief-of-the-staff and directed the movements of the army principally through his private letters to his generals'; which could create problems. Specifically at Talavera in 1809, Wellington's system led to faulty dispositions with, 'no man daring to correct them without his express command'.[42] For the cavalry Fortescue is less harsh than Oman, though he still criticizes them for having engaged in 'mad exploits'.[43] The artillery periodically receives mild praise, such as for excellent supporting fire at Roliça in 1808, but then more typically the cannon fire in battle at Salamanca is described as being unmistakably poor.[44] Wellington is forgiven for being dismissive of his artillery and having poor relations with his gunners, since they were, 'less immediately under his direct control than the rest of the army'.[45] Both artillery and engineers were under the direction of the independent Board of Ordnance; a body which receives criticism for a marked lack of skill.[46] Otherwise, Fortescue's assessment of Wellington's idiosyncratic command style is similar to that of Oman: he micro-managed his forces, but this got the job done effectively and despite the faults of others. Fortescue joins with his hugely influential forebears, Napier and Oman, in maintaining a steadfast lionization of Wellington's leadership. They are the pillars upon which subsequent study has been built. Only in recent times has the judgement of these expansive historians occasionally been questioned: author R.E. Foster facetiously considers that the romantic novel *An Infamous Army* by Georgette Heyer gives a truer perspective upon Wellington's army than Fortescue's 'adulatory assessment'.[47]

A precis of the work of Oman and Fortescue, writing after their subject's lifetime, would nonetheless certainly record that Wellington the commander was forceful in his language and autocratic in his manner, but also extremely hard-working, wise and without military peer. His subordinate generals were however mostly lax and dull-witted, and his troops deficient, especially the cavalry. The sweep of narrative history that built upon the foundation of these illustrious chroniclers of Wellington and his battles is of course enormous. Many works indeed fall far short of Oman and Fortescue to be mere recitations of Wellington's victories, apologists for the extreme class and cultural prejudices that he displayed. Nonetheless, other more recent works have emerged to enhance, perhaps unwittingly, the perception and understanding of Wellington's leadership, based upon the personal papers of the many involved individuals. Characterful insights may be gleaned from new information contained within certain biographies of Wellington's life, or the fewer such volumes that consider the lives of his subordinate officers. A first flattering biography of Wellington actually appeared as early as 1810–11 within the pages of a new publication, the *Royal Military Chronicle*.[48] The article is highly complimentary, and, thanks no doubt to key contributions from his friends and family, is totally supportive and solicitous of Wellington in the wake of the controversies he met in his early career. There have also been the abundant studies of Wellington's military campaigns and individual battles, from whence his approach to command under the stress of military action may be appreciated. Such works have tended only to atypically reference the multi-national and political criteria relating to the Iberian allies, or to the Prussians of 1815. Finally, there have been the studies which provide specific consideration of the troops and their intrinsic qualities, at best both British troops and foreign alike, that comprised Wellington's forces. From the time of Fortescue up until the present such works have addressed the sum of Wellington's command if not its especial constituent characteristics. What the subsequent chosen, but representative examples say, or do not say, with regards to Wellington's command is recorded by way of generalized corroboration to this critique. No criticism is intended, rather the intrinsic truth of the statement that, 'the events may not change, but how we see them does'.

An early campaign record, and uncommon analysis of the advance of Wellington's army in 1813–14 over the Pyrenees and into France, was Finlay Beatson's *Wellington* trilogy of works from 1914–31. They set out the importance that Wellington placed upon the communication services to ensure his commands were explicit. Yet, it is stated that the generals still managed to misuse them: 'The failure of Cole, Picton and Alten to keep up regular communication' caused command problems for Wellington.[49] Even the usually reliable Rowland Hill is here accused of letting down Wellington at the Nivelle offensive of 1813 by not following orders to the absolute letter.[50] Such observations again indicate how Wellington took full responsibility for all command decisions, regardless of geographic distance or other constraint. Beatson, as his immediate predecessors, deems this the only correct recourse. The subordinate generals were mere ciphers for Wellington, to be disproportionately blamed for any perceived setbacks. Of other contemporaneous historians, Douglas Bell, despite penning a work entitled *Wellington's Officers* (1938), in fact says nothing about the officers' professional relationships and the issues associated with command and control. His book, as most other works up until the Second World War, is largely a narrative history of the Peninsular War and Waterloo, with Wellington the hero, and with only superficial reference to the ineffectual support of subordinates.

From the 1950s there appeared certain more insightful volumes from historians whose ideas are respected to today. S.G.P. Ward's *Wellington's Headquarters*

(1957) focuses upon the practicalities of command and control at Wellington's headquarters under QMG George Murray. Ward's book is detailed, yet blunt when observing the reality for headquarters staff: 'the weaker elements were ground out in the grim attrition [. . .] but the residue, though perhaps small, was by all standards very good'.[51] Ward applauds supposed practical collaboration between Wellington and Murray, but acknowledges that its true extent, even its very existence has been obscured, since Wellington always took the final decision.[52] Unlike the contemporary and evolving Prussian army organization, Wellington's headquarters had no designated chief-of-staff; up until 1815 staff officers were of junior rank compared with their Prussian counterparts and their duties were solely to execute Wellington's explicit orders. But, Wellington's relationships within his administrative headquarters must certainly have had an impact upon army effectiveness. J.F.C. Fuller again confirms in his *Decisive Battles* (1954) that for Wellington's centralized command: 'obedience and not initiative was required of subordinates'. He indicates that Wellington was the 'supreme tactical artist', but one who did not 'rely upon second-hand information' from subordinates.[53] Fuller pointedly recognizes the rare 'intelligent disobedience' of General Henri–Georges Perponcher, who disregarded his commander-in-chief's orders before Quatre Bras in 1815; a well-nigh unique event.[54] This has been studied further by David Chandler in *The Campaigns of Napoleon* (1966), and dissected by other insightful recent historians.[55] Chandler highlights further mistakes made by Wellington in 1815, as when 'wasting valuable men' deployed remotely from the main area of battle. Only on the actual Waterloo battlefield was his centralized leadership style exhibited with 'barely a fault'.[56] Fuller and Chandler both contiguously question Wellington's command and control capability relative to specific incidents in 1815, but markedly do not develop the argument any further.

Other popular twentieth-century authors would firmly stick with the familiar unswerving reverence for Wellington. Jac Weller in *Wellington in the Peninsula* (1962) both records and supports Wellington's centralized command style by questioning ironically whether his job was not to win battles, but rather act as a military schoolmaster.[57] He notes Wellington's prescience for introducing the autonomous division to the British army in 1809, which instigated enhanced infantry effectiveness by including designated artillery and cavalry support.[58] This, though, is regrettably an example of inaccurate myth-making, since British divisions had first been used by Sir Ralph Abercromby in Egypt, in 1801. Objectively, army numbers meant that the division may nevertheless be said to have been something of a novelty for several years. One historian reports that in 1807 Sir John Moore supposedly still queried what a division actually was, but since Moore served under Abercromby in Egypt the tale is certainly apocryphal.[59] Weller's reverential tone would duly be continued within *Wellington at Waterloo* (1967), where the unerring Wellington is praised for routinely ordering an 'astonishing number of battalion and brigade manoeuvres himself', on his way to personal victory.[60] In 1969–72 Elizabeth Longford (Lady Pakenham) published a similarly populist two-volume biography of Wellington. The first part, *Wellington: The Years of the Sword*, concentrates on his time as a military commander and is also overwhelmingly commendatory of Wellington's command. Longford otherwise can again be dismissive of the generals and their troops, and is particularly unforgiving when describing Wellington's cavalry, whose leaders are accused of a 'nauseous mix of arrogance and incompetence'.[61] Longford absolves Wellington of any ill by damning others, just as Oman's standard narrative. The subsequent and similarly popular work of Michael Glover also tends towards the eulogistic. He says little by way of judgement upon Wellington's leadership and is wholeheartedly positive with regards to the outcomes. Nonetheless, in *Wellington's Army in the Peninsula* (1977), Glover idiosyncratically acknowledges: 'Not all Wellington's generals were incompetent', despite the fact that Wellington was 'terrifying to those who disobeyed his orders'.[62]

Two studies of the Battle of Salamanca display Wellington's command style specifically in the heat of battle. *Wellington's Masterpiece* (1973) by J.P. Lawford and Peter Young provides detail of Wellington's 'essential' control and management. He was on-hand at the Lesser Arapiles hill on the morning of the battle as the British and French armies manoeuvred in parallel, and supposedly alone recognized the importance of this hill as a hinge to the position. He directly arrayed Colonel McClean's 3/27th Regiment here and instructed with ostensible melodrama: 'You must defend this position so long as you have a man.'[63] Rory Muir's more recent *Salamanca 1812* (2001) hails Wellington's control of his army as 'nearly perfect'; unlike the tactical performance of his subordinates since, 'the local defeats of Cole and Pack in the centre [. . .] were significant blemishes on the victory'. Wellington was everywhere on horseback; he personally 'put every division into action that day'.[64] Salamanca may epitomise Wellington's centralized method of command, but both histories again fail to question any contradictions associated with the methodology. Wellington micro-managed his army, and thereby negated such potentially advantageous precepts as flexibility and responsiveness, positive co-operation, economy of effort, and enhanced morale.

Disappointingly, few hard questions are included within two studies which aim specifically to review Wellington's military leadership: *Wellington as Military Commander* (1968), again by Michael Glover, and *Wellington Commander* (1983) by Paddy Griffith. Glover here gives a dismissive account of Wellington's 'fumbling subordinates', and merely perpetuates the imperfect standard narrative. He harshly notes that Wellington's 'icy contempt for inattention to orders hurt many feelings, but they were almost always feelings which richly deserved to be hurt'.[65] In somewhat more objective terms, Griffith supervised *Wellington Commander* as a collection of essays by seven military scholars. He observes that, 'Wellington failed to explain his decisions to subordinates, omitted to give due credit and [. . .] his private letters are full of criticism of officers'.[66] Yet, while Griffith sees contempt from Wellington for colleagues and allies alike, he goes no further than diagnosing perfunctory man-management skills. He makes no effort to identify either the real or neglected contributions that subordinates made. Griffith does nonetheless go out on something of a limb when scrutinizing Wellington's abilities as a general. He suggests that Wellington's victories were often more nuanced than the standard narrative: some were certainly harder, closer fought battles than had been previously recorded.

The Spanish Ulcer (1986) by David Gates is noteworthy for rightly presenting the Peninsular War as predominantly a Spanish war of national liberation, and for discarding what is described as the 'jingoistic bias' of previous English histories. The overall perspective is again of a dictatorial Wellington who 'heaped unjustified criticism on everybody in the army – except himself'.[67] This rigorous leadership style is accounted for by Wellington's experiences in India, according to both Gates and also by the contributing authors within the 1990 *Wellington* volume edited by Norman Gash. It is conceived here that the significant competition for advancement within the Indian army initially impelled Wellington to the extreme assertiveness that he displayed. Within Gash's work Wellington's character is reviewed unfavourably in comparison with that of his elder brother, Richard, Marquess Wellesley. The plight of Britain's Portuguese and Spanish allies is highlighted, and how they suffered from the 'haughty, intolerant' command of Wellington; in comparison with the judicious behaviour of Richard when Ambassador to Spain.[68] Yet, the detrimental impact that these same personal traits might have had upon Wellington's own army command structure is not explored. Charles Esdaile's *The Peninsular War* (2003) also positively encompasses the activities and the politics of Wellington's Iberian allies within its narrative. Despite being described as a military genius, Wellington's personality receives criticism, not least his obsession with the 'concept of order', which generated 'fear, contempt and loathing' for his own soldiers. Here, when referring to Wellington's army as 'never being quite the equal of the legend', for the first time is an undefined inference that Wellington's leadership in the Peninsula generated command flaws.[69]

In parallel, Esdaile also emphasizes the strong political background to Wellington's own character and leadership style. He describes politics as a driving force for command decisions throughout his career, such as when entering Madrid with his army in 1812. Esdaile champions the need to firmly pull together both the military and political threads of the conflict, for complete understanding; something that Oman neglected. Huw Davies in *Wellington's Wars* (2012) ambiguously extols Wellington's perceived political strengths, though also noting the flaws of 'dogmatism' and 'lack of discriminating judgement', to be seen in both his political and military life. His study thus underlines a theme of inconsistency throughout Wellington's military career, which could lead to either brilliance or recklessness.[70] He stresses Wellington's expert administration, though proficient intelligence-gathering might still be ignored. Davies accuses Wellington of hubris, in that he would never accept personal blame, but would discredit others and claim their achievements as his own; as he did with the Prussians after Waterloo. Much of Davies' analysis may certainly be sympathized with, though Wellington's authoritarianism is accepted without due focus upon any effect within the army. The consequences of Wellington's disposition still require amplification, as his seemingly brittle ego never faltered in the exertion of his own command supremacy. Wellington's principal victims were certainly the officers of his own army: he considered that he alone was fit to command.

In 1989 Philip Haythornthwaite published *Wellington's Military Machine*, one work among others which focuses upon the individual combat arms of the British army, in a thematic and descriptive, rather than analytical manner. Haythornthwaite indicates the genius of Wellington's leadership, but does acknowledge that by failing to delegate, Wellington probably impaired the development of capable generals.[71] In the subsequent biography *Wellington: The Iron Duke* (2007), Haythornthwaite also sees mild flaws and contradictions in his subject, but also notes: 'His dispatches are models of clarity and emphasize not only his breadth of vision, but the care he took over the most minor details'. Haythornthwaite declares without irony that total, unqualified deference to Wellington's viewpoint could even bring to a favourite, such as QMG George Murray, a degree of responsibility as de facto chief-of-staff.[72] Otherwise Haythornthwaite indicates that even the most well-meaning of Wellington's subordinates had only limited ability. *Inside Wellington's Peninsular Army* (2006), edited by Rory Muir, also looks closely at Wellington's troops and their generals, but the conclusion again is that there was an abundance of poor quality subordinates. Some operational mistakes by Wellington are noted, but with extenuating circumstances provided, such as Wellington's lack of confidence in a cavalry arm that was sub-standard.[73] These works provide practical information about Wellington's army, but again make no real attempt to address the questions surrounding Wellington's command style and effectiveness.

Two specific volumes are most noteworthy for positively re-examining the attributes of Wellington's cavalry and artillery. Written in support of the cavalry, Ian Fletcher's *Galloping at Everything* (1999) is titled to reflect Wellington's furious criticism after the combat at Maguilla in 1812. The book is a partial rebuttal of much adverse comment upon the cavalry, which Fletcher considers to have originated from Oman. The cavalry is indeed recorded as being constantly paralysed from Wellington's own severe control.[74] Several infamous incidents are examined and logical evaluations provided which, all told, give a more positively nuanced perspective upon overall cavalry performance. For the artillery, Nick Lipscombe's

Wellington's Guns (2013) is similarly significant in reporting the perennial disputes between the RA and the conservatism and high-handedness emanating from Wellington. The official Waterloo dispatch penned immediately post-battle by Wellington, when recording the artillery's performance, is noted as quite extraordinary in its unfairness.[75] Lipscombe records how more artillery commanders were replaced during the war, at Wellington's behest, than senior officers in any of the other arms; Colonel George Fisher was pressurized into resignation by Wellington in 1813 in just one unsavoury command incident. Lipscombe here blames a clash of personalities, and despite the effective leadership qualities that Fisher actually displayed. Suffice to add that five other commanders of the Royal Artillery were also disposed of before Wellington fixed upon Lieutenant Colonel Alexander Dickson. Fletcher and Lipscombe exhibit fresh thinking in the treatment of their subjects, though it may still be felt that Wellington's unsettling influence extended further. The work of Frederick Myatt is an additional source that covers the activities of the RE, within *British Sieges of the Peninsular War* (1995). Peninsular siege works were some of Wellington's least successful military activities. Myatt implies that because of the pressure Wellington exerted, his engineers tended towards over-optimistic compliance. As a result the onerous, but ultimately successful siege of Badajoz 'did not reflect any great credit on Wellington or his professional advisers'. Otherwise at Burgos in 1812, Myatt blames over-work by Wellington, rather than the usual ineffective subordinate for the failure.[76] Wellington is recorded as having railed against any officers of the RE who showed initiative, just as he did with those of the RA. It might be supposed that it was a perfectly understandable impulse for the brow-beaten engineers, as others, to placate or simply crumble before Wellington in his overbearing demands; many individuals appear cowed by Wellington's dominant authority.

Only Albuera, in recent years appears worthy of stand-alone record, as a battle managed by one of Wellington's subordinates. The necessity for action here at all resulted from what Guy Dempsey in *Albuera* (2008) calls a major operational failure by Wellington. He records that Wellington expected Marshal William Beresford to follow his orders implicitly even when remotely located. During the battle Beresford reputedly 'lost his nerve', but nonetheless achieved a tactical victory.[77] Other such battle accounts may be contained within a biography; for example, *Wellington's Right Hand* (2013), by Joanna Hill, about her forebear General Rowland Hill. Joanna Hill astutely questions what her relative might have achieved in the field if he had not always been kept at Wellington's side. In battle at St Pierre d'Irube in 1813, Hill commanded the British forces. General William Stewart fought as Hill's immediate subordinate and later assumed that they received no official praise due to the fact that Wellington disliked him.[78] Despite the importance of this battle, Wellington failed to report it as a major engagement and it is thus little known today. This actuality is of significance when observing and confirming Wellington's self-absorbed command.

Such battles as St Pierre are otherwise important indicators of the capabilities of the generals when distant from Wellington.

Of course, the battles of Quatre Bras and Waterloo in 1815 have generated an enormous amount of literature. Mark Adkin's *Waterloo Companion* (2001) is noteworthy in that the book specifically contains a section entitled 'Command and Control' that covers all three armies present. Wellington's autocratic personality is again described here, followed by campaign plans for 1815 and the practicalities of command upon the battlefield. It is reiterated that Wellington rarely delegated authority to a subordinate, save for the 'strange exception' of the Earl of Uxbridge's cavalry command at Waterloo. The conversation Uxbridge held with Wellington on the night before Waterloo is recounted. When asked about plans for the forthcoming battle, Wellington responded: 'Bonaparte has not given me any idea of his projects; and as my plans will depend upon his, how can you expect me to tell you what mine are?' This was hardly an illuminating response to his second-in-command. Wellington 'paid scant regard to the normal channels of command', but rather employed a hands-on style that worked defensively, but not offensively, Adkin states with insight.[79] Others, in support of Wellington have suggested that this story is nothing more than 'a red herring', but the tone certainly fits the bill.[80] Beyond such analysis as Adkin provides, in recent years the rare historian has applied new research or challenged the traditional interpretation of Wellington's leadership, specifically for Waterloo. Noteworthy are the two contentious volumes of Peter Hofschröer's *1815: The Waterloo Campaign* (1998–9), which focus strongly upon Wellington's culpability for flawed inter-Allied communication in 1815. Among other transgressions, Wellington is accused of misleading the Prussians to fight at Ligny on 16 June, in order to buy time and to compensate for his own previous command errors.[81] Of other recent books published to coincide with the anniversary of the 1815 campaign, Tim Clayton's *Waterloo: Four Days* (2014) is also noteworthy in its observations of Wellington's command. He writes that despite the perceived problems surrounding Wellington's dialogue with the Prussians: 'Communication was something that Wellington's armies generally did well'.[82] Nonetheless, for Wellington the commander, 'if his own reputation was in peril, he could be caustically critical, which was resented' by subordinates.[83] Clayton otherwise describes Wellington's command style as 'eccentric and pliable', with Wellington giving 'orders to particular units as he saw fit'.[84]

Finally, in the most recent past Rory Muir has published his exhaustive two-volume biography *Wellington* (2013–15), which is likely to prove the most influential work since Longford. Muir is again clear in his esteem for Wellington, considering him the essential ingredient to victory, even though noting that his 'whole approach to command was ill-suited to delegation', with his intemperate 'sharp tongue and ready scorn'.[85] Wellington is recorded as perennially conservative in outlook: 'The British army is what it is, because it is officered by gentlemen.'[86]

He excuses Wellington of several leadership incidents, such as at Almeida in 1811, uniquely due to the political pressures placed upon him that emanated from the government in London. The Almeida incident notably led to the suicide of Lieutenant Colonel Charles Bevan.[87] Archie Hunter details these events admirably within *Wellington's Scapegoat* (2003), noting that the regimental history of Bevan's 4th Foot records that he 'was a good officer and had the sympathy of the whole army'.[88] Muir rightly observes that Wellington would neither back down, nor allow any incident or quarrel to interfere with the efficiency of the army as he saw it; even to this extent. He pre-empts any disapproval of Wellington's command style by acknowledging that he is sometimes accused of failing to recognize the efforts of his subordinates, but again counters with Wellington's description of the typical officer who, 'must never cease to be [. . .] obedient, subordinate to his superiors' in the execution of his duty.[89] However, it may reasonably and otherwise be considered that 'duty' meant extreme subservience to Wellington's command and control in a manner that he markedly never himself showed to his own superiors, and should not be taken unquestioningly as the standard of the day.

The precepts that derived from the comprehensive works of Oman and Fortescue have influenced the subsequent literature with regard to Wellington's command of his army, its subordinate leadership and the performance of his troops. These original proponents of Wellington's leadership, writing after his lifetime, were driven by the bequeathed strength of the Duke's personality, the enormity and legacy of the Waterloo victory and the strong patriotic social inclinations of their time. Despite their huge amount of detail, they were written from an unapologetically British viewpoint that now disappoints in its one dimensionality. Too many authors have since reiterated this same viewpoint such that the reported attributes of Wellington's command during his campaigns against the French have remained uniformly preferential. Wellington was undoubtedly a successful commander, but a marked unwillingness to delegate authority and decision-making assuredly did have the potential to generate a loss of efficiency by not making optimum use of the resources available. Wellington's ultimate success in both 1814 and 1815 has precluded forthright reconsideration of his degree of effectiveness from an all-arms perspective. It has indeed specifically been written by historian Lipscombe that 'details of that synergy have been largely ignored in the histories of the Peninsula'.[90] While the Waterloo campaign has otherwise been examined by historians in much more detail than events in the Peninsula, its inclusion here better enables consideration of whether Wellington's disposition, outlook and influence changed over time and location.

As consistently recorded, the Duke of Wellington was certainly a forthright and domineering personality. He appears to have had the need to be fully in control and personally to manage every situation he met. He micro-managed his forces throughout the war and severely criticized those he could not manipulate. Wellington's personal workload must have been unfailingly heavy as he alone saw to all aspects of command. His directing leadership style in fact pre-supposed low competence among his officers, and many otherwise talented individuals would have been de-motivated. The Peninsular War veteran Captain William Bragge confirms this when commenting upon what he saw as the three-stage demoralization of Wellington's senior officers.[91]

- The Duke of York would order a general, inexperienced in Wellington's command, to Portugal.
- Inevitably some perceived blunder would be committed and Wellington bluntly spoke his mind to the general.
- The offended officer would never again bother to exert his judgement, and slackness resulted.

The on-going recurrence of this repressive and dispiriting theme should be borne in mind for the events recorded hereafter. The compatible parallel proposition is that some officers were tainted as incompetent after they had displayed rather too much independence for Wellington's liking: 'Wellington is not a little disposed to repress all strictures on his conduct etc., it would not be altogether safe to say all one might think or know.'[92] That such a statement should be made at all speaks volumes. The historical narrative has certainly recorded the outward display of Wellington's personality, but any resultant operational impact has been neglected or misinterpreted. Hence the habitual statement: 'the officers of the infantry and cavalry were untrained and the generals inadequate. These factors were immutable.'[93] Yet, having clarified and amplified the actuality of Wellington's personal disposition, amendment to the standard narrative is surely overdue. A more dispassionate portrayal of Wellington's leadership needs to be acknowledged, and its impact upon the perception of numerous subordinates, as well as upon active operations in war, made fully clear.

Within the next chapter the background to Britain's army command structure and the relevant military tools at its disposal will be considered. Thereafter in chronological order, the major events which form the context of Wellington's leadership will be reviewed, with consideration of the evidence of command effectiveness. Events will be recounted in terms of three perceived interwoven strands, each requiring reappraisal within the existing narrative.

- To provide a more measured evaluation of Wellington's subordinate generals, to ascertain whether they were really all ill-trained, unskilled and of limited capability. Were they and other staff officers purely gentleman amateurs to be closely supervised by Wellington, or could he have benefited by providing them with greater latitude?

- To clearly re-evaluate the competency and inter-relationship between Wellington's troops, to ascertain whether Wellington relied principally upon his infantry through necessity. Was his low estimation of the cavalry, artillery and engineers justified, or did he himself impede their effectiveness?
- To gauge the effect that Wellington's uncompromising leadership had upon his subordinates and hence whether his personality impeded the effectual command of his army. It is hard to imagine officers who were overawed, if not intimidated by him being fully effective in their personal roles. To consider also whether Wellington's command style altered, for good or ill, over the protracted and intense eight years of warfare.

To attribute solely to Wellington's military genius, the forging of a winning army from sub-standard subordinate leadership and ineffectual combat arms is frankly an unlikely and inadequate explanation. No substantive evidence exists to indicate that Wellington ever in fact effectively tutored and encouraged his essential subordinates; he commanded from on high, rather than guided his men through training and teamwork. Esdaile's suggestion that the Peninsular Army was never quite as good as history would ascribe is therefore a valid consideration. Wellington's approach to command has to have played a part in any such perception. Definition is required to consider the effect upon others of the acerbity that surrounded his personality and his unwillingness to delegate any authority.

Wellington's leadership nonetheless proved successful over time and certainly deserves esteem for its focused inimitability; his battle record is prodigious.* Yet overall effectiveness can involve diverse ingredients, each having an impact. The initial conjecture is clearly that Wellington's leadership generated deficiencies in the maintenance of morale among his generals, and soured co-operation among the component parts of the army. Wellington's micro-management also potentially generated a defensive mindset, and an attendant failure to exploit his victories. These are the key postulated shortcomings; the explanation for others more specific, such as a failure to concentrate forces in 1815, will also be considered on the path to a reasoned denouement. While a famous victory, the culminating Battle of Waterloo may easily have had a negative outcome for Wellington's command; it was indeed a close-run thing.

---

* See Appendix A, for Wellington's battle record.

Chapter 2

Wellington's Army, 1808–15

'Above all, be careful never to promote an intelligent officer; a brave chuckle-headed fellow will do full as well to execute your orders.'[1]

The Duke of Wellington's effectiveness as a general and as a leader of men was founded upon what today the professional military would term 'command and control'. This has been somewhat expansively defined as: 'The exercise of authority and direction by a properly designated commander over assigned and attached forces in the accomplishment of the mission.'[2] To exercise his own authority and accomplish his mission in an efficient manner, Wellington needed to be the focus for 'receiving, processing and transmitting information in a way which [would] yield the maximum gain for the minimum cost'.[3] Information generated Wellington's strategic and operational planning, and from this foundation to subsequently command with adroitness he was required to ensure the management of people and supporting systems through effective communication. There is of course in addition the leader's less tangible, but equally important intrinsic elan, that reveals his initiative and combat ability. It is the sum of such positive, but diverse parameters of command that existed both then and now. It is also these parameters that require consideration to ensure that 'confirmation bias' does not dominate the record of Wellington's achievements. The very success that Wellington gained has ensured that his generalship has been reported in the most glowing of terms, with few questions, and in ways which confirm the hypothesis of excellence that his own dominant personality promoted.

Wellington's individual attainment of operational objectives throughout the war, either by battle or manoeuvre, certainly equates to a positive level of effectiveness. Yet, in doing so he always displayed an inordinately strong need for individual mastery, while personal popularity with his fellows was incidental in its achievement. Wellington's acerbity would mean that he both inter-communicated with individuals and managed subordinates questionably. He would demonstrate nevertheless that his strongly applied command could get excellent results from the tools that had been provided. These tools were the military systems and apparatus of Great Britain that should be seen as largely established and set in place, not involving sweeping initiatives fashioned by Wellington as is sometimes asserted. Wellington's command was successful, with victories that would in themselves enhance the morale of his army, and in turn facilitate further success, but it is reasonable to question whether victory might have been achieved more effectively. The true practical evidence of effectual leadership by Wellington may only be assessed by the degree to which his forces not only achieved their objectives, but did so in a timely fashion with an acceptable level of casualties.

The army's leaders were expected to exhibit courage, commitment and integrity, discipline and loyalty, just as all professional armies still require today. The notably strict discipline imposed by Wellington aimed to generate an automatic response in his subordinates; they were expected to do exactly as he ordered. In contrast modern predispositions emphasize training to develop clear thinking and resolve, so that the correct action is taken when under duress. This is termed 'mission command': the empowerment of subordinate leaders to use their initiative with speed and freedom of action within defined constraints.* Through such command flexibility and responsiveness, the benefits of positive co-operation, economy of effort, and enhanced morale are generated. There is no tradition of Wellington ever allowing his generals to think independently, nor was he a great trainer or mentor of his men; these were shortcomings in an otherwise professional organization.

> I am far from questioning the zeal [. . .] of the Officers of the army; and I am quite certain that if their minds can be convinced of the necessity of minute and constant attention to [. . .] the orders which have been issued [by me] for the performance of their duty [. . .] they will in future give their attention to these points.[4]

Is initiative a purely modern tenet? Wellington was not necessarily alone in his beliefs. The Prussian General Karl von Müffling wrote: 'The general alone should oversee the whole battle [. . .] he did not look for staff officers or subordinate commanders to conduct his business for him'.[5] Yet, Wellington went much further than even Müffling intended, he removed many of the superintending responsibilities that his subordinates could reasonably have expected as their prerogative. Wellington's leadership was symptomatic of eighteenth-century warfare, not the innovative, enhanced professionalism espoused by the Duke of York, as Commander-in-Chief of the British Army. It adhered to an old tradition and firmly suppressed the new, as epitomised by Napoleon Bonaparte and Sir John Moore. Wellington's conservative leadership, if not totally anachronistic, certainly

---

* See Appendix B, for principles of mission command.

had no visionary elements and would rather inhibit subsequent British military thinking.

An involved and valued subordinate generates loyalty and respect. Where there is limited respect, then loyalty weakens; leadership indeed degrades command effectiveness if it is overly controlling. Wellington, even as a junior officer, rarely delegated responsibility and again has been described as 'assertive, opinionated and extremely touchy'.[6] In reality he was a brilliantly focused personality, but one who failed to make those closest to him feel at all valued. No disobedience, perceived disloyalty or use of personal initiative could be tolerated by him, and any setback was always blamed on another. This was very, very far from enacting those attributes involving development and guidance that our contemporary leaders require; to consult before making command decisions and to encourage feedback, while also recognizing the stresses and feelings of individuals.[7] The end result for Wellington would be subdued and discouraged subordinate generals, intrinsically less effective than they might otherwise have been. This scenario may be recognized in the events of 1808 to 1815.

American military theorists and wargamers have greatly developed the concept of quantifying the variable factors that generate military effectiveness; to identify those contributing ingredients to combat success or failure.[8] Key variable factors within battle that author T.N. Dupuy identifies relate principally to the leadership and initiative of generals, and the combat effectiveness and morale of the army.[*] A failure by any one of these factors could be critical; if, for example, Wellington's subordinate generals had ever completely lost heart, then their cause would have been lost. Upon at least one occasion in the Peninsula this very nearly occurred. The physical and mental state of the men, their experience, training and logistics all play a role in how soldiers behave in battle. The resilience and mindset of the army, its morale, are of equal importance to material resources when determining how well these men would withstand the stresses of battle. Factors of secondary weight are those such as the provision of intelligence and the effectiveness of weapons. Other factors such as combat terrain and weather can be of a more individual or generic nature, specific to a particular battle and which often relate equally to both sides. Command and control upon a Napoleonic battlefield has been described as a 'very limited geographic concept'; but the true lesson of Dupuy's analysis is that each and every variable had the potential for decisive impact in battle.[9]

Prior to his appointment to army command, Wellington is recorded as having only limited connections among the leading soldiers and military cliques of the day,

---

[*] See Appendix C, for variable factors of military effectiveness.

but rather more association with fellow Tory politicians. He was cognizant principally with his own perceived path to advancement. Wellington would command an army of just 10,000 men in 1808, with his idiosyncratic personal dominance in place from the start. As the war progressed he was increasingly compelled to delegate authority, due to the growing size of his army and the geographic separation of its parts. This presented him with a major problem: he could no longer bypass his generals to deal directly with formation leaders and expect positive results. The traits that Wellington valued within his subordinates were always quite specific. Yet, the desired unquestioning compliance, in accordance with his strict control, now rather worked against those generals who on occasion needed to display initiative. The ideal whereby Wellington the commander could give orders and then leave the practical execution to a capable subordinate was undermined by the army leader himself. Army size and disposition were certainly factors that impacted upon Wellington's effectiveness. Indeed, these were most crucial issues, often misdiagnosed by the insinuation that his tactics were intrinsically defensive, or that he was only effectual as a general when defending in battle. The criteria associated with the enhancement of the scale of operations will be seen within the subsequent narrative. Otherwise, the context of Wellington's command consistently and essentially involved the army's leaders, the fighting troops that they led and the systems for communication and intelligence-gathering that Wellington routinely employed. The background to these fundamental elements requires consideration, as all were of inherent influence within Wellington's command. All certainly had the potential to limit the capability of battle to achieve its ultimate strategic purpose, namely the destruction of enemy forces and the subsequent winning of the war.

Army Leadership

To prepare an expeditionary force for landing in the Peninsula was a task of some complexity, involving disparate parties. The army's regulatory structures were outside of Wellington's control, but would place limitations upon his effectiveness. Wellington's degree of authority or persuasiveness with the bureaucracy would nonetheless alter, and to his benefit, through the course of the war. At the commencement of the Peninsular War in 1808, the Commander-in-Chief of the British Army alone was responsible for the provision of all infantry and cavalry officers and troops from his base at Horse Guards, London. HRH Prince Frederick, the Duke of York was Commander-in-Chief from 1795–1809 and again from 1811–27; Sir David Dundas was Commander-in-Chief from 1809–11. The Duke of York would subsequently be credited with having done 'more for the army than any one man has done for it in the whole of its history'.[10] Dundas was responsible for the first officially sanctioned British manual of infantry tactical doctrine, *Rules and Regulations for the Formations, Field-Exercise and Movements of His Majesty's*

Forces, published in 1793. He would additionally, in 1796, write the *Instructions and Regulations for the Formations and Movements of the Cavalry*, based upon his own experiences, and with which he aimed to ensure a standard system of training for the cavalry. Neither York nor Dundas was a dilettante. The independent Master General of the Ordnance (MGO) otherwise allocated artillery and engineering support; while the Treasury appointed Commissariat staff and arranged the funding for supplies. Troop deployment within Great Britain involved the Secretary for War, while sea transport abroad was the responsibility of the Admiralty. The Paymaster General, Medical Board, Apothecary General and Storekeeper General were all additional stakeholders. Finally, the Foreign Office was responsible for specific information pertaining to the theatre of war, such as mapping and local intelligence. The Commander-in-Chief thus delegated his authority to Wellington, as commander of the army expeditionary force to Portugal, in accordance with the *General Regulations & Orders*, last updated in 1804.

The Duke of York, when Commander-in-Chief, is accredited with three pre-eminent reforms to the Regulations:

- The standardization of training for all troops.
- The exclusion of patronage to senior military ranks.
- Ridding the army of incompetent officers.

York also may be given great credit for ensuring that order prevailed during the period of enforced major expansion of the army that the Peninsular War precipitated. Between 1808 and 1814 the original 'disposable force' for overseas operations grew from 10,000 to over 70,000 men. The army had previously held no permanent formations larger than the regiment and the generals within this army had all, in the most recent past, commanded no more than a brigade of 2,000 men. With organizational experience of large formations overwhelmingly lacking among the army's officers, it would be a challenge for all those who would, before long, become responsible for up to corps-sized formations of 20,000 men. They have received only limited acknowledgement or credit for the commission that they accepted and fulfilled: commanding major formations upon active service and under Wellington's difficult and hyper-critical leadership.

The Duke of York established the Royal Military College (RMC) for infantry and cavalry officers in 1801 at High Wycombe. His effort here has again rightly earned him the accolade of being a 'superb administrator'.[11] The College would duly produce high-quality leaders, if initially their numbers were limited to just thirty-four per year. The cynical and anti-intellectual Wellington is recorded as being distinctly prejudiced against such graduates. In turn, personal dislike for Wellington from York and indeed his father King George III has been recorded. Beyond a standardized military education, York's reforms enhanced professionalism by such measures as designating a minimum timescale for service at each rank. Commissions up to the rank of lieutenant colonel could nevertheless be purchased. Wellington himself pre-empted the tougher rules when quickly and progressively purchasing rank up to lieutenant colonel; which he gained in September 1793, aged just 24. While most senior officers had similarly progressed in an era of unrestricted purchase, younger men were now becoming more truly professional army officers. The aristocracy never dominated the army, and it is certainly unfair to generalize, as has been stated, that officers were all gentlemen amateurs. Wellington himself revealed his distain and indeed belligerence for his superiors when stating: 'Horse Guards looked upon me with a kind of jealousy, because I was a Lord's son [. . .] who came into the army more for ornament than use'.[12] The great majority of officers were rather themselves the sons of officers or clergymen, minor gentry, farmers and merchants. Unfortunately, by 1815 still only 4 per cent of total infantry and cavalry officers had passed through the RMC. Wellington otherwise habitually preferred 'family, fortune and influence' over individual merit; he had an intrusive hand in the selection of William Beresford in 1809, and as he would subsequently with sundry others. Those officers of little money, regardless of the compensation of a military education, he dismissed as 'coxcombs and pedants'.[13] Wellington himself had nevertheless studied briefly in France when in his teens, as had two of his favoured generals, Beresford and Rowland Hill, who both attended the Military Academy in Strasbourg.

Unchanged within the Regulations was the traditional reliance upon seniority for highest rank. All appointments for command above the rank of lieutenant colonel were based purely upon seniority. Ordinarily no British general officer would willingly serve under another whose achievement of senior rank was more recent than his own. This system would at first preclude the participation of certain officers of proven effectiveness from Wellington's command, such as General Sir John Hope: 'the ablest man in the army'.[14] Hope in fact did graciously offer to accept demotion during 1810 in order to serve in the Peninsula, but was denied by Parliament upon the grounds of maintaining military protocol.[15] Initially, in July 1811, General Edward Paget bluntly declined to serve again under Wellington, due to perceived issues of seniority.[16] During the Napoleonic Wars, the only exception to promotion above major general other than by seniority was Wellington himself when he was appointed Field Marshal in 1813. The rank of Field Marshal had only been in place since 1735 with the inauguration of Lord George Hamilton, and Wellington became the twenty-fourth such holder. Under the rules of seniority, he would not otherwise have become a full general until 1819. This maintenance of the protected status of those of the most senior rank was a hindrance to efficacy that some have used to damn all ranks of officer. Military Secretary (MS) Henry Torrens wrote in 1810: 'you will recollect my dear gen'l that we have not the most choice set to select Genl officers from!'.[17]

Torrens would be making reference to the unavoidably limited pool of available general officers as much as any criticism of individuals; but likely coupled also with his insight into Wellington's predilections.

The purchase system should not be seen as inherently detrimental. Purchase officers accounted for only 20 per cent of Peninsular War officers, and proved indistinguishable from those who rose in other ways. The cavalry held the greatest percentage of purchased commissions: from 1810 to 1813 it was 45.1 per cent, while the figure for the infantry stood at 17.7 per cent.[18] The cost of serving within the cavalry precluded 'three-fourths of the young men in England'. They were the most well to do and not necessarily the best qualified.[19] This has been cited as a reason why the British cavalry performed more poorly than the infantry during the war, if this reflection of the cavalry's performance is indeed to be accepted.[20] Certainly some individuals, likely those who primarily desired a smart uniform, may have found this an attraction in comparison with the more stolid infantry. A view of some lax discipline within the cavalry is backed by the derisory court-martial of Colonel George Quentin in 1814. Spurious charges were shown to have been brought by Quentin's subordinates in retaliation for the severe discipline he imposed, at Wellington's behest. Yet, while competition for commissions within the cavalry does raise questions, it does not automatically imply irresolution from any individual. A cynical view of the overall purchase system is given by a British sergeant when contrasting it with the appointment of French officers: 'No [French] man, however elevated in rank or connexion, had any chance of promotion, but by passing through the various grades, commencing with the lowest.'[21] For it to be claimed, as has sometime been stated, that the rank and file actually preferred aloof, aristocratic officers may rather be stretching a point. The British system ensured an intellectual mix of keen, if privileged young officers, with Wellington himself an example of someone who could attain high command at an age when still physically vigorous. Comparably, at the Battle of Salamanca in 1812 all British lieutenant generals present had received early promotion through purchase and patronage, but their average age was less than 42. Not a dissimilar outcome to that promulgated by the French, though certainly tainted by privilege.

Within his 'modernizing' parameters, York looked to encourage officer promotion by merit, regardless of money; a sentiment that left Wellington more than somewhat unmoved. Wellington indeed always vehemently opposed officers being promoted from the ranks, telling an enquiry in 1836, 'they do not make good officers; it does not answer'.[22] Wellington's autocratic attitudes were retrogressive; unlikely to have enhanced morale and professionalism, despite any argument that this was still the inveterate standard of the times. His personal preferences were shown by his extensive employment of the sons of dukes as his headquarters staff; a practice even Napier describes as, 'the cold shade of aristocracy'.[23] It again explicitly displayed the anti-intellectualism of Wellington's nature that was in marked contrast to, for example, the growing professionalism of the Prussian military staff, in response to their defeats by Napoleon in 1806.

Established in 1741, the Royal Military Academy (RMA) at Woolwich provided technical training for engineer and artillery officers. The course targeted a two-year education, but there were exceptions: the complexity of the final public examination meant that Major General Edward Borthwick, a future Commander of the Royal Artillery (CRA), took four years. For the RA and RE promotion went fully by seniority; there were no purchased commissions, and scarcely any officers of private means. To maintain their army income few officers ever retired, so the most senior officers were found to be ill-suited, generally too old for active service; technical officers in the Peninsula were of a lower rank than they had a right to expect. The Commanders of the RA and the RE on campaign were administrative, not command posts; they took their operational orders from Wellington. Yet, the independence of the Board of Ordnance proved problematic to communication in Portugal, with field officers often asking sanction of their Master General before an unapproachable Wellington. This division of command was anachronistic; a tradition that impeded effective command. Wellington battled clumsily with this scenario throughout the war, and to the discomfiture of many officers.

Wellington's generals can thus be said to have been mostly men of independent means, though all would be aware of York's reforms and it is to be hoped respected the principle of army professionalism. It was to Wellington's detriment that he markedly superimposed his own notions of class and property upon his army: he expected the army's leaders to be, 'both able and wealthy'.[24] In 1808 Wellington's forces had room for seventeen generals, with the number rising to over forty by 1814. Wellington somewhat contrarily stated: 'I wish to see officers possess [. . .] a cool discriminating judgement in action [. . .] and act with [. . .] vigour and decision'.[25] Relations between Wellington and his commanders would likely provide an impediment to this: 'It is difficult to have an order obeyed by the officers, if it affects their own convenience.'[26] It was 'do as I say, not as I do'. Wellington's stark personality and inability to credit subordinates could only provide restrictions and discord:

> You do not know Lord Wellington's private character. He has no idea of gratitude, favour or affection, and cares not for anyone however much he may owe him or find him useful.[27]

Wellington's robust leadership style firmly discouraged the show of initiative among his subordinates, and it is likely that Beresford, Craufurd and Hill were the only generals with whom Wellington ever 'condescended' to talk freely.[28] He eroded the confidence of subordinates, and in parallel failed to generate *esprit de corps*. Cohesiveness of command was fractured by his authority. There is otherwise no organizational reason why the generals should have lacked skill, commitment or integrity. Wellington's own conservative conviction that he alone should take command decisions worked against efficiency. Men in the ranks, such as Rifleman Edward Costello, might perceive officers as belonging to either 'the come on', or 'the go on' types, but this must invariably be the case, and the Peninsular Army was unexceptional in this regard.[29] British generals in 1808, though of limited active experience beyond colonial service, were both prepared and capable in their responsibility for superintending the commands for logistics, manoeuvre and battle tactics. It would certainly be Wellington's officers who never failed to positively provide the essential sustaining leadership and motivation that helped the rank and file of their respective formations to endure the difficulties of campaign and battle over the years 1808–15.

For reference, a succinct narrative for the army leadership is provided, which aims to omit the numerous temporary commands that occurred during 1808–15, as generals took short-term leave for health or personal reasons throughout the war.[*]

Training and Tactics

Battle rarely achieves decisiveness by generating a clear turning point in war, such as happened at Waterloo in 1815. Even here it has been argued that the Battle of Waterloo was less a single decisive event than rather the exhaustive culmination of over a hundred years of attritional warfare between Britain and France.[30] Cavalry, infantry and artillery may all claim to be the decisive military arm, though the period army saw cavalry as indispensable for reaching decision; Napoleon stated that it was impossible to fight anything other than defensively without them. Others have argued that infantry fire has always been the decisive factor in warfare, or alternatively that: 'Artillery conquers and infantry occupies.'[31] The contention has additionally been offered that, 'the use of manoeuvre is what makes warfare especially of this era at least as much an art as it is a science'.[32] Certainly operational manoeuvre deserves consideration as a war winner, when losses from attrition routinely exceeded combat losses during the Peninsular War: in 1813 three officers died of sickness or accident for every one that died in battle.[33] The performance of each military arm throughout the war requires scrutiny to gauge their individual contributions to overall army effectiveness. The backdrop for the British army immediately prior to1808 is easy to devalue, and certainly the actuality for many troops was largely limited to the experience of colonial service. Yet, despite early war failures, the army trained its scratch-built volunteer forces generally better than the conscripts that made up most European armies. The continuity of its regimental system most notably ensured

---

[*] See Appendix D, for army leadership, 1808–15.

excellent group cohesion, and its soldiers were provided with exemplars of the contemporaneous weapons of choice. Certain military lessons from the American War of Independence, which had formally finished in 1873, had been imbued thanks in part to Dundas' updated regulations. These lessons had subsequently been reinforced by the perceived performance of French forces on the Continent with, for example the standardization of artillery, as originally instigated in France by General Jean-Baptiste Gribeauval, and the employment of copious light troops.

Infantry formed the heart of all armies, giving tactical solidity and sustained firepower; though the standard smoothbore musket of the time could incredibly require from '3,000 to 10,000 cartridges as the proportion to one man killed or wounded'.[34] Potentially, after a volley nearly a quarter of the muskets could be found to still be loaded, owing to the often 'inferior quality of the flints then supplied'.[35] Wellington inherited infantry that was noted for its steadfast qualities; it had demonstrated an ability to stand in line and defeat a more numerous French opponent most recently at Maida, Italy in 1806, where General Sir John Stuart defeated General Jean Reynier. The tradition of the defensive British 'thin red line' was already in place by this date and stretched back at least to General James Wolfe in Canada of 1759. Disciplined line formations yet emphasized marksmanship; soldiers were taught to withhold their fire until the last moment. Thereafter the bayonet was wielded to maximize enemy casualties quickly and force their retreat; a tactic that on the face of it would prove largely irresolvable for the French. Static fire fights were to be avoided within British doctrine; they engendered indecisiveness and such heavy casualties as would be encountered for example at the Battle of Albuera in 1811. The full character of British infantry is most interestingly assessed in some detail within *All for the King's Shilling* by Edward Coss, which dispels assorted common myths, and stresses the huge significance of the group dynamic.[36] In contrast to British troops, the standard of the opposition French infantry by 1808 was already in decline, after twenty years of warfare. Napoleon reintroduced regimental artillery in 1809, since: 'The more inferior the quality of a body of troops, the more artillery it requires.'[37] Wellington himself stated: 'We may not manoeuvre as beautifully as they [the French] do, but I do not desire better sport than to meet one of their columns en masse, with our lines.'[38] Such commentators as Esdaile have emphasized Wellington's predominant focus upon the infantry; they 'had evolved a series of procedures that [. . .] made them an exceedingly dangerous enemy'.[39] Nonetheless, he urges recognition that near identical tactical systems were used by both the British and French armies of the period, despite the common picture of French columns slavishly attacking British line formations.[40] The French ideally preferred *l'ordre mixte* in the attack, which consisted of two battalion columns in open order, flanking one central battalion in line. In the Peninsula, with either conscript troops or the loss of those more experienced, it is likely that to ensure order, basic columnar attacks were mostly prevalent. Extraneous factors of a strategic or logistical nature so often necessitated French use of the offence, as was the case at Talavera in 1809. Wellington was thus understandably confident to stand on the defensive as both strategic and tactical necessity regularly created an attacking straightjacket for his enemy. It is otherwise simplistic to contend that the French somehow failed to understand the tactical nuances of columns attacking line; the scenario had, for example, been discussed by French military theorist the Comte de Guilbert thirty years before the Peninsular War.[41]

Prior to his death in 1809, General Sir John Moore had an unequalled reputation as an innovator and trainer of troops; notably a full division of light infantry using the latest principles learnt from the French. Light units were armed with rifles, unlike their French equivalent: Napoleon had ordered their withdrawal in 1802. Moore established an experimental Rifle Corps at Horsham in 1800 and with the first use of the renowned Baker rifle taking place when training within Windsor Forest. One of Moore's immediate subordinates here was Lieutenant Colonel William Stewart, who would join Wellington's army in 1809. Dissatisfied with the previous rigidity of tactics, Moore taught personal responsibility and professionalism; training light units to think and fight as individuals. Soldiers were now permitted to use their initiative, which unsurprisingly enhanced motivation and improved morale. Moore improved tactics and originated the 'thinking fighting man' for the British army. Wellington in 1808 and thereafter would ensure at least a numerical equality of skirmishers with the French; he rightly maintained Moore's initiative. The initiative of Stewart however would prove another matter.

The training that Moore had instigated meshed with the strong regimental system fundamental to the British army, and subsequently with Wellington's own strategic capabilities. The combination of these factors generated success. One notable, elite establishment within the army was the King's German Legion, or KGL, which was founded in 1803 by refugees from the Electorate of Hanover. KGL troop numbers would peak at about 14,000 officers and men in 1812; posted mainly within the 1st Division. Wellington would also eventually combine large Portuguese elements into all other divisions, ten brigades by 1811, and which troops, with training, would be largely indistinguishable from their British counterparts. For Wellington's Dutch and German troops, within the army of 1815, the short timescale of the Waterloo campaign precluded extensive priming. Any differences between troop nationalities would be highlighted by Wellington, most notably if a scapegoat for blame was ever needed. Wellington essentially won his battles with disciplined line infantry; the cavalry and artillery components were subordinate to it. With this in mind, the Peninsular War, in accordance with Napoleon's words, may be considered as predominantly one of attrition: the prescribed strong cavalry and artillery contingents, required for a battle of annihilation, were for a long time lacking within Wellington's forces.

In theory an army with effective cavalry was most capable of winning a battle by favourable casualty rates and associated psychological advantage sufficient to achieve strategic decisiveness. This was, in fact, always problematic: cavalry exploitation was often just an ideal, with both sides, post-battle, too damaged for effective pursuit. General John Le Marchant notably advised the RMC on cavalry training from 1801. Here was learnt such skills as an improved sword drill, though the practical skills of patrolling and picquet work, for which no regulations existed, were harder to acquire. Patrols were for reconnaissance and communication: 'Picquets may be established for two purposes [. . .] whether to watch the enemy or check him'.[42] Nonetheless, in 1809, Lieutenant Colonel Frederick von Arentschildt of the 1st Hussars published *Instructions for Officers and NCOs of Cavalry on Outpost Duty*, so the practicalities of the field were certainly being learnt and communicated. British cavalry ostensibly consisted of either dragoons – heavier cavalry for the charge, and hussars – light cavalry for patrols and reconnaissance. Wellington indicated disappointment with both throughout the war: 'the nature of the service precluded the tight autocratic control that he was accustomed to exercising over his infantry'.[43] Significantly, 'the majority of the successes achieved by British cavalry [. . .] were won when Wellington himself was not present'.[44] The opposition French cavalry in the Peninsula, both light and heavy, was in fact often poorly mounted and poorly equipped, but they had, as Austrian Archduke Charles commented, 'experience and élan'. The rugged terrain of the Peninsula, with bad roads and limited forage, in actuality somewhat curtailed effective cavalry usage and enabled Wellington to pronounce that, 'the peninsula is the grave of horses'.[45] Yet, Wellington's perennial and confounding antipathy for the cavalry arm notably impeded the attainment of combined arms benefits in combat; it reinforced his strategy of cautious erosion of the enemy rather than seeking annihilation. For it to be stated that Wellington's forte was in the use of cavalry in pursuit of a beaten enemy, now appears simply bizarre; rather, 'the cavalry was often relegated to a secondary role and had its accomplishments and contributions neglected'.[46]

Due to its segregated leadership, Wellington's desired control over the artillery was not as straightforward as for the infantry and cavalry. Yet, Wellington made little effort to influence the size and quantity of guns. He seldom concentrated artillery in battle; nor were his guns to be used for counter-battery fire, but instead to work in tandem with the infantry to seek enfilade shots against attacking French columns. The French increasingly employed heavier 8 to 12-pound guns, termed Napoleon's 'beautiful daughters' and which were supplemented by the provision of indirectly firing howitzers. In order to enhance their assaults, they would ideally look to open up intervals between units and drive artillery right up to the front line. This assault tactic most effectively combined artillery with infantry to potentially devastating effect upon opposing troops. That is, unless a suitable defensive counter-measure was employed, such as Wellington's use of reverse hill slopes. On the other hand, British artillery in the Peninsula consisted largely of 6-pound cannon, whose manoeuvrability otherwise compensated for the lesser weight of shot. This combat methodology successfully supported British linear defence and is, therefore, hard to fault; more and heavier guns would have added greater logistical load, and at a financial cost. The Board of Ordnance was nonetheless not without technological successes when employing rockets, improved gunpowder and shrapnel shells; none of which their French opponents were able to match. Rockets were designed and developed by Sir William Congreve in 1804; based upon those seen in Mysore, India. Congreve with Richard Watson, the Bishop of Llandaff, also developed an improved charcoal needed for gunpowder production. The new powder proved better by a notable 100:60 ratio.[47] Most significantly, Colonel Henry Shrapnel's shells were hollow projectiles containing bullets; designed to explode in the air and shower the target with missiles. The first ever such rounds had been fired in anger at Fort Amsterdam, Dutch Guiana as recently as 1804.[48] In battle shrapnel shells targeted infantry at a range between that of shot and canister; this was the highly inconvenient point at which an attacker ideally aimed to deploy from the more manoeuvrable column into *l'ordre mixte* or line of battle. These innovations would enhance British morale and combat effectiveness to a notable degree. Colonel Shrapnel at the time specifically wrote: 'the invention should not be made public in any way, lest its importance should thus be signified to the enemy'.[49] This secrecy, plus the isolated criticisms that Wellington inevitably made, have obscured the true force-multiplying effect of shrapnel. Skill and experience was required to fire both shrapnel shells and rockets effectively. The fact that performance was sometimes affected by limited expertise should certainly not detract from their importance.

Less successful in the Peninsula were the siege operations directed by the all-officer ranks of the Royal Engineers; their only recent prior experience had been the reduction of hill forts in India. 'Ours was perhaps, the only army in Europe which possessed no corps of sappers or miners, nor any body of men peculiarly trained to carry on the more intricate details of a siege.'[50] Wellington's limited success as a siege commander may have facilitated the formation of the Royal Corps of Sappers and Miners in 1813, but he was not directly responsible, as is routinely stated. The Corps had existed previously as the Royal Military Artificers, and was reformed in 1812–13 under Captain Charles Pasley, RE; an individual who had both written and lobbied regarding the needs of the service since 1809. Nonetheless, from 1813 mobile artificer companies became available, and elements of five such companies would first attend at the siege of San Sebastian from 11 July 1813.[51] Yet, the small number of engineer officers overall could neither meet nor contradict the demands Wellington made upon them; he likely believed his own experience from India exceeded that of his specialists. As with the artillery, organizational practicalities and sheer expense thus 'conspired against the effectiveness of the army's technical branches', and in turn upon Wellington's command.[52] His stated outlook was, 'to do the best I can with the instruments that have been sent to assist me', but here again his own judgement always took precedence.[53] Lieutenant Colonel John Burgoyne, RE wrote of Wellington: 'he never pays anyone the compliment to insinuate he took their advice, though he may perhaps in a case of failure'.[54] Ideally, standard doctrine called for siege artillery to be fired from a position located some 100yd away from their static target, though for expediency they were more usually employed during Peninsular sieges when located at 300–400yd range. The standard iron siege guns used to pound enemy fortress walls, as made use of by Wellington, would fire shot of either 18-pound or 24-pound weight. In addition 10in brass howitzers would be utilized to lob shrapnel shells over fortresses walls as anti-personnel fire. Adjutant General (AG) Charles Stewart at the time succinctly agreed: 'Our Engineer officers were [. . .] equally able and scientific, but [. . .] they were few in number'.[55]

The quality of troops employed by Wellington overall is in reality hard to fault; though the cavalry, artillery and engineers initially showed a lack of practical experience and were never as numerous in the Peninsula as they should have been. Just as was the case for the artillery and the engineers, the British cavalry arm was limited by the specifics of government policy. This naturally centred upon the basic cost to the government to both recruit and maintain the troops; the Commissariat regarded maintaining a regiment of cavalry as comparable to feeding an infantry division. Cavalry training initially had some deficiencies, largely relating to operational applications, but the training of the technical arms ensured that they were accomplished. Otherwise the standard of infantry troops in the early Peninsular years may only be questioned relative to the prevalence of regimental second battalions, after many first battalions were wrecked at either Coruña or during the Walcheren expedition, both of 1809. Coruña saw the end of Sir John Moore's Spanish intervention, while the Walcheren invasion unsuccessfully tried to open a new front against the French in the Netherlands. The Duke of York's reforms had nonetheless provided a uniform system of training which increased the professionalism of all arms. Wellington had robust and professional forces under arms, though no reputation as a trainer of either officers or troops himself. The British forces in the Peninsula would perform with routine excellence against the French, even when led by deprecated battle commanders such as William Beresford at Albuera 1811, or John Murray at Castalla, 1813. The context of such conspicuous British tactical success, which certainly stretched beyond Wellington's influence, should be seen against what has been described as, 'ten years of almost unbroken victory on the field of battle', for the opposition French forces.[56] Yet, for Napoleon's disheartened forces in the Peninsula their fundamental obstacle and overwhelming difficulty was the vigorous activity of the Spanish guerrillas.

The local French commanders could never discern the whereabouts of an enemy army until direct contact was made by their outpost troops; strategic surprise for them was nigh impossible.

The demand for reinforcing troops of all types was always considerable within Wellington's army. Due to battle, disease and desertion losses during the war were never less than 16,000 each year, and reached a peak of 25,000 in 1812.[57] Overall 55,000 British soldiers died of disease during the Peninsular War compared with 27,000 who died as a result of battlefield wounds.[58] These figures provide a higher ratio of loss to the actual numbers serving than occurred during the First World War. This harsh reality was understood and acknowledged by Wellington: 'It is my duty, and that of every General and other Officer in command [. . .] not to expose the soldiers to contend with unequal numbers in situations disadvantageous to them'.[59] Yet, in overall terms the British soldier in the Peninsula has always been considered through the prism of Wellington's damning characterization that has shaped perceptions: 'We have in the service the scum of the earth as common soldiers.'[60] Analysis has shown that not a single contemporary study supports the concept or supposition of the British recruit-as-criminal.[61] Similarly, with regards to their supposed illicit activities, they plundered basically because of the continued failures of the Commissariat. While the men may have received more regular supply than their French opponents, contrary to the writing of most commentators it has been intriguingly verified that a Venetian galley slave of the fourteenth century received better regular rations.[62] Theft of food was thus by far the most common crime within the army, for which Wellington invariably recommended the lash, and indeed resented any attempt to limit corporal punishment.[63] Larpent recalled how Wellington, 'fell into a passion about the Courts martial for not doing their duty by acquitting and recommending mercy'.[64] Overall it is hard to disagree with the summation of historian Edward Coss: 'Wellington's [own] derogatory appraisal [. . .] has prevented fair analysis' of his magnificent troops.[65]

Communication and Intelligence

No one who served under Wellington was ever in any doubt that it was he who was in charge; no advice was ever needed, just the ability to obey orders. Day-to-day directives radiated from Wellington, as intelligence-gathering converged upon him. If the army's strategic purpose was to efficiently degrade enemy forces and win the war, then information and communication were essential to effective leadership. Wellington discouraged the initiative of others, often down to the tactical level, because he had decided that subordinates were less likely to make good decisions than he was himself. In his work upon leadership, *On the Psychology of Military Incompetence*, Norman Dixon explains the likely quiescence of subordinates: 'The feeling of dependency induced by stress, successfully neutralize a person's normal antipathy towards the autocratic leader.'[66] Wellington's own very personalized and authoritarian command required him in practice to keep his forces as concentrated as possible, and then to have the horsemanship to personally be at any critical location. When practicalities precluded his personal supervision, then problems and controversy resulted. Despite the introduction of independent corps, even Napoleon failed to fully control huge Continental armies that for him grew to exceed 450,000 men in 1812–13. In 1809, Wellington established autonomous divisions to facilitate control, but he never effectively organized independent corps, which would have entailed further delegated authority. Divisions reduced the number of his immediate subordinates, and he could group divisions under a chosen general when geographic distance limited his ability to command in person. Wellington however would ideally give orders directly to his divisional commanders, and regularly to lower echelon leaders, or failing that wrote short, definitive instructions. The reverse scenario was that feedback to the energetic Wellington was difficult if his actual location was unknown and ever-changing. British army organization was intrinsically simpler than for the French, yet as strength reached 70,000 men in 1813, Wellington's centralized command style entailed formidable and problematic administration.

Command pressure emphasized the importance of Wellington's relationships with the independently appointed Quartermaster General and Adjutant General. By 1813 in the order of 350 officers served the staff of the combined QMG and AG, though only some twenty-odd were actually based at Wellington's headquarters; the rest were based with individual divisions. The QMG was responsible for organizing proposed routes and directions for the army, and its quartering. He has been described as the principal staff officer, as 'War is first and foremost a matter of movement.'[67] When Wellington once irritably told an officer to 'go to hell', the latter's friend sardonically muttered, out of hearing that he would 'ask the QMG for a route'.[68] With regards to Wellington's operational orders, the words of S.G.P. Ward cannot be overstated:

> It is certain beyond all reasonable doubt that no operational unit or formation was moved unless Wellington had given a previous order and that usually in writing.[69]

As QMG for much of the Peninsular War, at a pinch: 'On very rare occasions [George] Murray would during any short absence of Wellington, give some very obvious order to one body or another of troops; but this was a most unusual occurrence, for the Commander-in-Chief was very jealous of his own authority.'[70] Wellington's other instructions were passed through his AG, whose main duty was indeed to ensure that the commander's orders were carried out, while also attending to discipline and equipment. Neither the QMG or AG had responsibility for any operational function; as for so much else, Wellington solely retained responsibility. Wellington's MS recorded financial business and appointments;

of the three, only the MS fell under Wellington's direct command.* Often the ever busy Wellington would be personally writing orders while on horseback. He carried on his saddle a small box containing pieces of prepared hide instead of paper; to avoid the disintegration of paper if it got wet. Generals Hill, Beresford, Craufurd and Graham were the only officers to whom Wellington reputedly ever condescended to give an explanation regarding a command. Unexpectedly, even such a strong adherent of Wellington's leadership as Oman acknowledges that, 'the springs of self-confidence were drained out of men who had for long been subjected to his regime'.[71] Instances, therefore, certainly exist, from the commencement of the Peninsular War, where insight would have clarified Wellington's intentions and prevented command confusion; as for the misdirected General Ronald Ferguson at Roliça in 1808. Wellington's leadership style, 'prevented capable subordinates from displaying their best powers'.[72] If any officer had the temerity to act without Wellington's approval then severe censure, if not a court martial, could be expected.

The orders that Wellington issued from headquarters had to be written in longhand, and the MS would copy for multiple addressees. Movement orders for the following day were required to be written and dispatched by 5:00pm, to ensure a dawn start for the relevant formation. An early trial use, in 1809, by Wellington of carbon paper appears to have been soon abandoned. This would be Ralph Wedgwood's 'carbonated paper', which had been invented in 1806. Once completed, an urgent order would be distributed by an Aide-de-Camp, mounted upon the best of horses. These officers made it a point of honour to ride at about 12 miles per hour, or say a 4-mile radius from headquarters within 20 minutes. Non-urgent front-line correspondence was carried by letter party. These were dragoons stationed at intervals between portions of the army when separated. Wellington typically grumbled: 'I have never yet seen communications by letter parties upon which any reliance whatever could be placed.'[73] Letters to addresses along the supply route from Lisbon were carried by members of the locally raised Corps of Guides: 'As my letters frequently remain some time at the post-office, I beg you will write "immediate" upon such as are of importance.'[74] Other non-important mail was sent by the mules of the Portuguese civilian mail, which might cover some 50 miles per day.** Later in Spain and France the army relied solely upon military mail. All transmission methods were of course subject to natural hazards as well as enemy action. Hence by 1814 General Stapleton Cotton complained about the extent to which mail provision depleted the strength of his available cavalry.[75] Communication overall was most effectively systematized under Wellington's capable organization, but held an intrinsic flaw in its over-centralization.

---

* See Appendix E, showing the administrative offices of the army.
** See Map 1, for the key centres and communication routes within Portugal and western Spain.

From 1809, Wellington fully employed the services of seven ADCs as a minimum, in addition to his MS; notionally any British commanding general had previously been allowed just three. Lieutenant generals would routinely employ two ADCs and for major generals there would be one alone. Hence, for a division the staff might consist of two ADCs and two officers acting as divisional AG and QMG, as well as appropriate assistants. It has been argued that Wellington's administrative staff pool was small in number compared with comparable European armies: 'having a staff so small it would have been insufficient for a French Corps commander'.[76] This statement is disingenuous however, reliant upon the renown of French Corps commanders for keeping large staff numbers. During the post-war period, 1815–18, Britain, Russia and Austria all kept an equally sized army of occupation within France, each of 30,000 men, and HQ staff numbers were 78, 36 and 48 respectively. Furthermore, when George Murray arrived to become chief-of-staff to this army, he would hold the rank of lieutenant general, while his Austrian counterpart was a mere major. While Wellington's command has been accredited with seeming frugality or 'Spartan virtue' by some, his system of control in reality ultimately entailed expansive supervision throughout his army.

The gathering of intelligence, while a vital function, had no recognized staff post associated with it. Located at a distance from the Peninsular Army were 'Observing officers', who rode ahead to report upon enemy movements. One most notable intelligence officer in the Peninsula was Major Colquhoun Grant, who in 1810 was appointed to the army's staff as an 'Exploring officer' to range far afield and well behind enemy lines. He would subsequently, in 1815, become a British agent in Paris during the Hundred Days of Napoleon's return to power. Other 'Sketching officers' were employed to improve understanding and mapping of the countryside. Initially maps of the Peninsula were unavailable to the accuracy of those otherwise in existence for Western Europe. Wellington obtained copy of the best that were available, the decidedly inconsistent maps of Portugal by Tomás López, dated from 1778. Thanks to these sketching officers, by 1810, ¼ in to the mile scale plans existed for all operational areas of Portugal. Finally, at the most local level, light cavalry outposts surrounded the army and reported intelligence matters directly for Wellington's attention. The most notable and significant Peninsular intelligence was nonetheless that provided by Spanish guerrillas, including information gleaned from the capture of French dispatches. Wellington's methods of intelligence-gathering were comprehensive and far superior to those of the enemy in the Peninsula. A French intelligence coup of 1809 consisted of the latest British newspapers containing printed troop dispositions; Wellington of course was furious. Wellington was always the hub of British intelligence-gathering; reports might be collated by his staff, but they were always processed by him. This led to one particularly unfortunate circumstance, when Wellington lost the keys to his box of papers for a week in May 1811. Subsequent to this event, Wellington seemingly did increase the involvement of the QMG's department in intelligence matters. This though may have been purely coincidental since concurrently the French had begun to make greater use of their *Grande Chiffre* coding system. Assistant Quartermaster General (AQMG) George Scovell would become a code-breaker of renown, able to read all coded enemy messages by November 1811.

Responsibility for communication and intelligence lay with Wellington; this was a monumental pressure and emblematic of his huge ability for hard work. Nevertheless, even Wellington himself, in a rare admission, stated: 'It is quite impossible for me to superintend the detail of the duties of [all] these departments myself.'[77] However, communication emanating from Wellington alone was hazardous: without his presence, through illness or incapacity, the fabric of administration for the army would have totally broken down. That he failed consistently to keep a second-in-command abreast of his intentions was at the very least injudicious. It was in the organization of administration that Wellington was prodigiously efficient, but a consistent lack of delegation meant that there was a resultant, substantive question mark against his effectiveness. It was certainly fortuitous that no major breakdown through illness or injury ever occurred; an unrealized disaster that has subsequently, by and large gone unacknowledged.

Thus through consideration of the army's leadership, the character of the troops and the practicalities of communication and intelligence, we gain an enhanced picture of the administrative backdrop to Wellington's command. Constraints associated with the intrinsic army bureaucracy caused some restrictions for Wellington, though his idiosyncratic leadership would soon overrule and dominate. All troops and notably the technical arms were in actuality most competently trained and led by the contemporary standard, if initially lacking somewhat in practical experience. Actual troop numbers within the army would gradually increase, subject to other governmental commitments and basic cost. Communication and intelligence-gathering were both superbly organized, thanks in no small part to the benign cooperation of the Allied nations, but they were overwhelmingly subject to the major limitation of personal responsibility imposed by Wellington. It may be adjudged overall that there were limited organizational parameters that affected the practicalities of Wellington's leadership in the field. Once the army had landed in Portugal he was mandated to freely organize and deploy the resources to hand, and these resources are hard to criticize.

Having reviewed the established administrative parameters, as well as appraising Wellington's own application of command, an enhanced perspective upon his leadership begins to take shape. The following factors that hindered Wellington's effectiveness as a commander may initially be seen to include:

- Officer designations impacted by Wellington's own prejudices, as much as any issues of seniority or organizational disengagement.

- Wellington's over-centralized and conservative command style, which both discouraged and disparaged the initiative of subordinates.
- The problematic practicalities of command associated with army size and dispersion, as Wellington always eschewed delegation.

Napoleon himself in 1812 would overstrain his ability to command and control the huge forces he led into Russia and which for him brought firstly catastrophic retreat and ultimately defeat. No military commander is ever faultless and without mistakes; waging war is certainly not an easy occupation. Wellington had drive, ambition and the clear appreciation that British military resources were hardly inexhaustible. The underscored attributes that brought a degree of ineffectiveness to his command will all be considered further hereafter, while additional factors impacting upon positive command and control are also appraised. It was however this imperfect system of military organization that Wellington had either inherited, or personally promoted, upon first arrival in the Peninsula in 1808.

Chapter 3

Wellington's Initial Command in Portugal, 1808

'As I am determined not to give up the military profession [. . .] I can be of no service in it unless I have the confidence and esteem of the [. . .] army'.[1]

In November 1807 the French General Jean-Andoche Junot, at the head of 22,000 men, would invade Britain's oldest ally, Portugal. This was with the connivance of Spain, an ally of France since 1796. The operation that Britain instigated in response was surely audacious in light of previous setbacks against Napoleon's Continental empire. Any British counter-move, in the long war provoked by the French Revolution of 1789, had usually been adjudged to require the parallel involvement of a Continental ally of the first order. With this latest overseas expedition the aspiring and determined Wellington would assume distinct command of a European army for the first time. It would take eight dedicated years of near continuous land warfare against the French before Wellington's ultimate victory at Waterloo in 1815. The partisanship that resulted from the overwhelming relief and acclaim generated by Waterloo is thus unsurprising, but should not preclude the requirement for a dispassionate assessment of the essence and effectiveness of Wellington's leadership over these long war years. His 'command and control', from the earliest clashes with the French, was surely impacted by both his marked personal idiosyncrasies as well as assorted extraneous criteria. For the armies that he led upon campaign, there is a requirement for a distinct and non-partisan reassessment of how effectively the often criticized generals and the individual arms of the army all performed. Wellington himself had first entered into military service twenty years prior to the Iberian expedition of 1808 and it is appropriate to briefly consider those years in so far as they help to define his approach to command.

The aristocratic teenage Wellington spent the years 1785–6 in military training at the *Académie Royale d'Equitation* at Angers in France, before being commissioned as an ensign of the 73rd Foot in 1787. The unmistakable influence of Wellington's older brother, Richard, Lord Mornington since 1781, gained Wellington his commission and the position of ADC to the Marquess of Buckingham, the

Lord Lieutenant of Ireland. The youthful Wellington would certainly recognize that merit alone was insufficient for prominence, and he would soon display his own fierce ambition. At that time and in the wake of the American War of Independence, army rank and political connections still very much ran side-by-side. Wellington won promotion from ensign to lieutenant, but required Richard's money to advance by purchase from captain to lieutenant colonel of the 33rd Foot in 1793. After Revolutionary France declared war on Britain that same year, Wellington's first command on active service was to lead his battalion in the unsuccessful Flanders campaign of 1793–5. For this expedition royalty was still to be found in a senior leadership role, courtesy of the 29-year-old Prince Frederick, Duke of York, the second son of King George III. Here a British army of 25,000 men joined with forces from Austria and Prussia, which had been fighting the French in the Low Countries since 1792. Wellington's thankless lot, in June 1794, was to arrive at Ostend, within the Austrian Netherlands just in time to be part of a rearguard as the town was evacuated; the Allies were soundly defeated at Fleurus on 26 June. The army was in retreat from the French, firstly to the River Maas in the Netherlands, then the River Waal, and ultimately by April 1795 as far as to Bremen in Hanover on the River Weser. Lieutenant General Sir William Erskine, the father of the future Peninsular War general, commanded the army's right wing, and the whole army in the absence of the Duke of York during the winter of 1793–4. With little credit to anyone involved, the surrender of the Austrian led garrison of Luxembourg on 7 June 1795 meant that the French conquest of the Dutch Republic and the Austrian Netherlands was effectively concluded, and the end of the campaign thereby marked with French success. The Duke of York, as the future Commander-in-Chief of the British Army, pointedly observed that, 'no officer should ever be subject to the same disadvantages under which he had laboured [in Flanders]'.[2] Wellington had experienced the vigorous realities of war, had personally suffered debilitating illness, and it is certainly likely that the harshness of the winter campaign reinforced upon him the importance of logistics to keep an army in the field. There was also of course the enduring regimental drill and duty of these early years which were themselves an education; an ingredient in the strength of the British regimental system which would bind Wellington to the 33rd Foot for life. His more scholarly training would come principally from the purchase of some 200 books that would accompany him to India upon the subsequent departure of the 33rd in 1796. The British government had decided to send substantial reinforcements to its Indian possessions, destabilized by war's declaration and despite the ready surrender of French Pondicherry in August 1793. Wellington at the age of 27 may be seen as a confident and capable, if an unproven young officer, certainly ambitious in the extreme and cognizant both of the status he felt was his due and of the practicalities of advancement.

Wellington arrived at Calcutta in February 1797, to begin an eight-year stay in India under the mandate of the East India Company; his regiment would be attached to the Madras Army led by Lieutenant General George Harris. As politician Horace Walpole had joked in 1783: 'No man ever went to the East Indies with good intentions'. Wellington likely expected career opportunities in India, but both his financial expectations and his prospects for advancement were spectacularly transformed with the news of July 1797 that his elder brother, Lord Mornington, had been appointed Governor General of India. Personal recommendation and patronage could be anticipated. Lord Mornington would arrive in April 1798, to immediately face the problem presented by the evidence of French advisors having been posted within neighbouring Mysore. The potential thus certainly threatened for an active alliance between Mysore's ruler, Tipu Sultan, and France. Perfunctory negotiations took place, but Mornington quickly decided to pre-empt any continuing crisis and ordered immediate military action. Under Harris's overall control, 2 columns of troops, a main force of over 20,000 men under Major General David Baird, and a subsidiary column of 17,000 troops under Colonel Wellington, would invade Mysore from Madras on the east coast. About 5,000 of these troops overall were European, the rest Indian. A third smaller force under Major General James Stuart would attack Mysore independently from Cannanore in the west.

Commencing the advance on 3 February 1799, the combined forces led by General Harris, including Wellington, readily brushed aside the enemy at Malavelly on 27 March. They then speedily covered the remaining 30 miles, of the overall 270-mile march, to reach Tipu's capital of Seringapatam by 2 April. Here they were also joined by the Mysore Army led by Stuart, as Harris's forces concentrated. In generally closing upon the city walls of Seringapatam, a night attack at Sultanpettah Tope on the 5 April, led by Wellington personally, went wildly amiss; to the extent that it likely predisposed him to avoid any combat at night in his subsequent career. The British assault notably experienced attack from the Sultan's rocket troops; giving Wellington a first taste of this exotic weaponry. One participant of the Sultanpettah Tope attack reported: 'so pestered were we with the rocket boys that there was no moving without danger'.[3] Wellington would become hopelessly disorientated in what was a darkened palm grove beset by heavy fire, and indeed would somehow lose contact with his own troops as the attack disintegrated. He personally retreated back to headquarters 'in a good deal of agitation'.[4] He has subsequently been excused by historians, courtesy of youthful inexperience, or because perhaps he was ill, or possibly having been hit by a spent musket ball, such that the full reality of the debacle is hard now to fathom. Yet, it is simpler to surmise what reception any colonel in Wellington's own Peninsula Army would have received if he had lost or abandoned his troops and retreated back to headquarters alone. The opinion of Lieutenant Richard Bayley, present with the

12th Regiment, was that, 'so palpably glaring did Wellesley's misconduct appear [. . .] everyone was persuaded that a Court Martial would ensue [but] He was the brother of the Governor-General of India'.[5] After this attack another contemporary sardonically commented that 'Wellesley is mad at this ill-success'.[6] Such measured words most likely reflect a degree of *Schadenfreude* by way of observation upon both Wellington's pronounced supercilious nature, as well the preferential treatment he received. The aloof Wellington is indeed already described during this period as someone who 'could not brook anything approaching opposition'.[7] Lieutenant Bayly would further express his belief that a tribunal should have occurred to 'clear' Wellington's character of the implied 'stigma of cowardice'. It is reasonable to concur with at least one historian that as a junior officer, who would report directly to his brother the Governor General, Wellington was detested by his brother officers.[8] Lieutenant Bayly indeed somewhat confirms this viewpoint when he notes that some older officers would never speak to Wellington again after Sultanpettah Tope.

Yet, nonetheless overall militarily the energetic assault that Harris led across country to swiftly capture Seringapatam on 3 May 1799 can be seen as both an influence upon Wellington's own early independent operations and specifically his later approach to siege works. Wellington's unapologetic presumption would unsurprisingly appear to have caused a further major rift with General Baird immediately after the siege: Wellington now inveigled for himself the inaugural appointment of city governor for Seringapatam, rather than the more senior brigade officer. The arrival of Lord Mornington as the new Governor General had certainly cast a distinct shadow of nepotism over Harris's command. Indeed, the Duke of York snubbed the unfortunate General Harris over the incident two years later in England, after asking, 'Pray, General Harris, what reason had you for superseding General Baird in the command of Seringapatam and giving it to a junior officer?'[9] Harris stammered an excuse, but the Duke knew there to be no reason other than favouritism for Wellington, propelled by his powerful brother. This event appears to confirm a degree of hostility from the Duke of York towards Wellington that was still evident in 1815. While in India, when emulating if not surpassing the drive of his elder brother, Wellington clearly displayed a temperament with the strongest of aspirational attributes, and which would brook no hindrance to the progress of his chosen military career. His associated aloof personal reticence doubtless made it all too easy for his contemporaries to see only an aristocratic military amateur whose small successes could readily be explained away as the result of political favour.

In April 1800 Wellington, with a garrison of seven battalions of troops based at Seringapatam, was faced by rebellion in Mysore. He was opposed by an army of up to 40,000 men, formed largely from remnants of Tipu's forces and led by the charismatic leader Dhoondiah Vagh. In chasing down Dhoondiah, Wellington in his first operation as an independent commander practised what he described as 'light and quick' operational tactics.[10] He captured various hills forts from Dhoondiah, and with a first success in the field, stated on 30 July: 'I have taken and destroyed Doondiah's baggage and six guns, and driven into the Malpoorba [where they were to drown] about five thousand people'; his belligerent ambition certainly outweighed moral rectitude. Indeed, recalling the events in 1841, the *Chartist Circular* newspaper referred to Wellington as a 'cold unfeeling monster'.[11] On 1 August 1800 Wellington with 1,000 troops caught up with Dhoondiah himself at Conaghul, to kill him and defeat his remaining force of 5,000 men. Wellington has received much praise for the energetic campaign, in which he certainly displayed an attention to the importance of mobility and logistics, as learnt from Harris, and which in turn allowed unremitting aggression. These attributes would be seen again in India just three years later.

In 1803 as a recently promoted major general, Wellington was given command by Lord Mornington of an army to oppose the hostile Scindia of the Maratha Confederacy. The Marathas were a major independent Indian power made up of five ruling princes that had regularly engaged in civil war. Once again Wellington's command came at the expense of a more senior officer, this time the newly promoted Lieutenant General James Stuart, who had succeeded General Harris. With the news of Wellington's appointment Stuart informed the Madras government that he would resign, due to the implicit lack of confidence shown. He was not alone: General Baird also was sufficiently aggrieved to resign in disgust and prepare to return home. It may be seen that such blatant partiality was not automatically accepted as admissible by Wellington's contemporaries. In the subsequent campaign, as the unabashed Wellington advanced from Madras with 10,000 troops, a secondary contingent of 9,000 men under Colonel James Stevenson would advance from the more northerly Hyderabad province. Wellington was ordered to link up with Stevenson as soon as possible and to avoid hostilities; the Governor General believed a mere show of British force would bring peace to the Marathas. Wellington otherwise felt the situation more ambiguous, and since he had been awarded discretionary powers by his brother, was soon disingenuously writing, 'I offered you [the Marathas] peace [. . .] you have chosen war, and are responsible for all consequences'.[12] Wellington's mixed British and Indian army firstly captured the enemy fort at Ahmednuggar on 8 August, to ensure a convenient supply base. Here Wellington first encountered the young Lieutenant Colin Campbell who would become something of a friend, as well as an ADC in Portugal. Without waiting for Stevenson, Wellington thereafter duly raced to converge upon and subsequently defeat the main Maratha force of 50,000 men at Assaye on 23 September. He had just 7,000 regular troops, though supported by 5,000 irregular cavalry. This was Wellington's first major victory, but at the cost of approximately 25 per cent of his engaged troops; far greater losses than the British were accustomed to suffering in India. Wellington's intelligence-gathering, or the interpretation of it, had been deficient and he had certainly misjudged his enemy. He disingenuously wrote: 'These circumstances, and the vast loss which I sustained, make it clear that we ought not to attack them again, unless we have something nearer an equality of numbers.'[13] His leadership here has been described as showing 'cognitive dissonance': namely he preferred his preconceived enemy to that reported by the available intelligence.[14] Wellington's disesteem for his native opponent coupled with unmistakable impetuosity when striving for both a victory and personal distinction meant the battle was the closest of engagements. Yet, Scindia was confounded by the defeat at Assaye and with the forces of Wellington and Stevenson having combined, there followed an easy British victory at Argaum on 29 November. The war was subsequently brought to an end by taking the Maratha fortresses of Gawilghur, with great bloodshed, on 15 December 1803.

Wellington was certainly, if temporarily, shocked by the British losses at Assaye; as proportionally heavy as any he would ever encounter in the Peninsula. Yet, in his cool conceit he also likely concluded from the events of 1803 that swift aggression could offset many, if not all shortcomings. His Indian experience had doubtless given him a huge range of experiences and responsibilities beyond his years. War in India had made the man: 'I understood as much of military matters as I have ever done since or do now'; Wellington would reflect in 1838.[15] Yet, his correspondence regarding India and its inhabitants is routinely unsparing in its reactionary tone, just as his future correspondence would be with regard to the people and environment of Portugal and Spain. Nevertheless, as a largely self-taught, original military talent, he had assimilated specific lessons regarding the employment of infantry, cavalry and artillery. Speed and aggression, backed by carefully administered logistics were his watchwords of command.

Wellington returned to Britain from India in 1805, still aged only 36. The fact that this coincided with Lord Mornington's recall was no coincidence. Mornington was replaced by Lord Charles Cornwallis, a previous Governor General from 1786–93, but asked now by government to specifically curb the expansionist and unprincipled activity instigated by the Wellesley brothers. Wellington knew that with a new and less sympathetic Governor General, his victories would hardly assuage the bad feeling of his fellow officers in India; retribution was a strong potentiality. Yet, thanks to prize money received, Wellington was financially secure, a major general and newly a Knight of the Bath. With his elder brother Richard, now appointed Marquess Wellesley and certainly a rising star of the Tory party, patronage ensured Wellington's own entry into the House of Commons, and in 1807 he was further appointed as Chief Secretary to the Lord Lieutenant of Ireland. Otherwise his early political career was unremarkable; it chiefly revolved around defending Richard from the charges of corruption and high-handedness that had followed him home from India. Before long their younger brother William Wellesley-Pole, after a brief naval career, would be charged with covering up corruption within the Admiralty, where he served from 1807–9; so that the whole Wellesley family certainly had a more than somewhat questionable reputation. In parallel Wellington's career within the military continued, and he spent the three winter months of December 1805 to February 1806 again in Hanover, eleven years after his first foreign expedition had ended there. This British deployment was soon recalled without episode in the wake of news of the Emperor Napoleon's greatest victory over the Austrians and Russians at Austerlitz on 2 December 1806. Thereafter, in July 1807 Wellington was next appointed to command the Reserve of light troops upon a military expedition to Copenhagen, designed to neutralize the Danish fleet. This was an important and prominent role for him, though patently less impressive than the autonomy he had held in India. With some 25,000 men overall, the mission was led by Lieutenant General Lord William Cathcart, with Sir Harry Burrard as his deputy. They arrived separately from the troops, in a scenario which would unfortunately be replicated in Portugal in 1808. One other notable participant, as divisional commander, was Lieutenant General, now Sir David Baird, Wellington's nemesis from India, who was unfortunately wounded at Copenhagen. Also upon the expedition was Lieutenant Colonel George Murray, acting as QMG, a role he would conspicuously fill in the Peninsula. The light troops under Wellington's command were to be the same regiments that subsequently formed his Light Brigade in the Peninsula, and which in the Peninsula would be routinely to the fore. At Copenhagen they were conspicuous on 29 August when Wellington's reserves were dispatched to see off a Danish militia force attempting to disrupt the British position; Wellington readily undertook this task. With a subsequent bombardment of Copenhagen, the city duly capitulated on 7 September, and possession was taken of the Danish fleet.

During the timescale since returning from India, Wellington continued to go out of his way to enhance his prominence and personal reputation; to gain recognition for his military aspirations from the Tory government and specifically the Secretary of State for War, Lord Castlereagh. Indeed, he had threatened to resign his commission if not included upon the Copenhagen expedition.[16] Promoted to lieutenant general in April 1808, on 14 June Wellington was given command of the 9,000-man 'disposable force', based primarily at Cork, which became the nucleus of the expeditionary army for service in Portugal. Of the more than 130 lieutenant generals on the Army List, Wellington was fourth from the bottom, but his indefatigable ambition and lobbying had achieved its goal. His military credentials nonetheless rested principally upon his years of Indian service, which many of his contemporaries would certainly have judged as inadequate for the examination of leadership that lay ahead. He was scarcely known to Sir David Dundas, and was not among the influential group of young officers known as the 'scientific soldiers'. His contemporaries were thus still inclined to see him as an aristocratic amateur for whom contacts and political favour had ensured his success to date.

As France bestrode Europe, Britain's last remaining Continental allies were Sweden, Sicily and Portugal; all three countries led by monarchs of dubious mental stability: Gustav IV Adolph (1778–1837), King of Sweden; Ferdinand III (1751–1825), King of Sicily; and Maria I (1734–1816), Queen of Portugal. On 28 July 1807 France, backed by Spain, 'invited' Portugal to break her alliance with Britain. This implicit ultimatum was duly refused by a resolute Portugal. Thus, at the end of November 1807, 22,000 French troops would invade Portugal and occupy Lisbon, largely unopposed. The royal family and ruling elite of Portugal fled overseas to their colony of Brazil, where they would remain until 1821. Deceitfully, in March 1808 there followed the brazen occupation by French troops of Madrid and the Spanish royals were forced to abdicate. Napoleon would seize the throne of his erstwhile ally and install his brother, Joseph, as King of Spain in August. The key driving force behind these actions was Napoleon's Continental System, by which he sought to embargo British trade to the European Continent that he now dominated. Both Portugal and Spain thus appealed to Britain for assistance.

A message to the government sent by Admiral Cotton, RN, when sailing off the Portuguese coast, dated 30 June 1808, indicated that the French General Junot had only 4,000 troops actually at Lisbon, and that a superior force, speedily landed, could easily retake the capital. After various abortive proposals involving the dispatch of forces to South America, Lord Castlereagh now had a target for the 'disposable force' closer to home.* The choice of Lisbon also had strong support within the Royal Navy, due to the attributes of the Portuguese harbour and the potential ease of transport for supplies. The civilian government ministers had previously suggested that any expeditionary army should operate from Cádiz in conjunction with the Spanish forces being organized there under General Francisco Castaños. The Spanish had other field armies based in the north and east of the country which in 1808 would total in excess of 100,000 men and whose numbers would rise to some 160,000 by 1812. Despite repeated setbacks over the years of battle against the French, Spanish armies were always larger than the combined British and Portuguese forces. The Spanish initially in fact were to tell Wellington that they had no need of his assistance, just British arms, equipment and money. Theirs however was an outworn army of the eighteenth century, barely influenced by the latest innovations in warfare, yet their sheer numbers and unfailing resistance always tied down the French invaders. Meanwhile, Portugal's capital, Lisbon, beckoned to Castlereagh; it housed a tenth of the Portuguese population, it was the major port and location of the country's arsenal; indeed, it was the key to control of the country. The British government formally wrote to Wellington: 'His Majesty is graciously pleased to confide to you the fullest discretion to act according to circumstances

---

* See Appendix F, for the composition of the British 'disposable force'.

for the benefit of his service.'[17] Wellington went to war with command discretion, but his available forces and his personal authority both had limitations in relation to the context of subsequent years.

Major General Brent Spencer, described as a, 'good hearted, brave and gallant officer, but nothing more', would augment Wellington's force with his troops sent from Cádiz.[18] The two generals initially appear to have worked well together, though in time Wellington would write scathingly of him. As senior major general, Spencer become Wellington's second-in-command, but otherwise had no defined role in the Peninsular Army: 'I told him I did not know what the words "second in command" meant [. . .] that I alone commanded the army [. . .] I would have no second-in-command in the sense of his having anything like [. . .] superintending control'.[19] Arriving with Spencer, Wellington received Lieutenant Colonel George Tucker as AG, and Lieutenant Colonel James Bathurst as QMG. Both made a good impression; the quick-tempered Bathurst proved his efficiency by solving any and all logistical problems during the campaign and became Wellington's MS in 1809. Tucker died in a shipwreck on the way home from Coruña, Spain in early 1809. Wellington's MS in 1808 was Lieutenant Colonel Henry Torrens, known at the time as 'Happy Harry', and described as an 'immensely likeable man'.[20] Torrens would be promoted after 1808 to MS to the C-in-C, Horse Guards, where he continued to support Wellington for the rest of the war. He would placate many an argument; his discretion precluded any lasting rift between the acerbic Wellington and his superiors. Captain Colin Campbell, Wellington's compatriot from India, arrived with him as senior ADC. In 1808 all of these staff roles were professionally filled, and it is similarly hard to fault the individual generals of brigade.

Major Generals Rowland Hill and Ronald Ferguson were the most senior brigade commanders, while the remaining four brigades were led by brigadier generals. Hill received positive report from all parties, be they subordinate officers such as Ensign L'Estrange, who describes him as 'invariably kind', or enlisted men.[21] He lacked the self-importance of many, yet displayed the competence to become Wellington's best regarded subordinate. One of his notebooks quotes Proverbs 15.1: 'A soft answer turneth away wrath', and this appears to have been his outlook on life. He was always cool and courteous; self-effacing even to his own detriment.[22] Wellington had written to Hill: 'I rejoice at the prospect I have before me of serving again with you.'[23] They had previously served together in the 1794 Flanders campaign, and had last met in 1805, dining together at Mrs Chitty's hostelry at Deal, when both were en route to Hanover. Ferguson was likewise an experienced soldier, though known as a vehement Whig to Wellington's Tory; nonetheless, he and Wellington were close enough to travel home convivially together at the close of the campaign. Ill health would mean that Ferguson did not serve beyond the year. Otherwise Brigadier General Miles Nightingall of the 3rd Brigade impressed Wellington in 1808, so to be described as 'defeatist and hypochondriac' after the briefest return to the Peninsula in 1811 appears highly excessive.[24] He commanded a brigade within the 1st Division for just five months of 1811 before taking up a proffered appointment in Bengal. Barnard Bowes of the 4th Brigade was later praised by Wellington as an officer 'highly deserving of [. . .] confidence', but who heroically died in the taking of the Salamanca forts in 1812.[25] James Catlin Craufurd commanded the 5th Brigade until his death from fever in 1810. Wellington again thought enough of him to lobby the government to provide a widow's pension; contrary to the standard of the time, when a pension was normally paid only after death in action.[26] Lastly, the 6th or Light Brigade was commanded by Henry Fane, the well-connected, 29-year-old grandson of the Earl of Westmorland. This was his first campaign and he went on to serve throughout the Peninsular War, primarily commanding a brigade of cavalry and garnering praise from compatriots as a cavalry general of merit.[27] Wellington's brigade commanders can overwhelmingly be seen to be competent professionals, practised in the manoeuvre of troops.

Wellington sailed from Britain on HMS *Crocodile* on 12 July, for the start of almost six years campaigning in the Peninsula: the interlude over winter 1808–9 marked his sole return to England. On 1 August his 10,297 troops began to disembark at Mondego Bay, at the mouth of the Mondego River, some 100 miles north of Lisbon and halfway to the second city of Oporto. This was a largely safe and suitable setting chosen on the advice of Admiral Cotton, though the cavalry did struggle to land horses onto the open beach. The location also avoided the risk of immediate French opposition, as it was known that much of the country was increasingly up in arms and the distracted occupiers were concentrating upon the retention of Lisbon. Wellington's troops took 5 days to disembark; Spencer with 5,336 men would arrive on 5 August and take a further 3 days. The newly Combined force under Wellington in total comprised fifteen battalions of infantry, with only the 20th LD cavalry regiment led by Lieutenant Colonel Charles Taylor. The cavalry had to rely upon the provision of 60 Portuguese horses to ensure mounts for all 240 troopers. Effective artillery consisted of just three batteries, eighteen guns, led by Lieutenant Colonel William Robe, with other guns brought by Spencer immobile due again to the lack of horses. Robe wrote to Wellington on 5 August asking assistance with regards to the inadequacies of the transport provision organized by the Board of Ordnance. Wellington at this juncture replied that he could not interfere in Ordnance matters.[28] Captain Howard Elphinstone, the engineering officer present, purchased a local mule for transport, due to the dearth of horses. Yet, the army's morale was high: 'We have some of the finest troops that ever were seen and several well informed officers on the Staff that may be of great service in organizing the Spaniards [*sic*].'[29] Practical experience of campaigning was the chief deficiency.

As Spencer left Cádiz, he had forwarded revised intelligence to London indicating that Junot had now concentrated 20,000 troops at Lisbon, rather than the prior low estimate. Horse Guards reacted by immediately directing the troops of Lieutenant General Sir John Moore to Portugal from Sweden, with a senior lieutenant general, Sir Hew Dalrymple, designated to take overall command. Dalrymple would bring with him his deputy, Sir Harry Burrard, as well as Lieutenant Generals Sir John Hope and Alexander Mackenzie Fraser, all senior to Wellington. These troops with associated reinforcements would ultimately bring British strength in Portugal close to 40,000 men. Wellington was both angry and positively underwhelmed by the revised estimate of French strength, and his petulant ego was equally unimpressed to hear of the impending arrival of superseding authority: 'I hope I shall have beat Junot before any of them arrive, and then they may do as they please with me.'[30] However, Spencer's intelligence was certainly close to the truth, as subsequent events would show there now to be 26,000 French troops in Portugal overall, with Lisbon as their focus.[31] Wellington, exactly as had occurred in India, was predisposed to underestimate enemy strength; with unwavering ambition he continued to strive to advance his own personal agenda.

Wellington constituted his battalions into six brigades, each with a half-battery of guns attached. His general order for 9 August read: 'The army will march to-morrow [. . .] the mounted dragoons to lead, followed by the 3rd, 5th and 4th brigades of infantry [. . .] The reserve artillery and depot mules etc. will follow the infantry; then the baggage of the headquarters.'[32] The meagre 240 cavalry troopers were to patrol, form reserve and be employed as escort for the supply wagons on the road south to Lisbon. On 11 August the army met with the Portuguese forces of General Bernadino Freire at Leiria in central Portugal. Wellington had decided to stay near the coast and in contact with the British fleet, from where supply, and security, derived; Freire with 5,000 men wished to operate inland for his own supply. Wellington thus seemingly argued with Freire about future plans, with both being intent upon retaining freedom of action. Wellington swiftly and all too typically made a derogatory personal appraisal of Freire and warned London, 'If you should determine to form a Portuguese army, you must, if possible, have nothing to do with Gen. Freire.'[33] Freire nonetheless did graciously lend Wellington 1,700 Portuguese infantry and 200 cavalry, led by Colonel Nicholas Trant, a British officer in Portuguese service, and of whom Wellington commented: 'A very good officer, but as drunken a dog as ever lived.'[34] Wellington's relations with allies would be consistently awkward throughout the war. His focus was always upon his own perception of objectives, and lacked any empathy or compromise with others. One observer has gone so far as to accuse Wellington of subsequently inflicting severe, off-handed 'military despotism' upon Portugal; indeed, evidence of a political indifference and ineptitude exceeding anything he had demonstrated in India.[35] In 1808 his strategic judgement was correct, but he would certainly use his allies with disdain. It is assuredly not unreasonable to consider that the Portuguese and the Spanish allies would suffer in subsequent years, just as would his officers and troops, from Wellington's single-minded and unrelenting leadership.

With a shortage of cavalry, there was an emphasis upon the importance of light troops in the march south, though Wellington's intelligence of the enemy must have relied heavily upon the Portuguese. General Fane's Light Brigade duly led the advance to first contact with the French, which was made some 70 miles north of Lisbon. Indeed, Wellington combined the individual light companies of the line battalions at brigade level to facilitate command and maximize further the army's skirmishing ability.[36] The first shots of Wellington's Peninsular War occurred at Óbidos on 15 August when French outposts were encountered: General Junot had sent General Henri Delaborde with 4,400 men from Lisbon to observe and delay the British. The French troops of occupation have been described as 'skinny youths, sickly and in rags [. . .] others scarcely know how to hold their weapons'; no comparison with the soldiers of Napoleon's victorious *Grand Armée*.[37] Previously Junot had also dispatched General Louis Loison with 7,000 men to re-open severed communications with France. Loison had marched to the Spanish border before he received an urgent message recalling him. When exchanging shots with Delaborde's troops, Lieutenant Ralph Bunbury of the 95th Rifles became the first British officer killed in action during the Peninsular War. Fane's riflemen of the 60th and 95th Regiments again skirmished with the French *tirailleurs* on 16 August and Spencer, with the vanguard, had to retrieve the over-enthusiastic skirmishers from a sharp rebuff, after they had been drawn onto the French line infantry. Despite the previous words of Wellington, Spencer as second-in-command does appear to have assumed necessary control of the leading troops here, and to positive effect. After ambushing British skirmishers, Delaborde's further successful tactic was to make the British repeatedly deploy for battle before again retiring. This stratagem was undertaken in the 5 miles between Óbidos and the heights which rose some 100m above the approach road south of Roliça. Thereafter, on 17 August, in closing upon Delaborde, Wellington advanced in a wide arc with the wings of the army extended to ideally outflank and envelop the enemy. Having retired to the Columbeira heights, Delaborde chose now to stand and fight in this strong defensive position. The subsequent battle had Wellington outnumbering Delaborde by almost four to one, yet the French defensive tactics fought Wellington to a standstill; to the extent that contemporary French commentators called the battle a French victory.[38] Delaborde might well have expected that Loison with his troops would arrive from the east in time to provide decisive support, but this did not happen; it would be the day after the battle when the two forces actually united. Wellington still failed to use his numerical superiority to envelop the French army's flanks; to the west by Trant's Portuguese, or to the east by Ferguson's 2nd Brigade.

Wellington subsequently noted that: 'Mistakes prevented it [the battle] from producing the entire destruction of La Borde's Corps. The first that General

Ferguson was ordered to descend the heights instead of continuing his march to turn the enemy's left [. . .] This was not committed by me.'[39] Wellington had intended to assault the French centre only when both turning movements had developed, but now his centre led the attack. Ferguson abandoned the turning movement upon receipt of orders, of uncorroborated origin, but for which no subsequent criticism arose. On the other flank Trant's Portuguese wandered into the hills without coming to grips with the enemy. Wellington thus attacked the French position directly; somewhat more directly than intended. He had ordered a frontal advance by Hill and Nightingall, but then noted: 'The second [mistake] was that Lake [. . .] hurried his attack before [. . .] other troops ascended the other passes to support him. This I did all I could to prevent.'[40] Colonel George Lake, leading the 29th Regiment of Nightingall's Brigade, enthusiastically advanced up the wrong gully and in consequence combat commenced prematurely; he found his brigade under a rain of fire from both flanks. Hill and Nightingall both needed to use their initiative to hurry troops forward urgently in his support. It took 2 hours of concerted frontal assault by their respective troops to gain a foothold upon the crest of Delaborde's defensive ridge. During the attack Robe's artillery, provided supporting fire and directed two shrapnel shells at a French battery; the first such shots fired in the Peninsula. Colonel Shrapnel's new spherical case shot would have continued success, such that by 1813 regular ammunition stocks were 30 per cent such spherical case, to 60 per cent round-shot and 10 per cent common case.[41] This counter-battery fire is notable since Wellington later prohibited its use as being overly wasteful of ammunition. Wellington's control of events may certainly be seen as less stringent than would be the case in later years. The British troops persevered in the attack: 'The enemy made three more gallant [counter-]attacks [. . .] with a view to covering the retreat of his defeated army [. . .] he succeeded due to my want of cavalry'.[42] Such comment was disingenuous, since Delaborde in fact had only 300 cavalry to oppose Wellington's 240 troopers of the 20th LD, as well as the 200 Portuguese irregular cavalry. The British cavalry was 'shown' to the enemy, but otherwise took no part in the action. Wellington conceivably wanted to maintain this limited force of cavalry intact, while the battlefield terrain, beyond the main road south to Lisbon may in reality have proved more of a handicap for cavalry. Wellington's losses in battle were 479 men overall. Delaborde lost maybe 600 men, but including 226 Swiss troops, who in their long red coats deserted to the British.[43]

Delaborde was able to extricate his force successfully and was not pressed at all in the retreat. Wellington wrote to Lord Castlereagh praising the infantry, 'for the manner in which they conducted the different attacks'. No mention was made of the cavalry or of the artillery, beyond: 'I have every reason to be satisfied'; a perfunctory reference that became all too familiar as the war continued.[44] Wellington had failed to coordinate the envelopment of the enemy force's flanks. The primary eastern flank march was mistakenly aborted, and the lack of any subsequent rebuke suggests that the mistake involved Wellington himself; it is hard to see otherwise. He would have been aware that Loison might arrive unexpectedly, so faulty intelligence was potentially involved. This thus could be claimed as another's error. The subsequent frontal assault prevailed, but not before Delaborde's telling defence required initiative and tactical ability from Hill and Nightingall. Wellington attacked with the speed and resolve he had shown in India though his plan had unravelled; he was ultimately responsible for the mishaps. He thereafter made no effort to pursue, despite the eagerness shown by his fresh troops throughout the combat. Battle losses during the Napoleonic Wars were habitually equal, and hence battle inconclusive, unless a retreat was exploited.[45] Major John Colborne, Sir John Moore's MS, subsequently wrote home that, 'more bravery than generalship was shown'.[46]

On 19 August the first reinforcements, namely the brigade of Brigadier General Robert Anstruther, disembarked at Maceira Bay, south of Roliça, joined next day by that of Brigadier General Wroth Acland; together bringing a total of over 4,000 troops. Wellington, after the battle, had turned the army off the main road to Lisbon at Vimeiro in order to cover the new landings. Moore's 15,000 further reinforcements from Sweden were expected soon thereafter. Next day several French cavalry patrols came close to the British positions, and one even penetrated onto the beach where reinforcements were landing.[47] This doubtless alerted Wellington to the proximity of the main French army such that he issued orders for the troops to sleep at the ready and to be under arms at 3:00am on 21 August.[48]

When General Junot attacked at Vimeiro he had no more than 14,000 troops to oppose the 17,000 present under Wellington's command. He had felt the need to leave a large garrison of 6,500 men at Lisbon to maintain control over the unruly civilian population, and would also likely be unaware of the scale of British reinforcement.[49] At dawn on 21 August the French were seen to be approaching from the east; Wellington had posted his army on a line of heights facing southwards where the local roadway led to Torres Vedras and ultimately Lisbon. The brigades of Fane and Anstruther guarded the village of Vimeiro where the hills were cut by the River Maceira and the north–south road. The other brigades were either aligned to the west of Vimeiro or in reserve. At news of Junot's approach Wellington had to speedily redeploy his army to face eastwards, where in fact the more major road from Lisbon ran. Nonetheless, all French movements were suitably warned by either the limited cavalry vedettes or Fane's riflemen; no enemy surprise was achieved.

The French firstly attacked to pin Fane and Anstruther at the isolated mound of Vimeiro village and thereafter further north-east against Ferguson and Nightingall's brigades, still aiming to turn the British left wing. They attacked with a thick screen of *tirailleurs* preceding battalion columns, but nowhere with success.

French General Maximilien Foy later recorded that the British artillery's shrapnel was like, 'black rain' and, 'the shrapnel-shells at the first discharge struck down the files of a platoon, and then exploded in the platoon that followed'.[50] Since Robe could only deploy three guns per brigade, there is evidence here of the shock effect of shrapnel. Robe would write to Colonel Shrapnel: 'your Spherical Case [. . .] is admirable to the whole army [. . .] I told Sir A. Wellesley I meant to write to you [. . .] his answer was "you may say anything you please, you cannot say too much, for never was artillery fired with better effect"'. It would thus soon become a British artilleryman's dictum that: 'No [French] column could withstand a well-directed fire of shrapnel shells for twenty minutes.'[51] With the enemy repulsed, Wellington, possibly via Fane, ordered Colonel Taylor's dragoons and the Portuguese cavalry to attack the French left flank; though the Portuguese quickly fell back after receiving enemy fire.[52] Charging into the retreating enemy grenadiers caused appreciable damage until French reserve cavalry counter-charged, killing Taylor and defeating the outnumbered dragoons; a 'heroic' defeat observed eyewitness Rifleman Harris.[53] The 20th LD later admitted to misplaced enthusiasm, but with the limited available cavalry numbers it is easy to see how trouble resulted. Against French cavalry that totalled 2,251 troopers, in this instance it was a clear mistake to commit the 20th LD, and for which Wellington must take responsibility.

Yet, General Junot's infantry had been readily repulsed with heavy loss, likely up to 2,000 men, while half the British force was only lightly engaged and losses were only 720 men. Wellington wrote: 'This is the only action I have been in, in which everything passed as it was directed.'[54] Junot had relied upon surprise, mobility and the combat experience of his own troops to prevail, none of which proved significant; this was a battle against the odds for him. For Wellington, being attacked upon excellent defensive terrain by a smaller enemy force merely enhanced British morale; the hills that were defended, historian Dupuy suggests, enhanced the effective defensive strength by some 30 per cent.[55] For the first time in the Peninsula Wellington also ordered the use of reverse hill slopes to protect his infantry from enemy fire, a tactic that he would routinely use defensively thereafter; and the arrival of the forces of Anstruther and Acland had certainly been fortuitous. The hardest point of manoeuvre was to correct his initially erroneous dispositions; his brigadiers fully controlled the tactics of battle thereafter. They were the individuals who made the final tactical dispositions in defence at Vimeiro. It was the success of their endeavours that flowed back up the chain of command to ensure Wellington's success. Both troops and generals showed a level of effectiveness that confounded Junot; there could be no French claims of victory here.

Lieutenant General Burrard arrived during the course of the combat and subsequently forbade any pursuit of the beaten enemy, citing the perceived strength of the intact French cavalry arm. This order was confirmed on the morning of 22 August when Lieutenant General Dalrymple arrived and assumed overall command; admittedly his first active command for some fourteen years. Wellington did not act supportively or with any degree of tact, rather the opposite. His strident and opinionated nature immediately generated animosity with a superior officer somewhat confounded by arriving close upon battle, and of which he knew nothing. It has been recorded that Dalrymple received none of the letters that Wellington had sent to him since the start of the campaign.[56] Wellington commented: 'I had reason to believe [. . .] that he [Dalrymple] was prejudicial against any opinions which I should give him'.[57] He was keen not to be seen as alone in this opposition, writing: 'General Spencer and Sir Hew did not agree very well when they were at Gibraltar together; and poor Spencer is very low indeed.'[58] Yet, under the circumstances, it is unsurprising that Dalrymple judged the extremely forthright and impertinent Wellington with distinct suspicion. It may be noted that Wellington expressed his opinions in a manner that he never allowed his own subordinates to do in his presence. While not Wellington's military equal, Dalrymple had first-hand knowledge of the Peninsula and was known to have good existing contacts with Spanish generals such as Francisco Castaños.[59] It had been Castaños who provided the unexpected Spanish success at Baylen, on 19 July 1808, when a French army under the command of General Pierre Dupont managed to get itself surrounded and duly surrendered. Dalrymple's appointment was not simply crass misapplication by Horse Guards as it is usually adjudged.

Major General Sir Edward Paget, serving under Moore, wrote: 'Wellesley now wished to push on [. . .] with a view to cutting off from Lisbon the French corps. This might very possibly have succeeded [. . .] His opinion however, was overruled.'[60] The fact that both Burrard and subsequently Dalrymple expressed concern regarding the preponderance of the French cavalry and refused to advance has been routinely condemned. Yet, the large French cavalry force was undefeated, and Wellington would never subsequently show any predilection to incautious pursuit; his outrage in 1808 hints at self-serving bluster. Nevertheless, the French main infantry body was defeated, and also isolated from Spain by Freire's Portuguese troops. Thus, General François Kellermann contacted the British camp on 22 August to request terms for a truce, and from which the Convention of Cintra duly resulted: a ceasefire signed at the Palace of Queluz, Cintra on 30 August. The hugely controversial easy terms that were agreed provided the French with free repatriation to Rochefort, along with all baggage and booty; transported back to France by British shipping. General Hope oversaw the French departure between 10 and 22 September; in all 25,747 men out of 30,250 Imperial troops that had been sent to Portugal since 1807. It was Kellermann who suggested that Wellington actually sign the convention as both his equal in rank and also a British government minister: he was still the Chief Secretary for Ireland. But, by agreeing to do so Wellington was most heavily criticized at home; Cintra had quickly become a byword for folly in the press. Even in the contemporaneous poetry of Lord Byron, *Childe Harold's Pilgrimage,* one can read the line 'Britannia sickens, Cintra! at thy name [. . .]'. Wellington should not have been too surprised: eight years earlier, in 1800, the British government had rejected out of hand the proffered Convention of El Arish which sought to repatriate French troops from Egypt. The personal criticism he received would be the harshest of lessons for an apparently still callow Wellington, a situation that he would assiduously strive to avoid in all subsequent conduct. General Hope, in Lisbon, was just one military contemporary who criticized Wellington's actions as having 'outstripped all common rules and even the most necessary measures of prudence'.[61] Nevertheless, despite the ambivalent finale and hullabaloo, Portugal was freed from the French, who would now fully evacuate the country.

Wellington the military commander would probably still have been buoyed that he had the measure of the French at Vimeiro. Indeed, Napier rapturously and markedly over-aggrandizes the battle and Wellington personally with the comment: 'Notwithstanding the small numbers of the opposing armies, success would have ranked Sir Arthur high among the eminent commanders of the world, if he had never performed any other exploit.'[62] The British forces had certainly performed well and displayed effectiveness against a decidedly overconfident Junot. Wellington's own habitual and overbearing criticisms were here reserved solely for his superiors. His army had typically been concentrated, which readily allowed for the necessity of re-facing to block the true focus of the French assault. He appears to have spent most of the battle to the east with Ferguson and Nightingall, where he doubtless ordered the reverse-slope stratagem. Commentators again routinely claim this tactic as of Wellington's invention, and while it will forever be associated with him, it had been used previously by the Austrian army. Wellington had read Archduke Charles von Hapsburg's *Principles of War* where it is noted.[63] Weapon effectiveness and troop reliability had proved sound. His brigade commanders had worked well together, and the integration and co-operation between artillery and infantry ensured mutual support; Robe's artillery achieved all that was possible. The cavalry has subsequently been criticized for its charge at Vimeiro, but in reality it was a 'one-shot' weapon that should not have received such an order. The size of the cavalry force precluded both decisive action and the formation of a reserve; which later was Wellington's approved methodology in battle, to ensure the cavalry always had backup. It should not have been used at all, but rather kept intact. The cavalry's disordering subsequently affected screening and security; after the battle Kellermann was able to ride right up to the infantry pickets of the British army to request terms before being challenged. This very fact gives weight to General Burrard's concerns. The British government had historically penny-pinched with the cavalry, as well as with artillery cannon, and the shortages would take time to make good. The French dragoons had the conditioning and experience still lacking in their British counterparts.

Having been supplanted in command, on 20 September Wellington resigned and quit Lisbon, apparently untroubled by any perception of 'petulance' from his perceived unwillingness to be subordinated: 'I am aware that there is a party which will run me down for coming away; but I have never cared much for what people say of me [. . .]'.[64] He recorded his views upon the military situation in Iberia for Lord Castlereagh on 25 September; mutual confidence held sway between them. This proposition formed the basis for the official direction given to Sir John Moore for subsequent strategy in 1808–9: to co-ordinate action with the northern Spanish armies in Castile, aiming to sever communications between France and occupied Madrid. Oman lauds this communication as prescient of Wellington's genius in foretelling operations, but which yet harbingered Moore's death and the destruction of his army by Napoleon's forces. Dalrymple similarly and previously had proposed that a British army should operate in the north of Spain. He also pre-empted Wellington by some four years in recommending in parallel that: 'Accurate information should be obtained in regard to the communications leading to the ports of the Asturias and those of Galicia and the suitability of transporting troops and supplies along them from the coast to the Army.'[65] Again, it may be adjudged that in the record of Wellington's career, as a result of his successes, all good ideas have been deemed to be his alone.

The Convention of Cintra was duly and formally reviewed at a Court of Inquiry, which sat in the Royal Hospital, Chelsea between 14 November and 27 December 1808. Here Wellington again showed his antipathy and exasperation with Dalrymple and Burrard by cross-questioning both superior officers with 'acidity and a complete want of deference'.[66] For Burrard and Dalrymple, the specific case for their defence at the Inquiry was made by Lord Henry Petty. As recorded in *The Times*, he stressed that it certainly was not their fault that they had arrived at the climax of the campaign, with no knowledge of either the army or the country. Notably, the alarm they had felt at the strength of the French cavalry was reasonable and the British government itself should accept a degree of blame that there was a lack of cavalry.[67] Brent Spencer was among witnesses from the army, who firstly spoke loyally in favour of Wellington, but whose evidence was ambivalent in that he also defended Burrard and Dalrymple. His failure to give Wellington alone the unequivocal support he demanded has been suggested as reason for the subsequent dismal relations between the two men.[68] Wellington had otherwise earlier written of Spencer: 'There never was a braver officer or one who deserves [favour] better.'[69] Wellington's sometimes capricious personal assessments and poor relationships would impact upon his command judgment in ways which may be perceived many times over the following years.

All three commanding generals were ultimately acquitted, though Dalrymple as the senior officer was rebuked for the political actions contained within the Convention's articles; a scapegoat to assuage public opinion. For Wellington acquittal was a vital and critical personal vindication. His military victories had ensured that his political mistakes were overlooked; others would take the rap for the errors for which he was at the very least partially culpable. While ensuring the continuance of his active military career, the outcome would also reinforce his future inability to accept any degree of blame, and indeed fortify his steadfast belief in his own destiny. These were personal traits with credible negative connotations which would be displayed routinely in the future. A typical comment at the time about Wellington's public persona came from Samuel Whitbread, an Opposition MP: 'I grieve for the opportunity that has been lost of acquiring national glory, but am not sorry to see the Wellesley pride a little lowered.'[70] Neutral observers like Sir Walter Scott were also left with an impression of Wellington's arrogance, calling him 'a haughty devil', and indeed observing his perceived pique at the turn of events in Portugal, which Scott suggested as having distorted his judgement.[71] Yet, the inquiry also gave Wellington's name national recognition for the first time. He would be hero to some, while for others a villain; certainly a controversial figure. For Wellington himself the acquittal was altogether a triumph for his ego.

Upon Wellington's return to England his senior officers subscribed to him a silver plate costing 1,000 guineas; a very handsome gift. As in the future, Wellington might excite admiration from his subordinates, but he never excited affection. He was respected for his decisive actions; the officers could discern a winning general, and he appears to have alienated no one beyond his superiors. Indeed, surprisingly Sir John Moore noted how Wellington had often spoken with his staff upon the progress of events in Portugal.[72] Such sentiments disconcertingly brought about the accusation of Wellington 'indulging his troops'. The most unexpectedly vituperative letter was written by Lieutenant General Thomas Graham, who would join the Peninsular Army in August 1811. This accuses Wellington of both spreading discontent with Dalrymple, and also courting popularity with the army by showing extreme familiarity with every rank in order to achieve it.[73] A degree of truth surely applies to this observation. Wellington was immensely ambitious and motivated, and the lack of what would become his trademark criticism of subordinates in 1808 suggests a calculated drive to both build his own reputation and position within the army. His own words indicate a wish to generate 'confidence and esteem' for himself.[74] He possibly hoped to emulate Moore, the army's favourite officer, where to be 'one of Sir John Moore's men' carried a distinct cachet for his troops. No British commander was ever more popular with his officers; he was described as a man of the 'purest virtue'.[75] Moore would become Wellington's ultimate successor to the Iberian command, in 1808–9. Yet, the fact that Wellington's inexperienced forces performed as cohesively as they did in 1808, without the obvious overweening control and micro-management that would later only be too apparent, has been overshadowed in the record by the major controversy that surrounded the Cintra Inquiry.

Other recognizable elements of Wellington's leadership style were nonetheless evident from the start of the 1808 campaign, and would subsequently be repeated. He had circumspectly decided that the optimum operational plan of advance was to hug the coast from where supplies and reinforcements were to be expected, while placing no reliance upon the 'disreputable' Portuguese who had suggested an alternative route. Thus ensuring security of communication maintained the well-being of his force, before the confidence of his troops could be cemented by successful offensive action. The small army was readily concentrated for the advance; continuing the 'light and quick' style of operation adopted in India, and which also emphasized secure logistical considerations. Wellington was, therefore, circumspect and orderly in the approach, until the moment to initiate combat as swiftly as possible, in knowledge of his enemy, as at Roliça. This speed may indeed have precluded the conjoining of Delaborde and Loison's individual forces. Yet, faulty intelligence also played a part at Roliça: Wellington perennially felt that he knew better than others and was likely to ignore advice or intelligence. Caution would resurface immediately after this initial engagement as he made no effort to exploit the outcome. Wellington's subsequent careful use of the terrain in battle at Vimeiro was not the product of any inherently defensive mindset; he simply made effective use of the available topography, as Delaborde had recently demonstrated. On the battlefield itself he always presented a cool and detached demeanour, always in control as he deployed his forces to ensure every possible advantage. The countering of French battlefield strategy by a movement of his own, while both necessary and astute at Vimeiro, would become an integral facet of Wellington's defensive tactics; his battlefield awareness was exemplary. Dalrymple's untimely arrival disrupted the army's continuity before any potential counter-stroke by Wellington. It is easy to appreciate how Dalrymple would not readily take the advice aggressively put forward by a little-known Wellington. It was certainly the competent performance of British arms overall more than Wellington's generalship that surprised Junot the most at Vimeiro. Observers in Britain were nevertheless astonished and disappointed by the concluding agreement with the French, which Wellington had put his name to: 'The common cause has suffered most grievously by this expedition to the Tagus.'[76]

Regardless of the concluding act, Wellington certainly commanded the army of 1808 in an effective manner, despite shortages and inexperience. He encountered the typical problems that all overseas leaders of the era felt: remote political interference, testing relations with allies, questionable logistics, and unreliable intelligence. He treated his subordinate generals with respect, and they markedly responded with discernible professionalism. Yet, Wellington's oft-times incautious ambition was also apparent; he was embittered against the strictures of those he held little regard for, which here included his superior officers. In typical fashion he displayed an unerring faith only in his own ability. These were shortcomings of character, even if readily forgiven by most commentators as part of Wellington's innate '*hauteur*'.[77] It would certainly not be untypical if he did not routinely share all his intentions with his generals, and unclear expectations did apparently influence the effective control of Ferguson's troops at Roliça. Nevertheless, the small and centralized army best suited Wellington's leadership style: it enabled him to keep personal control over most aspects of campaign and battle. Under his strong direction, his 'green' troops thus largely achieved all that could have been expected. Wellington would return to the command of the Peninsular Army in 1809; the major identifiable personal traits associated with his command and control would be more clearly demonstrated during the tests of the ensuing years.

Chapter 4

Wellington's Attritional Command, 1809–12

'Really when I reflect upon the characters and attainments of some of the
General Officers of this army [. . .] on whom I am to rely [. . .] I tremble'.[1]

Early 1809 duly brought Wellington's return to Lisbon, at which juncture his
capability as a general certainly still remained unproven to many contemporaries.
There would follow three years of comparative equilibrium between the British
and the opposition French forces at war in Portugal and Spain. During these years
the always assertive leadership of Wellington would more distinctly achieve the
stereotypical aspect of authoritarian control and micro-management for which he
may be recognized. Nonetheless, in parallel all arms of his army would extend their
own individual experience and capability. Independent forces had now to operate
away from Wellington and their accomplishments are worthy of dispassionate
consideration and comparison. The events during these key years throw light
upon the capability of the generals, the efficiency of troops and operations, and
ultimately the effectiveness of Wellington's leadership.

In the meantime however, Lieutenant General Sir John Moore assumed
command of the army that remained within Portugal after the recall of Generals
Dalrymple and Burrard, post-Cintra. On 20 October 1808, having received
directions from the British government he advanced into Spain with 22,000 of
the total 32,000 troops then stationed within the country. A second, reinforcing
column of 12,000 men from England, led by Wellington's rival from India,
Lieutenant General Sir David Baird, was also landed at Coruña, in north-west
Spain. Both forces were to rendezvous near Valladolid with the aim of intercepting
French communication with Madrid. However, in parallel the Emperor Napoleon,
accompanied by his Imperial Guard, had arrived unbeknown in the Peninsula with
further major reinforcements, true soldiers of the *Grand Armée*, and was intent
upon overawing or overwhelming all opposition. This was now a French striking
force of veteran troops, over 152,000 strong, in comparison with the inexperienced
conscripts which were so often the standard for their arms during much of the
war in the Peninsula. The strength and scale of Napoleon's operation forced
the headlong retreat of British forces, crushing the hopes for Moore's meagre
Spanish expedition. The demoralizing flight ended back at Coruña, where in
ultimate tragedy Moore was killed in battle on 16 January 1809. Subsequently,

26,000 British troops in Spain were fortunate to be able to re-embark and escape for home, courtesy of the Royal Navy. In contrast to Wellington's typical demeanour, throughout his short, but extraordinarily difficult tenure Moore had been known to both respect the input and discuss his operational plans with his second-in-command, General Baird, and other senior officers. Calamitously, at Coruña, after Moore's fatal wounding, Baird would also be seriously incapacitated, with the loss of his left arm, which left Lieutenant General Sir John Hope to effectively lead and manage the eventual evacuation. Nevertheless, despite the apparent ill-luck and strategic failure of the venture into Spain, what was not immediately discernible was that Moore's campaign had played its part in quite disrupting the timescale and capacity for a swift French re-conquest of Portugal.

Napoleon felt himself forced to depart from Valladolid and subsequently the Iberian Peninsula on 17 January 1809; he urgently needed to face and deal with a renewed threat from Austria on the River Danube. Battle at Coruña he left to be fought by Marshal Nicolas Soult. Certainly not all reinforcements quit Spain with Napoleon: the reinvigorated French army that he left retained specific veteran units from the great victories of 1806–7; excellent troops in no way to be discounted. Nevertheless, Spanish resistance was spreading quickly and would proliferate among all sections of society. The Spanish guerrillas were beginning to generate and inflict a catastrophic havoc among the French, be they veterans or not. Napoleon appointed his brother, Joseph, in nominal overall command of Imperial forces within Spain, and as puppet king based at the capital of Madrid. Large-scale fighting between French and Spanish armies would however also now flare on several fronts within the country simultaneously. Indeed, during the year of 1809, there would be at least nineteen other battles, sieges and significant actions between the French and Spanish forces – from Uclés fought on 13 January to Alba de Tormes on 29 November – beyond the sole action within Spain, at Talavera that would involve Wellington. For Napoleon events would assuredly prove that the communication distance between Germany and Spain was just too great for his command to work as effectively as he desired. A dispatch took twenty days to travel over 1,100 miles from Vienna to Madrid, and invariably the contents, upon arrival, would be out of date. The disparate French commanders on the spot would be largely left to their own divisive degree of collaboration. The problems of command had already sown the seeds of inevitable French defeat.

A small British garrison yet remained at Lisbon, commanded by Lieutenant General Sir John Cradock, though after Moore's campaign he initially advocated the complete withdrawal of all British troops. As French forces advanced once again upon Portugal, a wholly unsung hero of the hour was Colonel Sir Robert Wilson, commanding the Portuguese Loyal Lusitanian Legion of less than 3,000 men. Upon Moore's defeat, the Legion deployed on the eastern Portuguese frontier to screen their home territory, while also occupying the Almeida border fortress, covering the main cross-border route. Wilson thereafter bluffed the advancing French division of General Pierre Lapisse onto the defensive as his imprecise intelligence overestimated Portuguese opposition. Colonel Wilson has been described as, 'a very slippery fellow'.[2] Nevertheless, from battle at Coruña Marshal Soult marched south and through Galicia to invade northern Portugal for a second time, duly reaching Oporto on the River Douro by the end of March 1809. Here, however, any further advance stalled with the necessity to disperse his forces to hold the recalcitrant countryside; the habitual problem faced by the despised French in both Spain and Portugal. Cradock was correct when he stated that Lisbon, the Portuguese capital, was the key to the country and that the French, 'were less likely to move upon it if the British force were kept compactly together [. . .] than if it were dispersed to hold isolated positions in advance'.[3] The British government, therefore, once again showed fortitude by dispatching reinforcing brigades to Portugal led by Major Generals John Sherbrooke and Rowland Hill, in January and March of 1809 respectively; they would soon establish their base at Leiria, north of Lisbon. The British government yet wanted an overall commander with a fighting reputation; Lord Castlereagh, Secretary of State for War and Wellington's firm advocate, recommended him. The choice was supported by Wellington's own latest, positive report upon the viability of Portugal's defence, which duly gave substance to the hopes that government held.[4] A soldier's letter home read: 'Sir John Cradock has [. . .] resigned the command to Sir Arthur Wellesley [. . .] We may now expect something decisive'.[5] Wellington's typically bold conviction when others were more circumspect ensured his renewed appointment.

The Portuguese government had previously requested a British lieutenant general to reorganize and take command of their forces, which the French had endeavoured to disband during 1807–8. They had Wellington in mind, but Foreign Secretary George Canning pronounced: 'Sir Arthur is thought too good for the Portuguese – Will Doyle do?'[6] However, Sir John Doyle, a veteran of the American War of Independence, was delayed en route to London from Guernsey, where he was Lieutenant Governor and the position fell to Portuguese-speaking William Carr Beresford. Beresford had been the governor of Madeira during 1807 on behalf of the Portuguese, before serving with Moore, and he was known as both a disciplinarian and an administrator; his combat record from prior service in South America was somewhat more questionable. Nonetheless, he had Wellington's recommendation, and later would be described by him as, 'the ablest man I have yet seen with the army'.[7] He arrived in Portugal on 2 March, with the Portuguese rank of marshal. This sequence of events proved fortuitous as Doyle was senior to both Wellington and Beresford, and his involvement would certainly have led to major complications of precedence within the Peninsular Army. Wellington himself would subsequently be made Marshal General of Portugal to ensure he suitably outranked Beresford. In due course Beresford reformed the Portuguese army, he sacked incapable officers and replaced them with British officers at an enhanced rank. In April 1809 6 such incapable officers were sacked, by June 100 had gone, and by the end of 1809 the figure reached 350. The war could not have been waged without effective Portuguese involvement; their organization was Beresford's triumph.

Wellington sailed for Portugal on 15 April aboard HMS *Surveillante*.[8] After the ramifications of the 1808 campaign, before leaving he now belatedly made a point of resigning his Chief Secretaryship of Ireland. Two of his chief staff officers, AG Charles Stewart and QMG George Murray, accompanied Wellington on board ship. Charles Stewart was the half-brother of Lord Castlereagh, Wellington's patron; he had also served as AG during Moore's campaign, as well as commanding a cavalry brigade in combat. The censorious Wellington would however later dismiss him in offhand manner as a 'sad *brouillon* [muddle-headed person]'. George Murray was known to be 'pleasant and imperturbable', and whose expertise Wellington had previously seen upon the Copenhagen expedition. Murray would notably demonstrate his competence over the following year, when, for example, he ensured the production of new maps of all the operational areas of Portugal at ¼in to the mile scale. There was also aboard ship a favoured ADC, Captain Lord Fitzroy Somerset; Wellington consistently, 'preferred ability with a title to ability without'.[9] The efficient Fitzroy Somerset became MS after Bathurst in 1810, and continued as such to the end of the war, personally rising in rank to lieutenant colonel. Further notable senior staff officers arriving in Portugal were Lieutenant Generals Edward Paget and Sir William Payne. Edward Paget was the younger brother of Lord Henry Paget, later the Earl of Uxbridge, and both brothers had earned great distinction for their skillful leadership during Moore's tenure. Sir William Payne had risen to general rank through various cavalry regiments and would duly take control of Wellington's own cavalry. He would immediately please Wellington by his steeliness and by specifically interrogating the Commissariat, in magisterial manner on behalf of his troopers and their horses. Already at Lisbon, the locally promoted, now Lieutenant General Sherbrooke became second-in-command of the army; Wellington initially described him as 'a very good officer, but the most passionate man, I think, I ever knew'.[10] The fiery Sherbrooke was acquainted with Wellington from India, as were other experienced newcomers, Major Generals Stapleton Cotton and John Murray. Of Cotton, Wellington commented that he was, 'Not exactly the person I should select to command an army.'[11] His future success as a cavalry commander under Wellington's command would appear to owe something to Payne's subsequent ill health and the unavailability of Lord Henry Paget; family scandal involving his re-marriage to Wellington's sister-in-law most likely interceded to preclude his appointment. Routinely dismissed as wholly incompetent, the subsequent events of 1813 have cast a long shadow over the earlier career of General John Murray. Nevertheless, in the early war years Wellington would consistently report that, 'Sir J. Murray is a very able officer'; certainly a more positive referral than that received by the otherwise successful Cotton.[12] Upon his own arrival at Lisbon on 22 April, Wellington planned to swiftly re-establish the momentum of the previous year by attacking the nearest French force of Marshal Soult at Oporto; he had once again, 'assumed command of the army'.[13]

The British army that marched north from Leiria consisted of 9 infantry and 2 cavalry brigades, 20,231 troops overall, including 3,000 Hanovarians of the KGL, as well as Portuguese forces totaling a further 7,000 men.[14] The quality of the regiments varied, and many lacked any experience of campaigning. The cavalry under Payne's supervision was again weak; just two brigades led by Cotton and now Fane, though by June the additional reinforcing brigade of Major General George Anson arrived. Lieutenant Colonel Robe had been in charge of the Lisbon artillery, but he was now superseded by the seemingly punctilious Brigadier General Edward Howorth, whom Captain Alexander Dickson described as, 'excessively irritable and dissatisfied'.[15] The compliment of guns had increased to five artillery batteries, with each battery normally holding five 6-pounder cannon and one 5½in howitzer. This still was hardly excessive for an army of 27,000 men: Napoleon would have expected three times as many.

Marshal Soult commanded the French *Armée du Portugal* located at Oporto. This was one of five corps of occupation within the Iberian Peninsula that through necessity the French maintained; the four others located to the north, centre, south and east of Spain.[*] Soult had entered Oporto on 29 March 1809 and had seemingly already displeased Napoleon by flirting with the title of King Nicolas I of Portugal.[16] Yet, all the occupying forces were never other than heavily taxed in maintaining merely a degree of control over their respective recalcitrant territories. Soult would be very sorely pressed. Wellington initially directed an independent force of 4,500 men under Major General John Mackenzie eastwards to watch Marshal Claude Victor-Perrin in southern Spain, though Victor already had his hands full with the Spanish army of General Gregorio García de la Cuesta. Mackenzie has routinely been accused of anxiety, and exaggerating French moves over the border, but Wellington gave him comprehensive instructions and no problems ensued: 'All you have done is perfectly correct in every part.'[17] Mackenzie indeed was not anxious, but rather disappointed not to see action with the main army.[18] Wellington then detached a second force under Marshal Beresford to block communication routes east from Oporto for the *Armée du Portugal*; this consisted of Major General Christopher Tilson's brigade as well as the 7,000 Portuguese troops. Wellington's

---

[*] See Appendix G, for opposing French commanders throughout the war.

advice to Beresford was: 'Remember that you [. . .] must not be beaten; therefore do not undertake anything with your troops unless you have some strong hope of success'.[19] Both these detachments achieved their aim of curtailing any French counter-moves. Despite commanding over 20,000 men centred about Oporto, Soult felt isolated and inclined to withdraw upon news of the British advance.[20] Indeed, reports show that there was concurrently serious discontent within these French forces, instigated by the *Philadelphes*, a republican secret society seeking to undermine and ultimately abolish the Imperial dynasty. Soult's own subordinates selected a Captain Argenton: 'You will go in secret to the English general and invite him to march on Oporto to rid us of this madman.'[21] Wellington confidently did not expect the French to stand.

Wellington, with about 18,000 troops in his main force, commenced the movement northward on 7 May 1808. He ostensibly divided the army into two 'wings' commanded by Generals Sherbrooke and Paget; though Wellington in practice continued to issue orders directly to the brigades irrespective of these commanders. Once again staying close to the Portuguese coast, on 11 May, as the British closed towards the River Douro and Oporto, Wellington decided to turn the right flank of the screening French troops by sending Hill's brigade by boat across a coastal lagoon. Local boats used for seaweed collection were requisitioned at Aveiro and the troops transported 15 miles to Ovar; they returned to similarly transport Brigadier General Richard Stewart's troops. The French, numbering 4,500 men here, duly withdrew and concentrated at the village of Grijó, but were again driven back by the threat of envelopment. Thus displaying considerable speed and elan, on 12 May the British reached Oporto and transport across the River Douro was procured, despite the French having looked to commandeer all boats. The already disheartened and mutinous French feared being further flanked, either by Beresford, reported to be to the east, or by another amphibious landing to the west. Wellington now ordered the brigade of John Murray to march 4 miles eastward to cross at the ferry point of Avintes. Awareness of the British actions led Soult to immediately evacuate Oporto, initially unmolested by Murray's comparatively small force, but eventually harassed by the 14th LD cavalry. Edward Paget lost an arm in the ensuing combat. Casualties were otherwise trifling for both sides, though the French had to abandon 1,500 sick in Oporto hospital, as Sherbrooke's troops continued to cross directly into the city itself. Soult fled north-east, but, 'finding Marshal Beresford [. . .] he again altered his route [. . .] thus escaped into Galicia'.[22] Portugal was free of the French for a second time, while Wellington fleetingly effused: 'I cannot say too much in favour of the officers and troops.'[23] The degree of co-operation shown by all parties was fully reminiscent of 1808. The success was great, though when news of the engagement reached England, the continuing unpopularity of Wellington, post-Cintra would mean that the *Morning Chronicle* newspaper only reported the combat as a mere skirmish with the French rearguard.

Wellington pursued Soult northwards for just six days, until 18 May. Not everyone was satisfied with this effort: Major Edward Cocks thought more should have been done to prevent the French escape.[24] Stapleton Cotton similarly hypothesized greater success if Wellington had originally crossed all of the cavalry at Avintes.[25] Yet, rather John Murray's muted operation east of Oporto has been the feature most heavily criticized by historians. His ostensible caution is however understandable when it is recognized that he was isolated and sorely outnumbered; a severe mauling from a desperate enemy would have fostered far worse criticism. Speed and surprise had generated victory for Wellington and the inexperienced British forces, before Soult's ultimate escape. At home, Opposition politician Samuel Whitbread indeed accused Wellington of exaggerating the success, and the argument was only smoothed out by the intervention of General Ferguson, their mutual acquaintance.[26] General Hill now wrote, 'The French, having another force in the South of Portugal, under Victor, and knowing of our advance towards Soult [. . .] made our return to Oporto necessary'.[27] Upon the subsequent return march south, Wellington nevertheless showed that he was exceedingly unhappy with any hint of voiced dissent regarding his orders, or of perceived indiscipline. He bemoaned: 'The army behave terribly ill. They are a rabble who cannot bear success.'[28] Beyond the noted hints of criticism from officers regarding the pursuit, elements of the inexperienced rank and file did engage in looting, but this needs be taken in context. There was a perennial inability of the British Commissariat to properly feed the troops, and the stretched supply chain from Lisbon was critical. Supply problems were an actuality for much of the war, despite Wellington's administrative strengths and his repeated denunciation of looting; speed of operational movement created shortages. The French may usually have been in a far worse state, as they looked to largely live off the land through the requisition of supply, but it is a fallacy to believe that British troops were even reasonably fed; they were not.[29] Nevertheless, in this initial and successful campaign of 1809, the brigade commanders had led their troops effectively. Any perceptible faults derived from Wellington's own orders, including the misconception that Soult was beaten.

By General Order of 18 June Wellington now re-formed the army into four divisions, each of two brigades, or four initially in the case of the 1st Division, which combined the Guards and KGL.[*] In due course, Portuguese brigades were mixed into divisions, and subsequently artillery, engineers, medics, signals, mules and wagons added: 'each division was now fully a complete army with British and foreign troops [. . .] requiring [leadership of] discretion and sense, plus experience for management'.[30] Wellington initially argued with Beresford and

---

[*] See Appendix H, for the composition of the Peninsular Army, 1809–14.

resisted the mixing of nationalities, but once accepted the measure succeeded largely in avoiding the operational problems that the co-ordination of independent allied forces could have brought. Yet, of most crucial import it should be recognized that divisions were never used tactically in battle by Wellington; they were to be purely an administrative formation. Oporto had highlighted to Wellington inadequacies with the degree of command control that he wanted, or, alternatively, control entailed an unsustainable workload given the growing size of the army. Wellington's experiences had credibly taught him further operational lessons, namely that it positively boosted the 'green' Portuguese to be mixed with British troops, and that divisional organization assisted with the massing of skirmishers. Matching French skirmish numbers always helped protect the line of battle, while precluding close enemy reconnaissance.[31] The enemy French field formations had developed tactical sequences based upon the principles of mobility, offensive action, relentless pressure and combined attack. Their battle plan would develop through stages of bombardment, skirmishing, infantry and cavalry combat. Wellington's own defensive counter-moves swiftly coalesced about the use of reverse slopes, matching skirmish ability, disciplined infantry fire combat and artillery fire employing shrapnel and canister.

Each new British division had its own staff of eight, including ADCs, as well as assistant AG and assistant QMG, to speed communication and enhance control. Staff work was not for everyone: 'I cannot afford to have any but useful men about me, be they cousins or not.'[32] From this period developed the relationships between AG Charles Stewart, QMG George Murray and Wellington. Both these staff officers initially felt that Wellington impinged upon the independent traditional prerogatives of their office. Murray was the more compliant and gradually gained Wellington's confidence. Stewart aimed to maintain his independence, which generated conflict; his perceived, 'petty intrigues turned may officers against the Commander-in-Chief's policy'.[33] Wellington duly facilitated Stewart's resignation in 1812, when he would be replaced by Wellington's brother-in-law Edward Pakenham. Wellington's disdain for Stewart was voiced in typical comment: 'Gen. Stewart is a very gallant and very able officer [. . .] He labours however under two bodily defects, the want of sight and of hearing.'[34] For the departments of the AG and QMG, and also the artillery and engineers, Wellington would gradually browbeat the distinct commands to his own complete governance.

During early 1809, Wellington's army establishment thus went from brigades to the concept of wings, before the introduction of divisions; indeed, this was a reflection of European military development over the previous century. Lieutenant General Sherbrooke and Major Generals Hill, Mackenzie and Alexander Campbell initially commanded the four new divisions. Though Wellington was eager to retain him, John Murray now left the army amid a row concerning Beresford's seniority; while Hill and Cotton were among others who also complained.[35]

Beresford was of course both a Portuguese marshal and comparatively a junior British lieutenant general, but he gained precedence as Commander-in-Chief of Portuguese forces. In parallel, the service of British officers within the Portuguese army proved unpopular, despite enhancement of rank. This was compounded no doubt by the openly expressed disapproval and antagonism, as expressed by Wellington of Beresford's use of such officers to reform the Portuguese forces.[36] Major General Tilson also sought to 'be allowed to return to England if it is intended to employ his services again in cooperation with the Portuguese troops', and left temporarily.[37] Both Wellington and Horse Guards made extremely heavy weather of reconciling the wider issues of seniority for British officers in Portuguese service. Indeed, the ramifications could still be seen in 1811 and beyond, when, for example, artillery Major Alexander Dickson argued with Major Andrew Bredin regarding their respective seniority across the two armies.[38] Such events reached a boiling point in 1809 and coincided with a noticeable exacerbation of Wellington's high-handedness: 'I wish to god that Beresford would resign his English lieutenant general's rank. It is inconceivable the embarrassment and ill-blood it occasions.' Indeed, Wellington himself stated: 'From the highest to the lowest, dissatisfaction does now exist in the British Army.'[39] Efforts at conciliation even upset Beresford, who considered resigning his own position.[40] While habitually forthright, Wellington's oppressive approach to his organizational difficulties did not work with senior subordinates.* With such a backdrop he would now even more obviously embrace command autocracy; he very openly criticized and reprimanded his senior officers. General Mackenzie was berated for merely allowing a cart to breakdown; he publicly bemoaned that Fane's heavy cavalry 'has not yet done a day's duty'; and markedly snubbed and ostracized Howorth, his CRA.[41] Nonetheless, on 28 June, the rested and re-equipped army set out for southern Spain, but without the Portuguese troops that Wellington pointedly and tetchily declared were as yet still inadequately organized.[42] Beresford was left behind to defend Portugal with just 4,000 men and the responsibility to sort the perceived disorder. The army had begun to experience Wellington's oppressive censure. Previously, on 3 April, Lord Castlereagh had declared that the army 'should not enter upon a campaign in Spain without the express authority of government', but now due authority had been granted.[43] In the meantime, Wellington had written to General Cuesta to suggest that a combined operation between his army and the Spanish Army of Extremadura could defeat Marshal Victor in the south.

The British army of 22,000 men met with General Cuesta's Spanish army of 34,000, on 21 July in the River Tagus valley. Cuesta was eager for action, despite having been defeated by Victor at Medellin as recently as 28 March; his forces

---

* See Appendix I, for seniority of General Officers Commanding, 1808–14.

would aggressively skirmish with the nearby French on 22 July at Gamonal. Since one facet of the failure of Moore's expedition had been the uncertainties of Spanish support, Wellington should have been forewarned and circumspect in these initial direct dealings. Yet, the ensuing problems of inter-Allied co-operation, both operationally and logistically, have been described as the 'nadir of Anglo–Spanish relations in the war'.[44] Wellington had hoped to receive supplies from the Spanish, but they could not feed their own men, and the failure of goods to materialize had British troops on half rations after 23 July. It is unclear who was culpable for the subsequent failure to co-ordinate in attack upon Victor's small *Armée du Sud*, envisaged for 23 July; Cuesta is of course routinely blamed, but positive cooperation certainly stalled. Thereafter, Victor's 22,000 men would have time to conjoin with the approaching reinforcements of General Horace Sébastiani and King Joseph; French strength was increased to 46,000 men. A secondary Spanish force led by General Francisco Venegas with 23,000 men had failed in its task of keeping Sébastiani suitably occupied about Madrid. On 27 July, Cuesta had to precipitously retreat back upon Wellington's army before the now advancing French forces, and in the process the British brigade of Lieutenant Colonel Rufane Donkins, part of Mackenzie's 3rd Division, was surprised by French cavalry at Casa de Salinas and badly mauled. Wellington himself was nearby and came close to capture when he and his staff had to scramble out of the house they occupied. General Payne's subsequent use of cavalry would appear to have ensured the successful screening of all parties as they retreated to Wellington's chosen defensive battle position in front of Talavera. Here the Spanish were allotted the defence of the town itself, flanked by the River Tagus, where walls and enclosures would compensate for a perceived lack of quality; certainly some Spanish troops had never been in action before. Still, after dark the French pressed forward once again, opposite the British left flank, and temporarily captured the key Medellin hill, where troops had not been properly arrayed. Indeed, it was again Donkins who had had to position his command here on his own initiative. Hill needed to search for Wellington to question him regarding field placements, and was himself nearly captured when meeting the French advance.[45] Ultimately, Hill led a local counter-attack of Brigadier General Richard Stewart's troops to retrieve the situation on the Medellin. Wellington's army deployment showed major errors from a lack of clarity and care that day. Divisional commanders appear to have been fearful, rather than unable to deploy their own troops without direct input from Wellington. The battlefield dispositions that were established at Talavera nonetheless continue to display the overall principles of battle formation that can be identified from the first landing in 1808, with British forces in broadly traditional array, and with the 'position of honour' on the right wing held by the Spanish, within their home country.

Wellington personally deployed the artillery for battle at Talavera on 28 July. He now stated his belief that the CRA, Brigadier Howorth, was a 'ditherer', hence his own involvement: 'I said as much about Howorth as he deserves, for I believe myself lucky if he does not get me into a scrape yet.'[46] This antagonism initiated an enduring rift between the gunners and infantry. While Wellington sheltered his infantry behind hill crests, the artillery was exposed, and losses were proportionally higher than at any battle save Waterloo. Effectively working with Howorth may have avoided years of subsequent discontent for Wellington. After their own initial bombardment the French launched massed attacks upon the British centre that shattered Sherbrooke's 1st Division and all but broke though. The Guards here felt the necessity to counter-attack without Wellington's own specific orders, to relieve the intense pressure they were under. The French attacked in column, with exchanges of point-blank fire that left 1,700 French casualties here alone before they were repulsed. The ferocity resulted in British Major General John Mackenzie of the 3rd Division and Brigadier General Ernst Langwerth of the 1st Division both being killed. Sherbrooke's division in fact lost 40 per cent of its starting strength and was all but demoralized. Hill was another individual to receive a bullet wound at Talavera, but this was a spent round and he was only temporarily out of action. The key to repulsing the French attack and to victory again proved to be the dominant British defensive firepower, from both infantry and artillery. On the left flank, Wellington ultimately ordered a cavalry counter-attack when General François Ruffin's French infantry threatened, and which brought about the near destruction of the 23rd LD. The British cavalry encountered a hidden dry watercourse which brought disaster to the charging horses. Major Frederick Ponsonby observed: 'We had the pleasing amusement of charging five solid [infantry] squares with a ditch in their front.'[47] Wellington testily stated that the charge prevented, 'the execution of that part of the enemy's plan'.[48] The charge has otherwise been variously described as 'reckless', or a 'mad exploit', but its very instigation may be questioned when the main French assault upon the British centre had already been defeated.[49] Indeed, it has been stated that the French had 'no stomach for another assault'. In similar vein, the disparaged Howorth has otherwise been given credit for moving guns to the left flank to help forestall Ruffin's attack.[50] The British cavalry would nonetheless play some part in revoking any consideration of a final French assault, but at a cost, and the lack of subsequent recognition from Wellington doubtless affected morale just as had his treatment of the artillery. William Wellesley commented upon his brother's dispatch after Talavera: 'I never read so clear or so modest a statement. I have but one fault to find with it – you are not warm enough in praise of your officers [. . .] I think you are particularly cold in praising the Artillery.'[51] Wellington's command of both the artillery and cavalry resources at Talavera may be questioned upon the premise of having shown neither timeliness nor effectiveness.

As the day ended, news arrived that the Spanish Army of La Mancha, under General Francisco Venegas, was now moving upon Madrid. As a result Joseph called off any continued offensive action at Talavera, being resolved to protect his capital. This was a fateful moment, when Joseph has been accused of choosing the decidedly wrong course of action, 'the fate of the Peninsula hung on a thread, which could not have borne the weight for even twenty-four hours'.[52] Wellington and Cuesta were thus, by default, victorious in battle, but Talavera was still a pyrrhic victory. British and Spanish losses totalled 5,500 and 1,200 respectively over the 2 days; the French lost 7,270; typically the contemporaneous record exaggerates French casualties as 8–9,000.[53] The impetus had dissipated from the Allied armies, even though Wellington optimistically now expected to pursue Victor. He wrote to Beresford, 'We shall certainly move towards Madrid, if not interrupted by some accident on our flank.'[54] However, that accident was yet ready to happen, as Soult's rejuvenated *Armée du Portugal* now approached from the north. Wellington had totally misjudged this army, thinking it was ruined at Oporto, until coincidence clarified the misconception. French cavalry captured a British dispatch indicating Wellington's belief that Soult had only 12,000 men, while the same day guerrillas captured a French dispatch stating the true figure of 30,000.[55] The reality dawned for Wellington as reports of Soult's swift and strong advance now prodded him into urgent action. Wellington had previously reflected that the British army could not immediately move after all, from want of provisions and the sheer number of battle casualties. However, on 4 August Wellington was forced to march, to put the River Tagus between him and the French, and the following day Cuesta's Spanish army also crossed. Nonetheless, by 8 August Soult had located a ford over the Tagus and in a determined crossing likened to Wellington's at Oporto managed to catch and badly maul the Spanish at Arzobispo.[56] This could easily have been the British forces that were thrashed. If Joseph's army had maintained its presence, so that Wellington and Cuesta remained fixed in place, then outright disaster would have likely ensued. Both allies thereafter fled towards the Portuguese border, to end active British campaigning for the year. Wellington had failed to work effectively with the Spanish, and his 'light and quick' operations had ground to a halt. He had failed to reconnoitre effectively, he had underestimated his enemy and ignored intelligence to such a degree that he was fortunate to escape. In light of the precipitous flight, much of the English press refused to accept that Talavera was even a victory. Sir Henry Clinton wrote: 'If the newly created Viscount [Wellington] saves his precious self it will be lucky for him [. . .] this is the man who the country is to honour and ennoble and to call a hero [. . .] and thus John Bull is gulled'.[57]

At Talavera Wellington had endeavoured to win a defining battle, but co-operation with the Spanish had been woeful and disaster had certainly been courted. Wellington indeed raved that he would never again co-operate with a Spanish army, upon whom he poured both scorn and blame. Their inability to provide supply even for their own men had precluded any significant assistance to the British Commissariat while in mutual contact. Fortescue describes Wellington's actions at Talavera as 'impetuous and over-confident, not fully alive to the magnitude of the problems'.[58] Yet, while he certainly would never accept his own limitations as a diplomat, in time Wellington would realize that it was the Spanish who generated the quagmire of attrition in which the French armies found themselves. The ill-considered Spanish forces of Cuesta were, meanwhile, equally furious at the retreat and perceived desertion of British forces from their national struggle; they were committed to sustaining the fight regardless of setbacks. The Anglo-Portuguese Army was small compared with the total of French forces within Spain and had borne the brunt of the fighting at Talavera. This was unsustainable, since in losing 25 per cent of its strength it was almost a defeated army; it had hazarded its very existence in battle and this could not be sustained. Additionally, Wellington had generated mistrust with both the artillery, due to his relationship with Howorth, and the cavalry, courtesy of both ill-luck and undue expectation. Wellington's infantry may also, in this instance, be accused of having displayed shortcomings against seasoned opposition. They showed inexperience, being twice taken by surprise on 27 July, and the French pressure engendered waywardness, even among the Guards of Sherbrooke's 1st Division on 28 July. Wellington however cannot escape command responsibility for the original field placings and perceived on-going muddle. The divisional generals must share some responsibility by default, but it may be surmised that Wellington's command was overwhelmed by events, as he tried to supervise everything personally. 'While this showed dedication,' has tellingly been written, 'it also revealed a refusal to delegate responsibility [. . .] Fearing his anger, his subordinates [. . .] resented his constant checks and lack of trust'.[59] The generals appear cowed and estranged by Wellington's autocracy, which was exacerbated by stress. For Wellington himself the immediate lesson would appear only to have reinforced his inclination to resolve all issues personally. Talavera was the low point of Wellington's aggressive 'light and quick' command style; its application had won battles, but had not and was unlikely to generate decisive victory. Speed and attrition had worn down the British forces for no strategic benefit, and morale had suffered; some contemporaries such as Brigadier General Robert Craufurd and AG Charles Stewart indeed stated that the Spanish campaign was a waste of time and resources.[60] Opposition Whig politician Thomas Creevey commented that Wellington's 'career approaches very rapidly to a conclusion'.[61]

It has been suggested that a study of Moore's last campaign led to Wellington's subsequent adoption of a 'cautious system', an alternative strategic approach whereby the French would be harassed to defeat from a Portuguese redoubt.[62] If so, it was not implemented until post-Talavera, and indeed well into 1810. Beforehand many further lives were lost to fever as the army camped by the River Guadiana, in what was at best a political gesture to be seen to remain within Spain.[63] Wellington had refused point-blank to take part in the subsequent Spanish offensive that led to their major defeat at Ocaña, south of Madrid on 19 November.

British troop numbers reporting sick tripled to 27.8 per cent in December, and morale dropped proportionately.[64] Wellington might well recall Foreign Secretary George Canning's warning to Moore: 'The army which has been appointed by his Majesty to the defence of Spain and Portugal is not merely a considerable part of the disposable force of this country; it is in fact the British Army.'[65] Wellington vacillated and wasted human life by prioritizing the request of his brother Lord Richard Wellesley, now Ambassador to Spain.[66] Catlin Craufurd died from malarial fever, while Hill would similarly suffer over two winters and thereby missed battle at Albuera. Yet, Wellington had now recognized the asymmetrical advantage that his own concentrated force had over the dispersed French: 'In proportion as the French spread themselves [. . .] they at the same time weaken themselves'.[67] Spanish forces prevented French concentration and the guerrillas alone created a loss ratio which equated to 100 men per day.[68] French soldiers' graffiti about Spain would read, 'General's fortune, officers' ruin, soldiers' death'. Retreat and the lessons of Talavera engendered lower key, attritional warfare for Wellington. Indeed, it is suggested that the British fired 'not a shot' between 20 August 1809 and 27 February 1810.[69] Wellington's increasingly intractable command style however was such that all generals found it hard to meet his expectations. Wellington was blinkered when stating that he commanded 'an unanimous army'.[70]

Brigadier General Robert Craufurd's reinforcing Light Division, or initially more accurately a reinforced brigade, arrived just too late for Talavera. Wellington would describe him as, 'a dissatisfied, troublesome man'; his use of initiative would displease.[71] Otherwise as 1809 ended there was a shortage of senior generals: Mackenzie dead, Campbell wounded, Sherbrooke and Payne retired home due to ill health and Cotton on leave. Horse Guards therefore returned Spencer to Portugal to resume as second-in-command, though Wellington soon complained: 'I cannot depend upon him for a moment.'[72] New arrivals were Major Generals Sir William Stewart, Thomas Picton, Galbraith Lowry Cole and James Leith, to command the 2nd to 5th Divisions respectively. Stewart was highly experienced, notably with rifle troops, yet Wellington's negative utterances have made of him another controversial figure. None other than Lord Nelson had previously described him as the, 'rising hope of our army'.[73] As with Craufurd, Wellington also found General Stewart 'too venturesome' and would state, 'It is likewise necessary that General [Stewart] should be under the particular charge of somebody [. . .] with the utmost zeal and good intentions and abilities, he cannot obey an order'.[74] Further recorded criticisms of Stewart, to the extent that he was a 'valiant busybody', and that 'as a general he was a menace', all stem from Wellington's own highly personalized comments; most notably after the events of 1813 in the Pyrenees.[75] Looking beyond Wellington's negative commentary, the disparagement is once again harder to substantiate. The irascible General Picton of the 3rd Division was subsequently described as, 'the best executive Officer in the Army', but who again could never be classed as a Wellington intimate.[76] Similarly for the distinctly more urbane General Cole; though, 'a more truly gallant and enterprising soldier never breathed'.[77] Despite Cole being an experienced general – he was second-in-command to Sir John Stuart at Maida in 1806 – he has still been accused of a loss of nerve in 1813, merely for not doing exactly as Wellington dictated.[78] Finally, Leith was also reported as being 'a most excellent man [. . .] a better soldier I believe is not to be found among us'; he was another who had served creditably with Moore.[79] Unfortunately, Leith also soon developed fever in Portugal and only commanded his 5th Division from late 1810. All the reinforcing generals once again appear carefully appointed by Horse Guards for their experience, capability and discernible willingness to serve; yet Wellington could find fault regardless.

In December 1809 a third major French invasion of Portugal threatened. Wellington's subordinates at this juncture likely doubted their own ability to defend Portugal; even the usually stoical Hill wrote to his sister, 'I am confident we can do no good by remaining.'[80] Napoleon's defeat of the Austrians at Wagram in July 1809 left him free to dispatch large reinforcements to the Peninsula. Wellington thus expected the French to attack at their earliest opportunity: 'The enemy will probably attack on two distinct lines, the one south, the other north of the Tagus, and the system of defence must be founded upon this general basis.'[81] As Wellington's army guarded northern Portugal, he found it necessity to designate an independent force, to be led by General Hill to watch the southern Portuguese approaches: 'I will separate you from the army and from my own immediate command.'[82] He nonetheless provided Hill with instructions to cover all eventualities, as previously with Mackenzie, though in this case he singularly commented: 'If you are obliged to act in any manner without waiting for my opinion, do so with confidence.'[83] Wellington knew that Hill would 'do as he was told', and accordingly was first choice for detached command.[84] Hill was both skilled and dependable, and provided the right amount of deference for Wellington's taste: never seeking to challenge his superior or overturn orders. Hill's detached force in 1810 consisted of Stewart's 2nd Division, with a brigade of cavalry led by Fane, and all was managed without misadventure. They appear to have worked well in combination together without any of the fault finding that Wellington generated in his dealings with both Stewart and Fane, indeed most cavalry commanders.

Lord Liverpool, newly Secretary for War, commented: 'The whole military efforts of France will probably in a short time be directed against Spain', and, 'it must be our policy to remain in Portugal as long as we can remain there without risking our army'.[85] Napoleon's own orders urged that Marshal André Masséna with 65,000 men, within the corps of Marshal Michel Ney, General Jean-Andoche Junot and General Jean Reynier, should capture, 'first Ciudad Rodrigo and afterwards Almeida, and will thus [. . .] march systematically on Portugal'.[86] For his part Wellington looked to ensure the defence of Portugal from three standpoints. Firstly, that Lisbon should be heavily fortified. To this end he visited the city in October with Lieutenant Colonel Richard Fletcher, Commander of the Royal Engineers (CRE), to survey the intended defensive lines north of Lisbon at Torres Vedras, where the ground rose in places above 600m. The idea for the defensive lines is invariably stated to have originated with Wellington alone; plausibly this may not be the case, but rather the initial consideration came from the Portuguese engineer Major José Neves Costa.[87] Fletcher reportedly found that working with Wellington was uncomfortable; though the secretive engineering works were able to be immediately put in hand, almost a year before the French were to reach them. In conjunction Wellington moved artillery guns about Portugal without any consultation with the man responsible for them; he again showed no respect or consideration for the artillery command of Brigadier General Howorth.[88] The second element of Wellington's defensive plans was to ensure the availability and competence of Beresford's Portuguese troops. By the end of 1809 Wellington had accepted Beresford's organizational measures and was now actually impressed by the infantry. Not however with the Portuguese cavalry; as late as 1811 QMG George Murray reflected Wellington's ambivalence regarding their use: 'I am to observe, however, that Lord Wellington does not wish Portuguese cavalry to be sent, as suggested by Major General Crauford.'[89] Lastly, the French army entering Portugal needed to be starved of local supplies, while the Allied Commissariat worked efficiently, courtesy of the Royal Navy; scorched earth tactics would be implemented. These tactics overall addressed the subsequent battle of attrition that was to defeat Masséna. Yet, as the general officers were denied knowledge of the preparations put in place by Wellington, they should not be criticized for the doubts they duly raised. It was Wellington's choice to ensure his personal leadership stood fully aloof. Indeed, by this date the demands of his leadership style and the attendant pressures had most clearly hardened his personality and approach to command, with perceptible resentment and sarcasm.

Brigadier General Robert Craufurd had responsibility for British outposts along the northern Portuguese frontier, adjacent Almeida and the River Coa in early 1810. Behind him was Wellington with the main army in cantonment, his headquarters at Viseu. Beresford held a central reserve at Abrantes, and Hill watched southern Spain from Elvas. The Light Division repelled various French incursions, including a major thrust on 19 March, before it was attacked in earnest on 24 July by Marshal Ney with 24,000 troops; the French looked to trap and annihilate Craufurd's outlying force. That Craufurd contested the advance has been much criticized, since Wellington had previously recommended withdrawal if outfaced, and some commentators bluntly accuse him of disobeying orders.[90] Nevertheless, the prevention of an earlier French blockade of the Almeida fortress and of French penetration of the front during the first half of the year has been called one of the great achievements of the war.[91] Contemporaneous reports were likewise mixed, with both critics, and supporters such as future Lieutenant George Gleig, who gave praise for Craufurd conducting 'a most gallant defence of his post'.[92] The Light Division escaped intact, yet bruised: casualties were in the order of 500 for both sides. 'Lord W. was much displeased with Craufurd for the last affair, though I consider him the best outpost officer in the army,' stated Lieutenant William Tomkinson of the 16th LD.[93] Craufurd himself felt the need to write a vindicatory letter to the press insinuating that Wellington's orders had created the difficulty. 'I would not wish you to fall back beyond that place, unless it should be necessary,' Wellington had written.[94] Craufurd was a general who strived for greatness; he had shown ability and enterprise until outmatched by what was a surprise thrust by Ney. Wellington appreciated the competence, and indeed said so, but was palpably averse to the initiative shown.[95]

Craufurd had made his own decision to hang on at the Coa, but found himself isolated by doing so. His reputed misadventure was compounded by having asked in vain for the support of the nearest troops: Major General Sir Thomas Picton, newly commander of the 3rd Division, 'chose not to compromise his own troops'.[96] Picton in turn also involved Major General Lowry Cole, who also dared not quit his own position at nearby Guarda.[97] Here is evidence of Wellington's authoritarianism generating ill-feeling between generals and eliciting command inertia; individual commanders certainly did not feel able to use their initiative. Wellington stated, 'I consider that a part of my business [. . .] is to prevent discussions and disputes between the officers'.[98] Yet, his command style struggled to improve matters; in like manner, Picton and Craufurd subsequently quibbled about the latter's performance at Fuentes de Oñoro in May 1811.[99] Wellington stated, 'Officers have a right to form their own opinions upon events and transactions; but officers of high rank or situation ought to keep their opinions to themselves'; and subsequently, 'There is a system of croaking in the army, which is highly injurious.'[100] Wellington was also most likely to reinforce his own standards and requirements with regard to the formalities of staff work, as when lecturing Cole to always 'write your communications, notwithstanding that you think it proper to send an officer'.[101] The artillery under Howorth would continue to particularly feel Wellington's odium and the strain was common knowledge; Wellington 'through an aversion to [Howorth] unfairly disadvantages the group'.[102] Wellington's man-management was oppressive, divisive and tended to undermine morale; unit cohesion was weak. AG Charles Stewart observed, 'Lord Wn's temper [. . .] is more uneven than I had ever imagined or indeed witnessed until recently. One is obliged, therefore, to study him [. . .]'.[103]

The French captured the major northern Spanish border fortress of Cuidad Rodrigo, followed by that at Almeida within Portugal, in July–August 1810. The smaller Fort Concepcion on the border had been partially blown-up by the

British, though it was apparently in sufficient good order for Masséna to use as his headquarters while Almeida was taken, and where it even boasted a cafe. Subsequently, the French moved into the Mondego River valley, the route to Coimbra and thereafter Lisbon. The British retreated behind their cavalry screen that was for long periods the only force in daily contact with the enemy. On a sanguine note, General Lowry Cole's pet dog Dash was captured by the French on his own retreat from Guarda, but was returned under a flag of truce.[104] Relations between British and French forces could be surprisingly positive on occasion, just as Anglo–Spanish relations could equally be difficult. Wellington wrote regularly to General Hill, now amplifying what he had earlier expected from Craufurd: 'I rely upon your prudence and discretion not to engage in any affair of which the result can be at all doubtful. Retire gradually, if you find the enemy threatening you in too great force; and let me hear from you constantly.'[105] The corps of General Reynier opposite Hill would initially move westwards along the Tagus valley within Spain, but would then choose to march across country to the north-west to join Masséna's main force within Portugal, rather than continue due westwards alone. After initial skirmishing with Reynier, Hill was, therefore, free to force march to join Wellington by 26 September at Buçaco. Wellington's own comment was: 'The best of Hill is that I always know where to find him.'[106] At Buçaco ridge, sitting some 150m above the approach road, Wellington's army halted the French. If Masséna had instead chosen to take a more southerly route to avoid Buçaco, Wellington also had a defensive position with redoubts prepared at Serra da Atalhada, 15 miles distant. Wellington's reason for fighting at Buçaco was simply that he had such strong positions available to defend at minimal risk; he could win a battle at a favourable rate of human attrition. Joined now by Hill, Wellington had 27,000 British as well as 24,000 Portuguese troops. Masséna's own 65,000 troops attacked considering that Wellington had been overly tempted by the strength of the position, and because Napoleon would have criticized him for not fighting.[107] The Portuguese government had nonetheless previously taken marked exception to Wellington's refusal to fight the French on the frontier, and further, the unilateral implementation of a scorched earth policy within their borders. These were political issues, which again show a marked lack of tact, effective communication or diplomacy from Wellington: 'I will not suffer them or anybody else to interfere with [the operations of the army]. I am responsible for what I do, and they are not.'[108]

The Battle of Buçaco on 27 September 1810 would be the only major clash of the year and resulted in a French repulse with a substantial loss of men; 4,000 troops to 1,250 Anglo–Portuguese. AQMG George Scovell thought, 'the position of Buçaco [. . .] the strongest he ever saw'.[109] This was purely an infantry and artillery affair; there was no scope for cavalry on the hilly terrain. Buçaco, with Vitoria and Waterloo, were the only occasions when Wellington organized a concentration of artillery; once again situating guns personally. Nevertheless, Captain Francis

Duncan observed: 'In the battle Lord Wellington displayed an ignorance of artillery tactics.'[110] Two generals, namely Picton and Leith, subsequently argued as to which of them had won the glory of the victory; Lieutenant Colonel John Colborne, a strong adherent of Wellington, otherwise wrote some years after the event: 'The battle of Buçaco was gained solely in consequence of Hill's precise attention to Wellington's orders, for which he was always remarkable.'[111] Yet, despite being repulsed, Masséna marched onwards, outflanking the Buçaco defensive position to the north. At home Whig politician Lord Charles Grey felt that the battle resembled Talavera: 'A vigorous repulse of the Enemy, a post unoccupied which exposed our flank and rear, and the necessity of an immediate retreat.'[112] Indeed, Wellington contemplated blaming the Portuguese for this need to retreat if any great controversy had resulted at home: 'I should have stopped [the French] entirely if it had not been for the blunders of the Portuguese General [Manuel Pinto Bacelar] in the north'.[113] Wellington's caution was exaggerated and failed to exploit the success achieved. The opportunity of harassing the French rearguard as they marched away was ignored. AQMG George Scovell considered that the army was not yet a 'manoeuvering army' in order to accomplish this successfully.[114] He implied that Wellington's command and control did not yet have the requisite staff to always ensure the full implementation of his precise directions. Wellington obstinately adhered to his chosen strategy of circumspection, knowing that the defensive lines of Torres Vedras awaited Masséna.

Wellington's army entered the fortified zone before Lisbon on 10 October: 'The Lines were of such an extraordinary nature that I daresay there was no other position in the world that could be compared to them.'[115] They consisted of two lines of interconnected forts and batteries 20 to 30 miles north of Lisbon, as well as a third subsidiary line adjacent to the River Tagus estuary, from where any necessary evacuation would have taken place from the harbour of San Julian. In addition, fortifications were constructed west of and contiguous to the River Tagus to protect against a French flanking attack here. If the French had been able to cross the Tagus then Lisbon might have been bombarded from the eastern side of the estuary. By mid-October, when the French arrived, 126 redoubts mounting 249 guns were in position, while further additional redoubts were still being added. Beyond the fortifications, the finishing touch was the incorporation of a system of telegraph communication that could signal along the 15 miles from coast to coast in just 7 minutes.[116] Static semaphore signals would be used four times in all during the war: both at the Portuguese border and at Torres Vedras in 1810–11; at Campo Mayor outside Badajoz in 1811; and at Bayonne in 1813–14. The Torres Vedras fortifications were directly manned by 29,750 Portuguese militia and *Ordenança* volunteers, as well as some Spanish troops, to leave the British army free for manoeuvre. On 13 October Masséna, in testing the defences, partially penetrated the first line of fortifications at Sobral, but quickly withdrew when it became apparent that a second line of forts as well as Wellington's mobile forces awaited him. The French would also consider potential bridge construction over the Tagus, but were likewise thwarted by the heavy defences. Masséna thus did not order a concerted attack upon the Lines; the fortifications proved just too formidable. The French sat before them for a month, until on 15 November they withdrew to Santarém, 55 miles north of Lisbon, to winter. Wellington was on the alert and considered that Masséna must now be quitting the country due to supply considerations, and prepared to attack. The action was cancelled however after reconnaissance revealed the misjudgment. As the terrain was hilly, Wellington belatedly and disingenuously compared the French position at Santarém as being as strong as Buçaco: 'Massena is an old fox, and as cautious as I am; he risks nothing [. . .] Although I may not win a battle immediately, I shall not lose one.'[117] Wellington indeed further expressed professional admiration for Masséna and for the length of time the French remained at Santarém with the most limited of supply means: 'it is certainly astonishing that the enemy have been able to remain in this country so long'.[118] For the Allies, the Royal Navy was indeed the bedrock of Wellington's strategy. Without food, munitions and reinforcements, Wellington's position would quickly have mirrored the straits endured by Masséna's army. The new arrival of a Lieutenant William Lindsay, in October 1810, with a contingent of Congreve's rockets, certainly could not break the deadlock: Wellington was not impressed with the first test of these rockets in the Peninsula at Santarém.[119] Masséna's only stated hope for success at this juncture was that the Portuguese would revolt against the British, 'who have reduced them to the most horrific misery; or that Lord Wellington will leave his fortifications to offer or receive battle'.[120] Over the winter, 40–50,000 Lisbon inhabitants died of disease, 2 per cent of Portugal's population.[121] Even the Portuguese troops were so hungry that plundering occurred and Wellington needed to authorize the British Commissariat to intervene upon their behalf; though: 'It is desirable, nay necessary, that the army should be relieved [. . .] from the difficulty of providing for [. . .] persons [. . .] who can render no service'.[122] The rationale of a continued British presence in Portugal unquestionably had a counterweight in human misery that Wellington could not, or would not address. On a foggy 3 March 1811, with no initiative from Lisbon and his own army suffering terminal privation, Masséna did finally order the retreat; now catching Wellington off guard.[123] Wellington's success was prodigious, but his inability to support the civilian population of Portugal meant he had been very close to meeting both of Masséna's projected scenarios.

During that winter of 1810–11, Generals Hill and Leith went home to England with illness; Cotton and Craufurd departed due to 'personal concerns'. Wellington's irritation was on display when writing to Leith: 'Those who are obliged to go for the recovery of their health, are compelled to appear before a Medical Board, and I shall be very much obliged to you if you will go through that ceremony.'[124] Then to Cotton: 'You will have heard that the French crossed the Guadiana at Merida on the 8th [December.] You will, however, judge for yourself the priority of going home.'[125] As even Army Surgeon George Mitchelson, laid low with winter fever and disability, could not avoid death on 25 December 1810, Cotton decided to go. Otherwise Torrens at Horse Guards confessed to Wellington that they had found difficulty in finding experienced and willing generals to now serve in Portugal. Wellington, in the standard narrative, was thus 'allocated subordinates neither competent nor to his liking', though the likelihood must be considered that there were other factors influencing those officers with the requisite qualifications, even if their numbers were not extensive.[126] Three new arrivals were Major Generals William Erskine, known for having spent time in an asylum before the war, William Lumley and Andrew Hay. Wellington's reaction was typical: 'The first I have generally understood to be a madman [. . .] the second is not very wise: the third will, I believe, be a useful man'.[127]

When the French finally quit Santarém it was the Portuguese militia that alerted Wellington. Their men also blocked any major movement by Masséna's forces north of the Mondego River, from where enough supply to remain in the country might still have been sourced. In Craufurd's absence, perhaps surprisingly the subsequently discredited General Erskine received command of the Light Division which led the pursuit of the enfeebled French forces. Erskine, in this role and with Cotton absent, also appears to have received authority over the limited available cavalry, to form in effect a temporary 'advance guard'. Major General Sir John Slade would head the available three brigades of cavalry in the absence of Cotton, and worked cooperatively and effectively with Erskine. Skirmishes occurred daily; at Pombal on 11 March, Redinha on 12 March, Condeixa on 13 March and Casal Novo on 14 March; until 15 March, beyond Coimbra, when the army was brought to a halt due to the outrunning of supplies.[128] For Wellington's concentrated forces, logistics were perennially an issue and the Portuguese countryside had of course already been stripped bare of foodstuff. French overall strength dwindled to 49,000 troops in their retreat to the Spanish frontier, while the Anglo–Portuguese strength, with reinforcements received, now exceeded 46,000 better conditioned men within 7 divisions. A further division was also being formed, and Major General William Houston's new 7th Division duly combined with the army in March 1811.[129] The experienced Houston had suffered with the infamous 'Walcheren fever' from the 1809 expedition, and he would unfortunately be invalided home again in the summer of 1811. Wellington now stated, 'I have determined to persevere in my cautious system [. . .] and thus force them out of Portugal by the distresses they will suffer'.[130] He notably commended Erksine's actions, and did likewise for Slade.[131] Nevertheless, the pursuit struck no truly decisive blow against the adept Masséna, and for which Erskine and Slade, rather than Wellington, receive routine criticism. It is of course unreasonable that they alone should take such responsibility, while Wellington is absolved and the canny Masséna receives little commendation. The ambivalent pursuit resulted in one final combat at Sabugal on 3 April, which misfired in thick fog. Wellington could have called off the attack, but persisted in a venture that most closely resembled the night-time combat he had avoided since Seringapatam in 1799. Wellington was of course blameless; his justification: 'these combinations for engagements do not answer, unless one is on the spot to direct every trifling movement'.[132] Routine blame for the Sabugal muddle has again been retrospectively heaped upon Erskine, though Picton went astray in the fog as well; their exacting commander had set them both unrealizable objectives. Fortescue uniquely states that Erskine's only fault at Sabugal was to leave a brigade temporarily without orders; likely due to poor staff work and which would not have occurred, but for the fog.[133] Losses at Sabugal were in the order of 760 French to 179 Allied troops. Masséna's forces thereafter retreated successfully into Spain.

With the French army all but evicted from northern Portugal, Wellington now gave orders for Beresford to march to the relief of the southern frontier fortress of Badajoz within Spain.[134] Wellington himself with the main army would approach firstly Almeida and subsequently Cuidad Rodrigo either side of the northern border, as he continued to shadow the retreating *Armée du Portugal*. These frontier forts were all heavily armed 'star fortresses'; low-set forts capable of matching a besieger's firepower, and which had been built upon the principles of the Marquis de Vauban, the famed French military engineer of the early eighteenth century. With General Hill absent, Beresford became the preferred commander for the south: 'It is impossible for two people to understand each other better than Beresford and I do.'[135] By this time, Beresford's independent responsibility for the Portuguese army had markedly diminished. There alone existed the all-Portuguese Division of two brigades, led by Major General John Hamilton, and an independent brigade led by Colonel Denis Pack. Of the other seven Portuguese brigades now in existence, Wellington had integrated them into the eight British divisions that would exist for the rest of the Peninsular War. A further independent Portuguese brigade led by Colonel Thomas McMahon formed in July 1811. The Portuguese cavalry were ever to be judged by Wellington's opinion that: 'they are worse than useless'.[136] Beresford's subsequent southern command would consist of 20,000 men within 3 divisions. Due to the flatter terrain of Extremadura, Beresford was allocated 1,119 of the 2,700 total British cavalry then available.[137] A further reinforcing cavalry brigade followed in May commanded by Brigadier General Thomas Long; before ultimately Sir William Erskine also joined Beresford in June.[138] Indeed, by the summer of 1811 Wellington's cavalry had for the first time gained enough strength that it could be split into two divisions, led by Cotton and Erskine, if only for the short period of time until year's end when Erskine's health deteriorated.

However, as Beresford marched south, it soon critically transpired that Badajoz had surrendered to Marshal Soult on 10 March; an event described as one of the great strategic failures of the war.[139] Wellington had sought to control every operational eventuality in person, but had failed to prevent the fall of the fortress; his excuse of Spanish treachery is unfounded and clearly shows the spin upon events that Wellington employed. Indeed, Wellington's own officers criticized the miscalculations that had led to the loss of the fortress.[140] Wellington had been too risk-averse when following the retreating Masséna to ensure that Badajoz could endure. The circumstances surrounding the loss may even throw some light on Wellington's subsequent frenetic and compelling urge to regain the fortress. Wellington would visit Beresford in late April to clarify the situation in person, leaving General Spencer in charge of the main army with the ubiquitous memorandum of instructions.[141] These included how to avoid battle, and the need to keep in constant communication, to avoid such pettifogging observation as, 'I conclude that you did not find it necessary to write to me until last night', when Spencer went a day without comment.[142] He again described Spencer as, 'very unfit for his situation. He is a good executive Officer; but [. . .] I cannot depend upon him [if] the act recommended by him is disapproved of'.[143] Yet, when Spencer had pressed Wellington to explain his plans in case of an unforeseen event, the response was, 'I have no plans but to beat the French'.[144] As Wellington's brother-in-law and friend, it is hardly a surprise that Major General Pakenham should agree with Wellington: 'Sir Brent Spencer has charge of his corps, and is as good a fellow as to meet at a Country Club, but as to succeeding Wellington it is quite Damnation to him.'[145] Spencer had his own opinions, which if they clashed with Wellington's own patently unvoiced plans were castigated accordingly. Beresford and Spencer represented quite different outlooks upon leadership and command.

As Masséna's forces recovered their strength, Wellington's own main force fully blockaded the northern Almeida fortress on 9 April 1811; the garrison was by then the only French force that remained in Portugal. Wellington now had 23,000 British troops, as well as 11,500 Portuguese and 2,000 cavalry available here. Apart from the troops of Colonel Denis Pack who closely supervised the fort, the army was positioned at Fuentes de Oñoro to screen against any interference by Masséna. No heavy siege guns were available; a lack of forethought which could only be Wellington's responsibility. With the investment of the fortress it would then be standard practice for the commander, Wellington, to make a detailed reconnaissance with his CRA, Brigadier General Howorth, and his CRE, Lieutenant Colonel Fletcher, and issue orders and directions for a subsequent siege. But, as Wellington kept his plans to himself they could hardly have been fully prepared unless he had previously given direction. Only if the fort had been besieged hitherto, as Almeida had by the French in summer 1810, would it be the engineers' business to understand the specific details. Wellington's defensive screening of Almeida stretched some 8 miles, from the outlying remains of Fort Concepcion in the north to the village of Fuentes de Oñoro. On 3 May Masséna's revitalized army, composed of 42,000 infantry and 4,500 cavalry, directly attacked the crucial village, but without decisive result, though prolonged close-quarter bayonet fighting here was both unusual and reflected the severity of the assault. On 5 May Masséna attacked again, attempting to outflank the Allies to the south. Here Houston's new 7th Division had been pushed far south of the village by Wellington to defend against such a move, but he had totally underestimated the potential French effort. It has been suggested that Wellington's responsibility for this deployment was somehow diluted, since it had 'Spencer in particular supporting it', but this is immaterial; Wellington's control prevailed and he gave the orders.[146] Rather more to the point, Wellington, 'committed a fault by extending his right too much'.[147] Thus, on the southern flank, a large cavalry combat soon ensued: 3,500 French cavalry attacked Cotton's screen of 1,500 defenders, who risked obliteration. This cavalry cover for Houston consisted of the brigades of Slade and Lieutenant Colonel Friedrich von Arentschildt, the author of *Instructions for [. . .] Outpost Duty*, who temporarily commanded for Major General George Anson. French sources describe the British cavalry here as 'brilliant horsemen'.[148] General Slade would nonetheless acquire the label of incompetence just the following year, despite the truly effective cavalry performance displayed at Fuentes de Oñoro. Major Cocks wrote, 'I think that this day gave Lord Wellington a higher idea of the effect of cavalry as an arm in battle.'[149] This lesson was learnt: 'I am of the opinion that we cannot have too much British cavalry. We can certainly do nothing without them in a general action out of our mountains.'[150] As the cavalry fought, in parallel the support of Craufurd's Light Division enabled Houston's men to 'leap-frog' position back into alignment with a new south-facing British defensive line. Despite being forced back, the defence was maintained. Craufurd's own initiative was 'his finest hour', and described as 'one of the most polished displays in military history'.[151] Wellington stated, 'The movement of the troops on this occasion was well conducted, although under very critical circumstances.'[152] He acknowledged, 'If Boney had been there, we should have been beaten.'[153] The French ultimately withdrew without achieving a critical breakthrough; losses overall from the severe fighting at Fuentes de Oñoro were in the order of 1,500 Anglo-Portuguese to 2,200 French. The artillery's significant defensive contribution was ignored by Wellington, a fact lamented by Howorth and an attitude which has been described as 'petty and unprofessional'.[154]

Others had equally frank views: 'how easily England is duped; how completely ignorant she is of the truth of what is going on here. [Wellington] would lead you to think that the troops on the right were withdrawn rather than, as was the case, driven in; and then they give him what he himself never dreamt of claiming, a victory'.[155] Fuentes de Oñoro amply demonstrated the skill of the British divisional commanders, notably Craufurd, Houston and Picton, since the exposure of the right flank was, 'one of the most questionable moves that Wellington ever made'.[156] Wellington had assumed a frontal assault and was surprised when the French decided to do something different. Victory was, 'so dearly purchased, that in a sober estimate the day will perhaps be reckoned [more] among the disastrous than the triumphant ones'.[157] Unfathomably, the lesson that Wellington learnt from the battle appeared to be that even tighter control was needed when managing the army. Wellington had already written to Beresford: 'I have begun [. . .] to state in the orders at what hour each [unit] is to start and is to arrive at each place'.[158] All movement orders would now further state a specific route and not just the end point. Now despite his general's performance, that had positively showcased their initiative, Wellington's orders would state tactical dispositions on the field of battle for the first time. The role of the QMG was specifically extended to make no distinction between orders either before or away from the enemy.[159] Wellington notably curtailed the customary role that his divisional commanders would have seen as their prerogative. He now likely felt that he had finally organized his headquarters as he desired.

To Wellington's mortification, on the night of 10 May and despite a blockade supposedly being in place, the Almeida garrison of 1,000 men, led by General Antoine Brenier, escaped to leave the empty fortress in Allied hands. Wellington's huge annoyance might have been further exacerbated by the fact that Brenier owed him £500. This had been lent by Wellington when Brenier had been a prisoner in London during 1808–9; he had been captured at Vimiero. However, an in-depth review of the blockade by historian Archie Hunter has indicated misplaced pickets, late orders and a lack of co-ordination between individual units as being responsible for the debacle, and for which Wellington must share the blame; all communication between units had by necessity to pass via him.[160] Yet, once again, commentators have largely prescribed blame to Wellington's subordinates alone, principally Generals Erskine and Alexander Campbell, as well as Lieutenant Colonels Basil Cochrane and Charles Bevan. Others more discerning have stated that, 'it is too easy to follow the fashion and blame Erskine' for the fiasco.[161] Brenier's escape proved that the cordon around Almeida was insufficiently strong or tight enough, a responsibility that ultimately rested with Wellington who determined these factors. Nonetheless, he himself declared that the escape was: 'the fault of our Col. Bevan'.[162] Upon this accusation being made the unfortunate Bevan requested a court of inquiry, which was dismissively refused by Wellington, and Bevan's suicide followed. The fact that Bevan's family were initially told that he died of a 'violent fever' would only have added insult to injury. This series of events are just too much of a coincidence to give an 'unproven' verdict, as some historians have ascribed. Wellington was unwarranted to single out an individual for blame. His readiness to designate a scapegoat, coupled with his desire to avoid any personal blame, demonstrates his reluctance to learn from mistakes. This was an attribute that could only lower army morale and effectiveness, and indeed foster discontent among those involved. Oman's own synopsis states: 'Public opinion in the army held that he [Bevan] had been sacrificed to the hierarchical theory that a general must be believed before a lieutenant colonel.'[163]

In early May with Almeida fortuitously secured, Wellington's thoughts again turned to Badajoz: 'The first object of our attention must be to regain Badajoz', and 'It is impossible to do anything to the south till Badajoz should be again in our hands.'[164] Concurrently, Beresford's detached force now approached the strategic town, just 4 miles from the frontier within Extremadura: 'A mistaken notion [had] induced Wellington to undertake two operations at the same time, which was above his strength; and this error might have been his ruin.'[165] Beresford's force consisted of Stewart's and Cole's divisions, Hamilton's Portuguese Division, as well as two cavalry and six artillery brigades. This force has been described as 'an embryo corps', but as Wellington never employed corps in the Napoleonic sense, this is an irrelevance.[166] The cavalry arm was commanded by Brigadier General Robert Long; widely recorded as 'an active and most intelligent officer'.[167] The French here also had to contend with Spanish involvement: Generals Joaquín Blake and Francisco Castaños had agreed to support and supplement Beresford's command. Wellington's orders to Beresford stressed the need for a swift, aggressive advance, in what appears to be a return to 'light and quick' operations. He wrote: 'You had better lose no time in moving up to Portalegre and attack Soult, if you can, at Campo Mayor.'[168] Wellington expected his subordinate to follow orders implicitly, and also to co-operate closely with the Spanish; a task he had signally failed to undertake effectually himself. Any projected variation from orders would require dialogue with Wellington over a 48-hour communication link, putting an enormous weight of expectation upon Beresford.

On the march towards Badajoz, Beresford's not insignificant force of cavalry has been described as playing a purely insignificant role, inhibited without doubt by Wellington's restrictive orders: 'When the French cavalry advanced the Allied cavalry withdrew.'[169] As the British approached Campo Mayor on 25 March, the French garrison, including a sixteen-gun siege train, abandoned this minor fortress. Beresford did however agree to send the 13th LD cavalry on a detour to cut off the French, but a series of encounters ended with the exhausted dragoons repulsed by fresh French hussars, close to Badajoz itself, and the forces from Campo Mayor escaped in the confusion. General Long thought it 'a disgrace' that the French garrison had been allowed to retreat to safety and with Beresford making no reinforcement of the initial success achieved by the 13th LD. Beresford in turn blamed Long for the supposed faulty execution of his orders: they should have done no more than await the infantry's arrival. Wellington was furious with the report from Beresford and severely censured the 13th LD in a dispatch;

an outburst described as 'wrong, yet one of the most influential with historians'.[170] The Campo Mayor action should however be considered in light of Wellington's strict warning to Beresford to keep the cavalry, 'in reserve, [for] striking a decisive blow'.[171] Despite Long's pleading, Beresford would not support the dragoons, and 'through this error [. . .] the whole operation failed'.[172] Beresford feared the loss of the cavalry and thus wasted one of the finest tactical achievements of the war: the 13th LD had defeated a force twice its size and trapped large infantry and artillery contingents.[173] Beresford was crippled by Wellington's strictures. Wellington raged, and even with clarification refused to withdraw the reprimand. Nevertheless, the 13th LD received 'the unsparing admiration of the whole army'.[174] Evidence of the poor effect upon morale was manifest: 'The army [. . .] appear much discontented with this affair'.[175] Upon news of the debacle reaching London, Lord Henry Paget was even asked by Horse Guards, 'to inspect, report upon and in part reorganise the cavalry' in Spain.[176] Paget tactfully declined as it would have been 'insulting to the cavalry commanders' in the Peninsula; he patently felt their blame to be limited. Campo Mayor set the prickly Beresford permanently against his subordinate Long, and continued bickering meant that Wellington would dispatch Erskine to the south as a replacement cavalry commander; someone he again described as having 'prudence and circumspection'. Wellington at this juncture still most positively vouched for Erskine as a leader: 'You will find him more intelligent and useful than anybody you have.'[177] With such explicitly positive reference, it is again unreasonable that Erskine should be dismissed as an 'unstable, dim-eyed drunkard', while most unlikely, a supine Wellington is supposed to have done no more than 'made the best of a bad job'.[178] At this date Erskine was clearly well thought of by Wellington and had undertaken his duties to satisfaction. Wellington otherwise was the fount from which Beresford's problems had sprung; here again is evidence that his demands had extinguished the command initiative of subordinates.

Wellington arrived at Elvas upon his previously noted four-day visit, to confer with Beresford on 20 April 1811. He here stated his belief that it would take sixteen days for Soult to feasibly march from his base at Seville to intervene once siege operations commenced. Beresford's force duly advanced and isolated Badajoz from the position at Albuera that Wellington specified; three detailed memos dated 23 April 1811 dictated the siege and all on-going operations for him.[179] But only then were orders also given to assemble siege artillery. Beresford's siege guns had to comprise requisitioned antique Portuguese ordnance from nearby Elvas; the French guns that escaped from Campo Mayor would have been invaluable. As at Almeida, Wellington had failed to organize provision; the British siege train had sat for two years onboard ship at Lisbon: 'Hence the British army, in no single instance [. . .] sat down before a fortified place, but under disadvantages'.[180] By 11 May the museum piece guns opened fire; an event described as a 'farcical arrangement'.[181]

Marshal Soult with the *Armée du Sud* would depart Seville on 9 May with a relieving force of 24,000 men, and reached Albuera in just seven days, on 16 May. With their speed of advance, the French had hoped and anticipated being able to attack a day before the Spanish arrival. However, Spanish Generals Blake and Castaños with 14,500 men most fortuitously joined Beresford early that same day to bring the total of Allied troops to 35,000 men. They deferred to Beresford's overall command in the subsequent battle. The Allies' chosen position was undulating plain that was, 'easy for cavalry throughout'.[182] Major General William Lumley was given temporary command of the British cavalry that yet awaited Erskine's arrival. The out of favour and sidelined General Long astutely noted that a southern knoll was the key to the defensive position, and indeed General Hill made the same assessment when occupying the selfsame ground in 1812.[183] Beresford however left the knoll undefended and from here the French duly attacked. Some components of the Allied forces would be unseen where deployed adjacent to the dry watercourse west of Albuera village; Soult was initially unaware that the Spanish had actually arrived. However, no reverse-slope deployment was subsequently used by Beresford as the troops formed on the hills behind Albuera village, possibly hoping to overawe the less numerous French. With the French movement against the Allied right-hand flank the three defending Spanish divisions located here needed to re-face southwards before they were struck by the single, most massive attack of the Peninsular War: 2 whole French divisions with more than 8,400 men that advanced in one massive column with only a light skirmish screen before them. Virtually the whole French army save for one infantry and one cavalry brigade were soon attacking Beresford's refused right wing. Under huge pressure the defending Spanish divisions were supported in due course, from necessity by Stewart's 2nd Division. Beresford did position himself here where he was most needed, at the focus of the French attack; however, the Spanish generals were not readily to hand and no arrangement for inter-communication appears to have been made. Rain and hailstorm also limited visibility as Brigadier General John Colborne's right-most flank brigade was surprised and then routed by enemy Polish Vistula lancers, without, it would seem, Lumley's cavalry being able to intervene. Beresford's control floundered, and he now went personally to order General Hamilton to further reinforce the right. His absence led to accusations of panic; Major Alexander Dickson stated: 'The Marshal himself for a moment thought he was defeated', and to ride in person away from the focal point of battle was extraordinary.[184] However, Cole's 4th Division now belatedly came onto the scene. His ADC, Major Alexandre Roverea, stated: 'I was sent to the Marshal [. . .] to receive his orders [. . .] I received none'.[185] Cole advanced without Beresford's orders in support of Stewart. Such initiative was of course anathema to Wellington, but the French attack stalled, then gave way and the battle was won. Lieutenant Colonel Henry Hardinge, a deputy QMG, had urged Cole to advance and subsequently wrote to him, on 24 May: 'Your movement on the left flank of the enemy unquestionably saved the day and decided the victory.'[186] After the battle, unlike Wellington, Beresford graciously praised the contribution to victory from both the cavalry and artillery. Albuera would prove a tactical victory for the Allies, but a strategic victory for the French; the siege of Badajoz was halted, if only temporarily. After the battle Hamilton's Portuguese troops were quickly sent back to re-establish the blockade of the fortress, but in the meantime the garrison commander, General Armand Philippon, had taken the opportunity to sally forth and destroy the surrounding Allied fieldworks. The horrendous casualties suffered at Albuera – Anglo-Portuguese and Spanish losses totalled 5,915 from 35,356 men, while the French suffered 5,936 from 22,856 men – condemned Beresford's performance to his contemporaries: 'Beresford has entirely lost all hope of being considered by us lookers on as a general.'[187] General Pakenham wrote, 'Beresford is a clever man but no General; his Anxiety is too great, and he cannot allow an Operation to go through [. . .] without interference, which [. . .] mars everything'.[188]

After the battle Wellington once again laid the blame upon the Spanish for the costliness of the stalemate; their lack of maneuverability was said to be responsible.[189] This is clearly wrong; the Spanish divisions needed to redeploy in order to face towards the looming and monumental French assault, and of which the division of General José de Zayas resolutely bore the brunt. Even after Colborne's rout adjacent to their position, Zayas' troops remained steadfast. The Spanish themselves would nonetheless blatantly exaggerate when subsequently claiming that they alone had generated the victory, but they certainly played a most important role. Beresford had displayed dubious quality as a fighting general, but Wellington had placed him in an invidious position. He had been thrust into an aggressive campaign, with little time and inadequate British resource, but with much pressure to both defeat Soult and capture Badajoz. The expectation existed that he would co-ordinate the activities of the Anglo-Portuguese forces with Spanish forces, something Wellington himself had conspicuously failed to accomplish. Beresford was expected to faithfully follow the directions of his superior located 120 miles away. The observant Long complained of unnecessary 'mystery' from Wellington, saying it was 'high treason' to ask him any questions.[190] Wellington set aside caution for audacity, believing his own interpretation of the situation rather than intelligence reports. The risks taken were extreme and in underestimating the enemy, lives were wasted. After the battle, Wellington initially suppressed the news and subsequently distorted the reportage when stating to Beresford: 'write me a victory'.[191] Wellington himself observed, 'they would have written a whining report upon it, which would have driven the people in England mad. However, I prevented that.'[192] Yet, his perception of events only further exacerbated his wish not to rely upon subordinates.

On 19 May, after the reoccupation of Almeida, Wellington again returned south, now with two divisions of reinforcements to formally resume the Badajoz siege. Wellington wrote: 'When Hill comes he must return to his command, and I must confine Beresford to the management [. . .] of the Portuguese army'.[193] Hill returned to the army on 27 May. In organizing the antique brass cannon from Elvas, Major Alexander Dickson, RA now became a Wellington favourite, earmarked for future siege operations. Nonetheless, two assaults thrown against the walls of Badajoz, on 6 June and 9 June by troops of Houston's 7th Division, both failed. On 11 June the siege was again lifted with intelligence of a fresh French approach under the command of Marshal Soult, including numerous cavalry. General Picton here noted that Wellington had 'sued Badajoz *in former pauperis* [in the manner of a pauper]'.[194] Blame for this second failure descended upon the engineers. The next time, Wellington declared, 'he would be his own engineer'.[195] It may well be considered that he was already.

As a counterpoint to any criticism of Wellington's leadership, two instances from April and May of 1811 have intermittently been recorded by historians, in order to demonstrate supposedly that Wellington did indeed respond to the concerns of subordinates. They purport to show that Wellington was not merely a 'cold imperious upholder of military hierarchies'. Firstly, a Major Henry Ridewood complained of insufficient credit, within Wellington's dispatches, for his 1/52nd battalion of the Light Division after battle at Fuentes de Oñoro. Secondly, Major General Charles Colville complained that he received no commendation for his superintendence of fieldworks at Badajoz. In the first instance Wellington responded in writing that he had rather 'expressed dissatisfaction with none', and in the second case his solution was to invite Colville to dinner.[196] In neither case is in fact the recipient other than fobbed-off with platitudes. Wellington may have borne on his shoulders 'responsibilities that would have crushed a lesser man', but such examples still make it difficult to favourably amend the perception of his man-management skills.[197] In advancing the defeat of the French he yet routinely sought to safeguard, if not boost his own reputation regardless of the impact upon others; at a time when he was now distinctly being lauded at home, in the press and in the House of Commons.

By mid-June Marshal Auguste de Marmont, who during the previous month had replaced Masséna in charge of the *Armée du Portugal*, joined Soult to face Wellington before Badajoz. No attack resulted, though the French duly re-established contact with their garrison on 20 June. Meanwhile, General Spencer marched south with the bulk of the British army, to bring Wellington's concentrated forces to 54,000 men. Here has been recognized the turning point of the war: the point at which the French, despite numbering 60,000 men, passed the future initiative on to Wellington by failing to attack before Spanish resistance flared elsewhere. For Soult and Marmont logistics alone meant that their armies could not stay combined for long, and on 27 June, first Soult retired back towards Seville, and on 15 July Marmont crossed the River Tagus to move back northwards. Notably, on 29 June, Wellington welcomed the Prince of Orange to his staff as an ADC; the Prince's father was currently in exile in London. His companion and military tutor was fellow Lieutenant Colonel Constant-Rebecque, and both would gain prominence in 1815. On 18 July the British army also marched northwards shadowing Marmont, though now leaving General Hill with 13,000 men to again observe Badajoz and watch Soult's *Armée du Sud*. This Hill undertook most effectively. In October French General Jean-Baptiste Girard moved west with 6,000 men to pillage Extremadura. Hill intercepted at Arroyo dos Molinos on 28 October and trounced his surprised opponent. Hill's cavalry was very creditably led by the disregarded General Long. By such initiative Hill proved his leadership and command capability, including the effective control of subordinates. Sir John Murray courteously wrote: 'I feel a peculiar pleasure in this fortunate affair as it concerns yourself personally and assure you that I only repeat the sentiments which are in the mouth of everyone whom I have heard speak upon the subject.'[198]

Having been thwarted in the south, Wellington returned to Almeida and northern Portugal, still opposite Marmont's *Armée du Portugal*; with a view to once again blockading Cuidad Rodrigo with his main force of 46,000 men. In August, Lieutenant General Thomas Graham, renowned as the 'victor of Barrosa', arrived as reinforcement. The Battle of Barrosa took place on 5 March 1811, in support of the Spanish government base at Cádiz. Graham's troops here repulsed Marshal Victor, despite being abandoned by the Allied Spanish forces led by General Manuel Lapeña. As Graham was senior to Spencer this now allowed Wellington's ill-considered deputy to gratefully depart for home: 'Spencer has returned and not upon good terms with Lord Wellington.'[199] Graham was something of an oddity with regards to his seniority within the army. After the death of his wife in 1792, only at the age of 43 had he decided to serve as a volunteer, and he personally raised the 90th Perthshire Volunteer Regiment in 1794. In 1809 his services received recognition from the Crown when, 'His Majesty has been pleased to direct that the established custom of the army may be departed from by your being promoted to the rank of Major General'.[200] Graham 'left the highest character possible both for understanding and courage'.[201] It had also been Graham who had previously criticized Wellington's leadership in 1808. He clearly served from the highest standards of patriotism.

On 10 August Wellington moved to impose a blockade upon the fortress of Cuidad Rodrigo as he exploited his central position: 'The French armies have no communication and one army no knowledge of the position and circumstances in which the other is placed; whereas I have knowledge of all that passes.'[202] Nonetheless, the numerous French cavalry thereafter undertook aggressive forward scouting and harassment. Their aim was to ascertain whether Wellington now had the available siege guns for direct siege action. On 25 September such a foray by Marmont's cavalry at El Bodón caught Wellington with his army strung out, and enabled the French to ensure re-supply of Cuidad Rodrigo. The British cavalry's own defensive action here nonetheless enabled Picton's infantry formations of the 3rd Division to successfully retreat away from what might otherwise have been a disaster. Notable at El Bodón was the unique 'charge' made by the 2/5th Foot led by Major Henry Ridge, who advanced in line against opposition cavalry, to successfully recover four lost guns. El Bodón has otherwise been described as 'controlled and very business-like', as the outnumbered British cavalry fought hard and effectively to reverse the enemy tide, with no evidence of appreciation from Wellington. Also on 25 September a separate cavalry combat at Carpio is described as a 'brilliant little affair', and as being 'remarkable for its obscurity'.[203] Here the charge of the British cavalry, against French lancers for the first time in open combat in the Peninsula, was said to be one of the finest of the war. Aldea da Ponte on 27 September was a subsequent cavalry success under the pragmatic leadership of General Slade and Colonel George De Grey, before Wellington finally settled the army in a strong defensive position at Freineda, west of Fuentes de Oñoro. The French withdrew into winter quarters; they had seen no evidence of siege equipment. In point of fact, all of these autumn exchanges displayed a degree of caution by the more numerous French when advancing to the attack, and which likely saved the Allied formations from worse damage. The French had now become used to Wellington shielding his troops behind an available reverse slope; they were wary of unexpected surprises.

In July 1811 Howorth, the CRA, had finally had enough of his perpetual poor relationship with Wellington and returned home due to 'ill health'; their letters show the strained communication between the two.[204] Lieutenant Colonel Hoylett Framingham temporarily took command before Major General Edward Borthwick arrived in December. A gunnery officer, Captain George Jenkinson, wrote:

> My expectations of anything General Borthwick may effect for us are not very sanguine, and I must confess I pity him from the bottom of my heart, for I am convinced that were an angel to come down from Heaven he would not please Lord W., or remove from his mind, that rancorous hatred of our corps.[205]

In two years of strained command Wellington's relations with both cavalry and artillery had plummeted, and the lack of communication and trust could only have impacted upon the efficiency of both. However, also in July, Wellington had finally ordered the siege train forward from the coast, under the supervision of the trusted Major Dickson. As summer turned to the autumn of 1811 sickness again severely struck the army, as it had in 1809. General Houston retired home, to be followed by Pakenham who nearly died of dysentery; Wellington himself was unusually indisposed for a fortnight. Yet, Wellington's planned siege operation at Cuidad Rodrigo was able to unfold finally on 8 January 1812, to the surprise of the French in their winter quarters. By 19 January two breaches had been made in the defences, and the fortress was stormed that night. The perceived strategic imperative of speedily concluding the operation forced Wellington to spend his men's lives in a way he had avoided in open battle. Major General Robert Craufurd and Brigadier General Henry Mackinnon were among those killed, out of 1,120 British casualties. After the siege of Cuidad Rodrigo, Wellington praised Dickson, but not Borthwick, despite the fact that the latter was wounded. Wellington dismissed him as 'the walking target', and within weeks he was invalided home amid fresh scorn; Framlingham again assumed temporary artillery command.[206]

In March 1812 Wellington's headquarters returned south to Elvas, the Portuguese fortress town closest to Badajoz. Wellington had appointed Lieutenant General Carl von Alten to command the 7th Division in Houston's absence and he was now left to command in the north, with merely incomplete elements of that division. Alten's brief was to liaise with the Spanish, and ensure no direct enemy action against Cuidad Rodrigo. Marmont with four divisions of infantry would subsequently advance towards Cuidad Rodrigo, with the aim of diverting Wellington's plans, and understandably Alten found it necessary to temporarily retire before the superior French numbers. Wellington was thus once again typically scathing of his subordinate's independent leadership when commenting that Alten must have 'misunderstood, as he disobeyed my instructions in every point'.[207] Nonetheless, the fact that Marmont lacked siege guns proved to be the decisive factor; it signified a French inability to seriously threaten Cuidad Rodrigo again. Wellington undoubtedly had this intelligence; Alten's small force was there merely to observe, and it duly avoided any harm: 'murder and plunder [. . .] are the only fruits of Marshal Marmont's expedition'.[208] Wellington would subsequently, in May 1812, appoint Alten to command the Light Division; he was less talented, but more pliable than Craufurd had been.

In the south Wellington was now able to proceed to besiege Badajoz. The British siege train had not been able to move overland from Cuidad Rodrigo, apart from six 5½in iron howitzers, so Wellington was reliant upon sixteen new 24-pounders, and ships' guns offered by Admiral George Berkely, RN. These latter turned out to be of Russian calibration, so Wellington was unhappy, 'in consequence of the busy meddling folly of those whom I had been inclined to trust'.[209] This vitriolic sentence was edited from the published version of Wellington's dispatches. Wellington also now at Badajoz unaccountably bemoaned the shrapnel shells which 'must wound a great number of men, but probably none very materially'.[210] While siege works proceeded, General Hill led a covering force to the east at Merida, north of the Guadiana River, while General Graham commanded a similar force south of the river. Badajoz was formally invested on the 16 March, with Fletcher, the CRE, promoting an attack on the northern castle quarter.[211] Beforehand Wellington had sarcastically commented to Fletcher regarding his preparations: 'Probably it did not occur to you that a gabion 18 inches in diameter would not cover a man. Every man, even the smallest, occupies 20 inches.'[212] Unfortunately, three days later Fletcher was wounded and Wellington thereafter wholly directed the siege himself; he ordered the attack upon three breaches that he ensured had been made in the south-east perimeter wall. Marshal Soult was reputedly now 'on the move' in southern Spain, but there was otherwise no immediate need for urgency. There was in fact no French threat from outside the fortress that dictated the exaggerated speed that Wellington brought to the assault. Soult it transpired was preoccupied with Spanish attempts upon his own Seville base and Wellington would have been aware of these events. The storming of Badajoz on 6 April descended into chaos and near failure; eventual British casualties totalled 4,670 men, with Generals Picton, Walker, Colville, Kempt, Bowes and Harvey all wounded. However, diversionary escalades by Generals Picton and Leith were both successful and the fortress most fortuitously fell, almost despite Wellington's best efforts. Fletcher had advised Wellington not to cut corners, yet the blame for the heavy casualties still fell upon the engineers. Wellington told QMG George Murray: 'I trust [. . .] that our engineers will learn [where] to put their batteries'.[213] Public silence from Wellington was an added rebuke: 'You will observe that Lord W. had not mentioned the Engineers in the late actions; how I hate such capriciousness.'[214] The engineers were blamed again at Badajoz just as others had been before them, for no good reason other than Wellington's marked unwillingness to take responsibility for any errors. Badajoz had shown that Wellington's leadership was willing to risk all, if he believed it to be a military necessity; only afterwards might the cost be counted and regretted. The command failure of the previous year that led to the loss of Badajoz would appear to have been a part of that necessity. The practicality of a more leisurely siege should certainly not be discounted, while it might even reasonably be questioned whether the mere screening of Badajoz would have precluded the operations that Wellington subsequently undertook in 1812. Its capture primarily obviated the need for Wellington to place any reliance upon the Spanish field armies in Extremadura, and also neutralized any negative perception from the prior loss of the fortress. Nonetheless, the actuality of the event and the attendant dreadful losses at Badajoz did likely mark another step in the evolution of Wellington's leadership; the scale of the purely British casualties certainly rivalled Albuera and it was hard here to deflect responsibility. Badajoz plausibly re-emphasized the importance of methodical pre-planning for Wellington, while again accentuating caution to both his decision-making and the actuality of future operations; his own and Britain's winning progress needed to be maintained. The micro-management of measured progress would thus certainly continue to be seen, while future siege operations in particular would be steeped in trepidation.

Nevertheless, Portugal and its borders had been secured. Wellington was a winning general, and his position at home was unassailable. He was backed by commanders who had shown great forbearance, as well as professionalism and effectiveness. Craufurd, Spencer, Erskine and Beresford have unjustly borne the brunt of subsequent negativity for the generals, despite being constrained by Wellington's strictures. Only through strict adherence to his exacting standards could a general win approval, but yet no recrimination could touch Wellington himself. A subordinate was more likely to be discredited and sidelined than coached and encouraged. Of the troops, the infantry, with experience, surmounted some early fallibility to achieve disciplined precision; likewise the artillery, with field success doubtless enhanced by the successes of new technology. Criticism of the regularly outnumbered cavalry has been most harsh; the perceived shortcomings were largely confined to the actions under Wellington's personal command. The cavalry had certainly gained experience and 'in every conflict of the small bodies engaged, the Allies had the better'.[215] This would be the theme for the rest of the Peninsular War.

During 1809–11, Wellington successfully thwarted both the second and third French invasions of Portugal; the forces of Soult and Masséna respectively were insufficient for the task in hand. The period was a quintessential war of attrition: logistics wore down forces far more than combat casualties did. The efforts of the Spanish armies and guerillas in this regard should always be recognized for their profound impact upon the opposition French. Wellington fought an asymmetric campaign: cautiously withdrawing in the face of superior enemy forces, but always prepared to return to offensive action, preferably against a weakened enemy. He usually displayed an excellent eye upon the battlefield, once decided upon combat, and which he would as far as possible personally manage in his inimitable cool and detached manner. Yet, more than anything, he showed a passion and dedication for the minutiae of military life, all of which enhanced his personal control, regardless of the expense to relations with individual officers and even the Spanish and Portuguese allies. He gradually re-fashioned the practicality of his leadership command to achieve the notable degree of control that he desired. Nonetheless, in early 1812, the security provided by the ultimate British capture of the key fortresses on the Spanish frontier would facilitate a new phase of the war by providing a shift in the strategic options for Wellington.

Several characteristics of Wellington's command, initially perceived in 1808, are undoubtedly more clearly discernible during this period and would certainly have had some measure of impact upon the effectiveness of his army. These traits did not of course make him a bad leader, but he would have potentially been a better leader and a greater general without these negative undercurrents. His exaggerated reliance solely upon his own ability precipitated the micro-management of his forces, and meant that Wellington would ignore subordinates and allies alike; he alone knew best. Wellington's vexatious leadership only added to the inherent pressure upon his subordinates, for whom any failure only fuelled his self-perception of indispensability. He could likewise misinterpret intelligence if it did not align with his own defined ideas, while also manipulating news of events for home consumption. Such over-arching control would have failed to inspire his subordinates, while it equally may be considered to have stymied the exploitation of any disarray among his opponents. In his hands the balance between caution and risk-taking would always appear problematic. Yet, back in Britain Wellington was feted as a winning general; the means were irrelevant. Optimism was high for the forthcoming summer campaign of 1812. Even Horse Guards felt the need now to mollify Wellington when expressing regret for their 'interference' in the earlier choice of his subordinate generals.[216] However, such a boost to Wellington's ego would only serve to maintain the command faults that had influenced his effectiveness to date, and which would still be visible in the final years of the Peninsular War.

Chapter 5

Wellington's Dominant Command, 1812–14

'I am a very clever man [. . .] except when any gentleman happens to differ in opinion with me on any point'.[1]

Since their renewed intervention in 1809 the British forces under Wellington's command, with their Iberian allies, had spent almost three years largely in a war of attrition. Fighting had flowed back and forth as the strength of each side gained temporary advantage. The Allied forces had been unable to do other than gradually wear down their French opponent by whatever means possible. But, by April 1812, with firstly the capture of Cuidad Rodrigo followed by that of Badajoz – at the third attempt – Wellington's army had finally gained the strategic initiative. With dwindling capability the French faced an ever more difficult strategic environment. They were opposed now by well-equipped, experienced and formidable Anglo-Portuguese forces led by Wellington. This army indeed now truly provided an experienced cutting edge force to supplement the unremitting warfare of the Spanish regular troops and guerrillas. Meanwhile, the French armies in Spain, despite totalling almost 300,000 men, continued to suffer from the diffused command structure imposed by Napoleon, while their numerical strength withered as he withdrew formations for his great offensive into Russia. These unresolved problems would ultimately prove to be insurmountable. In early 1812 General Auguste Marmont's *Armée du Portugal* was alone in having the ability to conduct operations aimed at thwarting Wellington's initiative. Wellington's own leadership had in turn been discomforted and bruised by his recent experiences of siege warfare and his uneasy control would again impact upon army effectiveness during the subsequent campaign. Contemporary commentators, unaware of the scale of the problems facing the French, had been unable to discern a way forward to Allied victory: 'His Lordship seems rather to be feeling his way, than to be following any determined plan.'[2] In order to accelerate events, above all else, more effective co-operation with the Spanish allies would have been required, but this had proved problematic for Wellington. Yet, with the fall of Badajoz, the nearest French army, namely the *Armée du Sud* led by Marshal Jean Soult, had trouble mustering 15,000 troops.

With Portugal finally secure thanks to the capture of the key frontier fortresses, Wellington could now potentially strike with relative impunity at the heart of French power within Spain, and three main options for offensive action presented themselves. Firstly, he could march to the south-east, towards Seville, the capital of Andalusia and base of the *Armée du Sud*. This however was furthest away from France and into an area of high Spanish activity; close besides their centre of operations at Cádiz. Continued Spanish assertiveness here best kept Soult busy enough to prevent any French action outside of Andalusia. Indeed, no serious French attempt upon Portugal had come from the south, and which again emphasizes the secondary importance of Badajoz when compared with Cuidad Rodrigo. Wellington's expanded cavalry force could also now expect to warn of, and indeed baulk any aggressive activity from Soult. Two cavalry divisions had been established by Wellington in June 1811, as appropriate when his forces were split north and south. The success achieved by the newly arrived Major General John Le Marchant's heavy dragoons at Villagarcia, east of Badajoz, on 11 April, showed just how the augmented British cavalry arm could fight in the flatter southern terrain: this was a 'brilliant little affair'.[3] Indeed, surprise has been expressed that this action did not generate battle honours, purely because Wellington refused such credit where 'musketry' was not involved.[4] The second alternative option for Wellington would be to rather strike due eastwards towards Madrid. Yet, such an approach could be readily dismissed in the spring of 1812 as it would certainly both encourage and best facilitate the combining of the scattered French armies; just as would be demonstrated later in the year. The third option would be to advance north-eastwards towards the major city of Salamanca, to confront and ideally suppress Marmont's mobile force. Such advance would also preclude any possible thoughts of a further French incursion into Portugal along this least demanding of routes. The twin fortresses of Cuidad Rodrigo and Almeida of course also commanded the border crossing here and provided a limitation upon any potential French counter-move; this was the preferred course of action.

Wellington had gained the upper hand not only against the enemy, but had also enhanced the degree of control he demanded within the army. Many generals would again take leave over the winter and spring of 1811–12, and which has been described as an 'epidemic of applications' to return home.[5] Beyond the traumas of recent events, it is easy to credit that the markedly constrained atmosphere surrounding Wellington had to be a consideration; indeed, elsewhere it has been acknowledged that 'enormous resentment' had been generated among his subordinates.[6] Concurrent with the departure of General Picton and other officers wounded at Badajoz, AG Stewart and divisional commanders Houston and Cole all went home temporarily. Lieutenant General Sir Alexander Campbell of the 6th Division left permanently due to ill health, and despite Wellington's pronounced reservations was replaced by a former critic, Major General Henry Clinton.[7] The health of General Thomas Graham would also mean that he followed them home in July, to be absent until May 1813: 'his eyes poor fellow, have failed him'.[8]

Wellington likely reflected upon his own comment of the prior winter, that excepting himself, 'there is not one [general] in the country who came out with the army'.[9] This however was not quite true: Beresford also spent the entire war in the Peninsula. Theoretically with Graham's departure, Cotton was the senior lieutenant general and in line to become Wellington's second-in-command, but Wellington preferred Beresford and was now able in effect to snub Cotton until the post was filled by the arrival of Lieutenant General Sir John Hope in May 1812. Wellington always claimed to have no choice in his generals: 'I have nothing to do with the choice of General Officers sent out here or with their numbers'.[10] Despite Clinton's arrival, this statement is again not quite the truth, as he had in all probability a direct hand in the selection of Beresford, Hill, Picton, Craufurd, Graham, Houston, Leith and Nightingall, as well as many others of subordinate rank.

Wellington would immediately miss QMG George Murray, when he also left the army in May 1812: 'when I first heard of your intention to quit us my sentiments were not confined to concern and regret'.[11] An insightful observation upon this event affirms: 'It is a significant sign of Wellington's failure to create *esprit de corps* [. . .] that Murray was willing to go home for a mere desk job'.[12] Contemporaneously, Murray has otherwise been described as 'the life and soul of the army', beyond the personality of Wellington himself.[13] Other correspondence has shown that up to this date Murray had routinely been kept in the dark regarding Wellington's intentions, just as all others of Wellington's staff, and it would only be upon his return to the Peninsula in 1813 that he would gain a greater degree of confidence from Wellington.[14] Murray's replacement was Colonel James Willoughby Gordon, who naively observed, 'Our Officers are very bad indeed [. . .] they are dreadfully nervous upon all that regards what is called personal responsibility'. He also said of Wellington: 'he acts in person when he might often much better direct, but this he knows and he does so because his experience has shown him that he cannot safely depute'; he had apparently listened only to Wellington.[15] Gordon would subsequently find that for officers to act on their own responsibility was in fact the last thing that Wellington desired. Nonetheless, Wellington's concentrated force would now dictate the time and place for the next campaign to be fought. The depleted French forces in Spain, dispersed to hold territory, could merely defend. Wellington wrote in May 1812, 'I propose [. . .] to bring Marmont to a general action [. . .] I shall have the advantage in the action'.[16] The circumspect Wellington ideally needed to guarantee that the other French regional armies would not reinforce Marmont before battle. General Hill, left with 18,000 men in Extremadura, was directed to destroy the Tagus Bridge at Almaraz, to cut the direct line of communication between Marmont and Soult. This was duly undertaken on 19 May. Hill captured forts Napoleon and Ragusa, either side of the River Tagus, and destroyed the twenty pontoon barges that formed the bridge. Wellington commented with some appreciation: 'Hill has done it well and ably.'[17]

Hill had again certainly proved his capability; he executed 'difficult manoeuvres with imagination, skill and bravery'. Erskine's cavalry under Hill's command, meanwhile, effectively screened the *Armée du Sud*, and as Le Marchant had in April he repulsed three French cavalry regiments outside Villa Alba; described as 'a very handsome affair'.[18] This was a final flourish from the routinely disparaged Erskine, whose chief fault would appear to have been that he subsequently suffered a return of mental illness. Later in 1812 this first led to him being banished to Lisbon and afterwards to his unfortunate suicide. As might be expected, Wellington did latterly utter expressions of annoyance with a by then unfit Erskine, but he did so for all generals and any irritation appears only to parallel Erskine's mental deterioration; his subsequent representation has been poor.

However, there followed on 11 June 1812, at Maguilla in Extremadura, a cavalry action that paralleled in controversy that of Campo Mayor, the previous year. In defeat the previously successful Major General John Slade became the most controversial of commanders: 'a curse to the cause, a disgrace to the service'.[19] It should be noted nevertheless that this comment derives from Assistant Adjutant General (AAG) Hercules Pakenham, a brother-in-law and devotee of Wellington. Slade's brigade of 700 troopers within Hill's command had bumped into a French cavalry brigade led by General Charles Lallemand; likely just one of his two regiments. Slade got the better of the action and as it transpired, unwisely allowed the pursuit of the French for some 8 miles, before encountering Lallemand's second regiment which counter-attacked and overthrew Slade's now frazzled troopers. Poor leadership by Slade is portrayed in the standard narrative, though others have blamed troop disobedience for the pursuit. General Long for one certainly and notably sympathised with Slade for his ill luck and inability to 'be everywhere to control every individual'.[20] After the event, the irate Wellington made the infamous reference to, 'the trick our cavalry have acquired of galloping at everything'.[21] For most historians this forthright statement has fully damned the British cavalry in the Peninsula, and that General Hill also joined in the disapproval of Slade's leadership certainly gives credence. Prior cavalry success in the south had perversely led to the expectation of uninterrupted victory. Yet, analysis concludes that, 'Slade's responsibility lies less in his tactical errors [. . .] than his undermining of the regiment's morale' through irresolution.[22] Such awareness again highlights the fundamental importance of morale and *esprit de corps* for all parties within any army. Not all Wellington's generals could be consistently exemplary, especially when subject to his strictures and the reality of his displeasure. Slade's supposed disquietude can be seen as a feature among several of Wellington's commanders, most notably Beresford at Albuera, and conflicting instincts conceivably diminished his control at Maguilla. Slade's former successes are thus forgotten, though more discerning historians still refer to Maguilla as 'the unluckiest combat'.[23] The actuality was that the British loss of 150 men to 50 French troopers was more a rare embarrassment than a critical setback. Wellington typically overreacted to a deficit of the prudence he stipulated, as well as luck, among Slade's 1st and 3rd Dragoons; Wellington's own style of leadership generated unacknowledged pressures for his subordinates.

On 13 June 1812 Wellington's army of 48,500 troops marched to confront Marmont within Spain: 'Lord Wellington has now a great game before him.'[24] He had instigated all means possible to ensure the isolation of Marmont's army. The French *Armée du Portugal* could expect no reinforcement from Soult, with the *Armée du Sud* separated by the loss of Almaraz on the Tagus. Spanish forces were also encouraged to remain an incessant danger: 'Threaten as much as you can, but do not engage in serious affairs.'[25] Nonetheless, Marmont was forewarned by such discernible activities and duly concentrated his army in good time. General Graham had alerted Wellington regarding the lack of surprise: 'Marmont will have the means of getting sound intelligence of the movements of [. . .] the army, & will regulate his accordingly'.[26] By mid-June Wellington's target, the major city of Salamanca, was reached by the Anglo-Portuguese forces, and where it proved necessary to slowly reduce three heavily fortified, large stone buildings left by the French. These were the convents of San Vicente, San Cayetano and La Merced, manned overall by 800 French troops. All three had been fortified over the prior three months by French engineers in a move that would surprise Wellington. Once again there would be insufficient readily available heavy guns and the inconsiderable, yet irksome convents took ten days to subdue. While Wellington's losses at 430 men were hardly on the scale of Badajoz, they did again undermine confidence in his ability as a siege commander. Lieutenant Harry Ross-Lewin observed after an initial abortive assault: 'the result was precisely such as most officers anticipated – a failure attended with severe loss of life'.[27] Marmont was happy to stall and frustrate Wellington, while he had his own army approach Salamanca on 21 June, inviting attack. Warily, he would not attack himself, since his army of 30,000 men was appreciably the smaller; yet Wellington, with exaggerated circumspection, also declined combat. Wellington's failure to press the initiative he held could potentially have been a huge mistake, since within the immediate timeframe Marmont would gain major reinforcements, principally the division of General Jean-Pierre Bonnet, to bring equality of numbers to the opposing armies at approximately 50,000 men each. Marmont thereafter watched events and again invited attack from a strong position north of Salamanca and the River Tormes at Aldea Rubia. Wellington was determined not to lose the initiative and 'not to fight an action unless under very advantageous circumstances'.[28] Marmont still did not attack; he rather manoeuvred his army to initially retreat further north, over the River Duero and thereafter he swiftly and most skilfully counter-marched to threaten the now exposed British right flank and line of communication.

Wellington was compelled to fall back by necessity to the east of Salamanca and in a typical and emblematic narrative, he gallantly, 'galloped about his army [. . .] He took personal command of one division after another in preference to sending orders to detached, nervous generals'.[29] Wellington's micro-management is thus lauded in typical narrative, while experienced subordinates, with their initiative fully proscribed, are reproached for what can only be presumed timidity.

On 22 July, both armies marched further southwards, just 4 or 5 miles to the south-east of the city of Salamanca. Wellington continued with his display of studied caution, typically shielding his forces as far as possible behind the available low hills. As they manoeuvred and skirmished the British troops vied with the French for the occupation of any conspicuous terrain features; Cole's 4th Division occupied the prominent Lesser Arapiles hill, but failed to occupy the Greater Arapiles hill before French *tirailleurs* beat them to it. The speed and initiative shown by the French when manoeuvring did not surprise the watching British troops. Wellington would subsequently write to the recently departed Graham confirming: 'We had a race for the larger Arapiles.'[30] This hill with the French guns that were soon deployed upon it firmly sat as a threat to the British army's flank and Wellington at first considered an assault upon it. Uniquely, he indeed openly displayed apprehension regarding the situation and actually allowed Beresford to talk him out of the attack: 'Lord Wellington is so little influenced, or indeed, allows any person to say a word, that his attending to the marshal was considered singular.'[31] He subsequently settled for concentrating his own army and reinforcing his own position about the Lesser Arapiles hill; it was here that he directly ordered Colonel William McClean of the 3/27th: 'You must defend this position so long as you have a man.'[32]

After days of manoeuvre a now somewhat over-confident Marmont had possibly seen enough of Wellington to consider him a general who was loath to attack. He likely considered that Wellington's army would continue to retreat before him. Hence, supported by guns situated both upon and to the west of the Greater Arapiles hill, he would initiate combat as the division of General Antoine Maucune skirmished with Cole's 4th Division at the village of Los Arapiles. Yet, Wellington was thereupon provided with the opportunity for his own offensive action as formations of the French left wing continued to circle to the south. They most probably hoped to fully turn the British flank, while their nervous opponent was pinned in place at Los Arapiles. However, their lines were now grievously over-extended. Wellington stated: 'This will do at last, I think', as he readied the 3rd Division to lead the attack.[33] On that day he had certainly vacillated – from the expectation of having to fully retire, to subsequently anticipating a major French assault – before finally he now redeployed his own army for the attack. Wellington personally carried orders to each divisional officer: 'He told no-one what was going through his head until he decided what to do and even then he told only those he needed to'.[34] Major General Edward Pakenham was temporarily in command of the 3rd Division, after Picton's wounding at Badajoz: 'Pakenham may not be the brightest genius, when I tell you he is one of the best we have.'[35] The 3rd Division duly struck the exposed French left flank, followed critically by the charge of Major General John Le Marchant's dragoons; one brigade of which had been at Maguilla. It may certainly be considered most likely, if only from the ambivalence within Cotton's memoirs, that Wellington directly ordered Le Marchant's charge, just as he had ordered Pakenham forward. Cotton had in fact exchanged cross words with Le Marchant at the start of the battle, and which was blamed for the lack of any recognition for the heavy cavalry from Cotton post-battle, as well as typically from Wellington. Lieutenant Colonel William Clowes of the 3rd Dragoons wrote: 'I have never ceased to feel annoyed at our treatment, which [. . .] drove me out of the service'.[36] After this initial crippling assault, respective British infantry divisions attacked in classic oblique order, massing overwhelming strength against the left wing of the enemy. Le Marchant's cavalry provided the previously missing element of tactical decisiveness, as his charge routed eight French battalions, and dealt heavy casualties. Eventually, French losses would total 12,500 men, half this number being taken prisoner, while Wellington's losses in killed and wounded were in the order of 5,000 men. Events were brutally dynamic. The hero of the hour Le Marchant was killed, while the wounded included: 'Sir William Beresford, our friend Gen. Cole, also Leith, Alten, and others'.[37] Stapleton Cotton was wounded by friendly fire, which diverted historian Napier to state that he was 'unable to discover that [Cotton] ever [personally] once crossed swords with the enemy'.[38] The disfavoured Clinton was left as the senior unwounded officer after Wellington. These losses among senior officers at Salamanca were exceeded within the French army, where Marmont and his second-in-command, General Jean-Pierre-François Bonnet, were both severely wounded. That both Marmont and Bonnet were quickly *hors de combat* was a major contributor to the French army's initial desultory response to the British attack. They demonstrate the dangers then faced by all generals, and the importance of a robust chain of command.

Wellington personally sent into action every major Allied formation that took part in the battle; haphazardly at the close of the day, when attacking columns of Clinton's 6th Division suffered against a defending French line, as had occurred so often previously when roles were reversed. In addition the 1st Division, temporarily commanded by Major General Henry Campbell, sat without orders and complained of ill-use after the battle.[39] No substantive pursuit was organized until the following day: 'Wellington mishandled the pursuit and attempted to blame the error on his Spanish allies'.[40] Once in pursuit, the cavalry, now led by Major General Eberhardt von Bock with Cotton wounded, uniquely and brilliantly broke two French infantry squares at Garcia Hernández on 23 July. Yet, Cotton was always preferred by Wellington for overall cavalry command; as Beresford, he did exactly as ordered: 'He commands our cavalry very well [. . .] much better than many who might be sent to us and who might be supposed cleverer'.[41] This echoes his comments upon Pakenham, who similarly did exactly as he was told without deliberation. Inevitably post-battle Wellington grumbled to government with regards to the artillery: in this case that it had apparently proved markedly inferior to that of the French.[42] Salamanca was certainly Wellington's battlefield masterpiece, but marred by detail; true elan in the attack was limited to the initial manoeuvres of Pakenham and Le Marchant. Historians have routinely blamed Wellington's generals for a lack of spontaneity and 'the killer instinct in pursuing a defeated opponent', but the responsibility clearly lay with Wellington and the degree of command control that he exercised.[43] Nonetheless, with some good fortune Wellington had achieved his aim; he had neutralized the main French mobile force and fatally shaken their rule within Spain.

In defeating Marmont at Salamanca, Wellington had in fact inflicted upon the French their greatest battlefield defeat for a decade; a victory within Spain, which now incontrovertibly removed the war from Portugal.* The battle gave Wellington's army free rein to advance upon Madrid, the Spanish capital, military depot and hub of communications. The incumbent King Joseph had to speedily decamp, eastwards to Valencia on the Mediterranean coast, leaving only a small force of 2,060 men within the Retiro fortification. This was an old china factory within Madrid whose estate walls had been extensively barricaded and garrisoned to protect French supplies and ammunition stores. The Retiro only briefly threatened to be another Salamanca city fort as it quickly became apparent that the garrison was inadequate to man all the defences, and it soon fell to cursory fire. The ramifications of Wellington's entry into Madrid gave him huge and doubtless gratifying personal cachet, while as a political move on behalf of the Spanish nation there was also certainly a strong rationale. Soult's newly isolated *Armée du Sud* was now convinced to end the long French siege of the Spanish government at Cádiz and evacuate Andalusia; in effect the whole of Spain south of the River Tagus was soon liberated. The thus buoyant Wellington now stated his aim of taking Burgos, north of Madrid, 'and I hope before Christmas [. . .] to have all the gentlemen on the other side of the [River] Ebro'.[44] Capture of the Burgos fortress would allow Wellington to maintain his army in northern Spain and leave his French enemy behind the last major river before the French border. However, he would seem to have fully discounted the scope for the coming together of the discrete enemy forces; an option now just as at the start of the year's campaign. Despite Salamanca, there had otherwise been negligible impact upon French strength; there were still in excess of 200,000 French troops in Spain overall and the balance of forces had

---

* See Map 2, for the key centres and communication routes within eastern Spain and southern France.

only been temporarily affected. General Hill, meanwhile, was ordered to advance from the south to take charge at Madrid. As Wellington moved northwards to follow the *Armée du Portugal* he left the 3rd, 4th and Light Divisions at Madrid, so that when Hill reached the city there would be 40,000 troops here compared with just 30,000 actually with Wellington. French General Bertrand Clausel now commanded the *Armée du Portugal* and his candid words nonetheless confirm both the significance of the Salamanca battle and the demoralization that had resulted, when writing: 'It is usual to see an army disheartened after a defeat, but it would be hard to find one whose discouragement is greater than that of these troops.'[45] Wellington would appear now to include the Madrid forces of King Joseph and those of Soult from the south in a presupposition of a general French collapse within Spain. Yet, not for the first or the last time Wellington would be surprised at the speed of French resurgence, as Clausel and other generals rallied their troops to ensure that they again confronted their enemies.

Wellington continued to embrace presumption; he saw no need to attack Clausel: 'it is not our object at present to fight them'.[46] This was a mistake: he underestimated his enemy. Wellington's leisurely advance halted at Burgos on 19 September, where General Jean-Louis Dubreton held the fortress with just over 2,000 men. Yet, under this wily and obstinate leader the defenders could not be moved. Inexplicably, Wellington had with him just three 18-pound guns and five 24-pound howitzers, the surviving pieces that had been used at the Salamanca forts. His commanding generals were also depleted; three of the four divisions with him were temporarily commanded, with Graham of the 1st, Leith of the 5th and Alten of the 7th Divisions all absent. Furthermore, Picton of the 3rd, Cole of the 4th, as well as Beresford and Cotton were also unavailable. Events would assuredly reflect the missing contribution of their collective experience. Wellington decided to attack the fortress, but he did so falteringly and with just the resources to hand. He otherwise procrastinated outside the Burgos walls for five weeks without result, until 21 October. Despite the professed pre-focus upon Burgos, he was again ill-prepared for a siege, but unable to admit the quandary he was in or eventual defeat. Indeed, it can only have been the assumption by Wellington that all French forces would retreat beyond the Ebro that can explain the leisurely way that the citadel was approached and invested. Fortescue likens his siege attempt to the assault of an Indian fort; since he had, 'snatched away more than one Indian fortress by escalade, he hoped to do the like with Burgos'.[47] Pragmatism and the avoidance of self-deception could otherwise have ensured the availability of siege guns from Almeida or the Retiro depot in Madrid. It is not plausible, as Wellington subsequently claimed, that insufficient oxen were available to bring forward a dozen heavy guns. While he would later acknowledge responsibility for the failure, initially Wellington also claimed that: 'the fault [. . .] was not that I undertook the operation with inadequate means, but that I took there the most inexperienced instead of the best troops'.[48] The involved 1st and 6th Divisions were competent and experienced; this was again mere shifting of blame. A soldier of the 1st Division stated: 'If ever a man ruined himself the Marquis had done it. For the last two months he has acted like a mad-man.'[49] Oman suggests that Wellington's own pessimism about another arduous siege plausibly affected troop morale and sowed discord, but the initial reality at least appears rather to be overconfidence and presumption.[50] Lieutenant Colonel John Burgoyne, RE was just one who quarreled here with Wellington regarding his methods. There were however a mere five Royal Engineer officers and eight engineering 'tradesmen' available. Captain Hew Dalrymple Ross, RA otherwise noted Wellington's 'usual cold manner'.[51] While Dickson wrote: 'Thus ended the siege of Burgos in which the Artillery were put to more shifts and difficulties from want of means, than it is possible to explain.'[52] Wellington suffered over 2,000 casualties at Burgos to 623 for the defenders before the siege was raised. One notable casualty among this number, killed when assaulting the fortress, was Major Edward Somers-Cocks; an observing officer of renown and close protégé of Wellington.

By the middle of October General Marie-François Caffarelli's *Armée du Nord* had provided reinforcements to the *Armée du Portugal*. This re-energized French force, now with 53,000 men under the new leadership of General Joseph Souham, once again directly threatened the 24,000 men with Wellington. The *Armée du Portugal* would concentrate just 13 miles north-east of Burgos at Monasterio. Rather than continue to retreat to the Ebro, in a parallel operation, Soult's army from Andalusia would conjoin with Joseph's forces to total 60,000 men east of Madrid. They now threatened General Hill's designated position at Aranjuez, south of the city. Wellington had wanted to meet with Hill at Madrid, but could not bring himself to leave the disregarded General Clinton in charge at Burgos. The divided British forces were now in a state of 'hopeless inferiority'.[53] Wellington had split his troops such that he had superiority against neither threatening French army, while any communication took two days to pass between himself and Hill. Souham's French cavalry, with in excess of 6,000 horsemen, clashed with Cotton's troopers at Venta del Pozo, behind the British lines at Burgos on 23 October and Wellington at once saw the imperative of retreat. Indeed, at this date Souham's forces could easily have overwhelmed Wellington if not for the ever-unacknowledged Spanish, who judiciously attacked and re-took Bilbao, the Basque capital. This most fortuitously compelled the French to temporarily pause and detach troops to that city, 100 miles distant, which gave Wellington a head start in his retreat. On 31 October Hill also abandoned Madrid, and it would take a week of hard marching for his forces and Wellington to rejoin together again, east of Salamanca. By 8 November, King Joseph had available over 80,000 troops from 3 combined armies, all close upon the heels of the British. The only option for the Allied forces was to continue to precipitously retreat all the way back to Portugal in a march where morale and discipline finally unravelled into 'a debacle'.[54] Only bad weather prevented the French from overtaking Wellington and inflicting further misery, if not outright defeat. Indeed, General Maximilien Foy subsequently considered that this was the best opportunity the French ever had to inflict a crippling defeat upon Wellington.[55] The unlucky Lieutenant General Edward Paget, who only returned to the army on 11 October, was a notable loss among many, captured by the French on 17 November while on patrol. Wellington's campaign had failed operationally, yet he thereafter brashly distorted events: 'It is in fact the most successful campaign [. . .] and has produced for the cause more important results than any campaign in which a British army has been engaged for the last century'. Also, 'I have [. . .] made a handsome retreat [. . .] without material loss. I believe I have done right.'[56] Subsequently, and despite the ubiquitous blame for the Spanish, mistakes had to be acknowledged: chiefly the under-estimation of enemy strength and the lack of a siege train at Burgos.[57] Wellington also complained that new French codes had stifled his intelligence-gathering; a true reflection upon its importance to his success.[58] The British army lost 4,752 troops after Badajoz during 1812, to leave just 30,400 effectives in December.[59] As only 700 British soldiers were killed at Salamanca, it can be seen that death in battle was a fraction of that from other causes, including command hubris. Yet, Wellington still issued a damning circular condemning perceived misconduct on the retreat, which aroused enduring resentment.[60] Even those commentators who usually express naught but admiration for Wellington have struggled to make light of this. Oman more objectively observes: 'To blame the officers was simply not true. [Wellington] may easily underrate the privations of [he] who has faced the weather unsheltered and with no rations at all.'[61] QMG Gordon was blamed for misdirecting rations away from the army. Gordon was already under a cloud with Wellington, who had discovered that his correspondence included personal letters to both the Duke of York and Lord Grey, the leader of the government's Whig opposition. This was perceived disloyalty, worse than any action committed by say General Spencer in 1808. Three generals, namely Clinton, Stewart and the newly arrived Major General Lord George Dalhousie, actually ignored march orders on the retreat in a show of independence, much to Wellington's extreme ire.[62] They felt obliged to hold council to ensure unity, before deciding whether they would obey Wellington or not, before acting upon their own best judgement. Oman further states: 'It might have been expected that Wellington would at least show more regard for the feelings of his officers, however much he might condemn his rank and file. As a rule he did not.'[63] Wellington was harsh and possibly out of touch; he effectively lost control of events and distributed blame regardless of his own culpability. Major Frederick Robinson was just one of very many with a grievance; he felt obliged at this time to write to Wellington regarding the discrepancy between the rations received by the enlisted men compared with that of officers, but he received no equitable response.[64]

The specific scapegoat of the retreat was QMG Gordon: 'he has never in fact performed his duties, and I do not believe he ever can or will perform them'.[65] Gordon had hitherto floated the topical idea of becoming a chief-of-staff to Wellington, but both Horse Guards and specifically Wellington were quizzical and his expedited departure – due to 'ill-health' – now resolved the matter. Colonel William de Lancey became acting QMG. Other disfavoured senior officers such as the ailing Erskine, and notably from within the cavalry, Generals Slade, Long and Victor von Alten had already been sidelined and in time would gradually depart as Horse Guards now fully complied with Wellington's wishes. Permission to remove these specific officers was given to Wellington on 28 December 1812, though it would take until January 1814 before the last, von Alten, returned home, again ostensibly due to ill health. The principled though understandably cynical General Long, recalled in August 1813, declined an appointment to the Home Staff as it would be, 'wholly inconsistent with any principle of service to hold any military situation at home, the duties of which I have appeared to have not displayed satisfactorily abroad'.[66] Wellington would later untruthfully deny requesting the recall of Long, despite the recorded evidence.[67] 'By now Wellington had acquired such ascendancy over Liverpool and his ministers that [. . .] they were content to accept his decisions and demands'.[68] Wellington had overturned his former professed inability to veto his subordinates; an obstacle quoted by some historians as the sole limitation to his command effectiveness.[69] Yet, given the administrative disposition of the Duke of York, it is unreasonable to suggest that the Horse Guards had knowingly undermined Wellington with inappropriate staff appointments, as he might suggest, or that Wellington should be above accepting the regulatory checks and balances inherent to British governmental authority.

Wellington's army headquarters was subsequently established at Freineda, close by Almeida, Portugal between 24 November 1812 and 22 May 1813; AG Charles Stewart, before his departure, had described it as 'this miserable village, or rather abominable mudhole'.[70] The health and motivation of AG Stewart led to him permanently stepping down in February 1813. During his recuperation from the illness of the previous year Stewart had enquired of Wellington regarding the potential for alternative employment in the Peninsula, ideally in command of a cavalry brigade. Patently, Wellington did not want another independent thinker in such a role when he replied, 'although it might be more agreeable to you to take a gallop with the Hussars, I think you had better return to your office'.[71] The final scene from Stewart's face-to-face relations with Wellington supposedly consisted of the latter reducing Stewart to tears of apology for his errant behaviour. Such details are otherwise open to scepticism as the source for the story was Wellington himself, told in 1826 – with regard to a professed friend.[72] Again, the telling of the story clearly shows the discourteous, if not vituperative side of Wellington's nature. Lord Castlereagh otherwise observed with regard to his half-brother Stewart that

Lieutenant Colonel Macleod at Badajoz, by John Augustus Atkinson (1775–1833); the maelstrom of Peninsular War siege combat.

Arthur Wellesley, 1st Duke of Wellington (1769–1852).

General Sir John Moore (1761–1809).

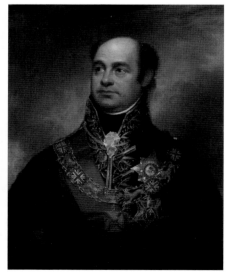

General Sir Hew Whitefoord Dalrymple, 1st Baronet (1750–1830).

General William Beresford, 1st Viscount Beresford (1768–1854).

General Sir John Coape Sherbrooke (1764–1830).

General Rowland Hill, 1st Viscount Hill (1772–1842).

General Thomas Graham, 1st Baron Lynedoch (1748–1843).

General John Hope, 4th Earl of Hopetoun (1765–1823).

General Stapleton Cotton, 1st Viscount Combermere (1773–1865).

General John Le Marchant (1766–1812).

General Sir Edward Paget (1775–1849).

General Henry Paget, Lord Uxbridge (1768–1854).

General Charles Stewart, 3rd Marquess of Londonderry (1778–1854).

General Sir George Murray (1772–1846).

General Sir Henry Torrens (1779–1828).

Colonel FitzRoy Somerset, 1st Baron Raglan (1788–1855).

General Robert Craufurd (1764–1812).

General Sir William Stewart (1774–1827).

General Sir Galbraith Lowry Cole (1772–1842).

General Sir Thomas Picton (1758–1815).

General Sir James Leith (1763–1816).

General Sir Edward Pakenham (1778–1815).

General Robert Ballard Long (1771–1825).

General Sir John Slade, 1st Baronet (1762–1859).

Wellington's masterstroke: British troops triumph at Salamanca, 22 July 1812.

Wellington's imbroglio: French defence at Burgos, September–October 1812.

he had, 'a high opinion of his good sense and discretion'. Stewart had always been prepared to argue with Wellington, even to the extent that Wellington had threatened to, 'send him back to England in arrest' for his wilfulness. It has been credibly suggested by at least one historian that, in fact, Stewart was condemned mainly for standing up to Wellington.[73] Regardless of Wellington's low opinion, in April 1813 the disparaged Stewart was deemed sufficiently capable to become British Minister to the King of Prussia. Wellington's brother-in-law, Major General Edward Pakenham, would be formally appointed the new Adjutant General in May 1813. By this date Wellington had fully purged his staff of 'double allegiance' with his strength of personality. For those needing to consult Wellington, 'some [. . .] are much afraid of him [. . .] I feel something like a boy going to school'.[74] Wellington now firmly and rigidly controlled all headquarters' operational functions; staff work became, as the new AG Pakenham would observe, 'insignificant clerking business'.[75] During this period, the newly promoted Lieutenant Colonel Colin Campbell, as an assistant QMG, was in charge of Wellington's household, superintending all practical arrangements for Wellington's accommodation and welfare. In thus supervising the headquarters for much of the war, part of Campbell's role was specifically to smooth relations between Wellington and QMG George Murray; Wellington doubtless grated with many astute subordinates.[76] In 1810, Campbell himself had complained of his role alongside Wellington and had procured a posting to Gibraltar. He confided in Torrens that he found his duties at headquarters 'irksome'.[77] Nonetheless, Wellington argued with Horse Guards to retain Campbell's services, an event that Torrens labelled: 'God's Curse'.[78] The only other individuals Wellington ever went out of his way to retain were the then Lieutenant Colonel Edward Pakenham in 1809, and, surprisingly, the otherwise disparaged AG Charles Stewart in 1810; which again appears to present something of a contradiction to the standard portrayal of Stewart's capabilities. Wellington was typically observed at this time: 'if his plans are thwarted [he] will be in a rage'; and again it is said that he 'raved like a madman' at any contradiction to his will.[79] After five years of war, the inherent pressures within Wellington's command appear to have stretched relations with even his closest of associates. While examples may be quoted of his loyalty and indeed affection towards some, for others he would be bellicose and overbearing; it may reasonably be adjudged that he struggled to inspire widespread devotion.

Once again over the winter of 1812–13, Generals Graham, Picton, Leith, Cotton, Clinton and Houston were all absent for a variety of so-called 'personal reasons'. Concurrently, Lieutenant Colonel George Fisher, RA arrived to assume artillery command from Framlington. Wellington was again unhappy, and, 'took care to let him feel that I thought him very stupid', and despite subordinate officers speaking well of him.[80] Such a difficult clash of personalities forced Fisher to resign within weeks. In May, Wellington pointedly passed over Lisbon-based

Lieutenant Colonel Charles Waller, RA, and blocked the arrival of Sir George Wood from England in favour of Lieutenant Colonel Alexander Dickson, his seventh artillery commander.[81] Waller duly wrote to Wellington to complain of his treatment, but Wellington made it clear that he would appoint whomsoever he wished.[82] This behaviour caused sensation at the time, and illustrates Wellington's now unassailable authority, despite, 'a tense atmosphere at headquarters'.[83] Further insight reports: 'There is much obsequious, time-serving conduct to anyone who is in office.'[84] Wellington's headquarters was completely subservient to its commander, whose autocratic command could not be gainsaid. Wellington now had full control of and responsibility for the composition of his staff: 'To conciliate whom [Wellington] is the only road to popularity'.[85] Torrens observed, 'Ever since the Army in the Peninsula has been of such an extent as to furnish its own meritorious candidates for the vacant staff employments upon its establishment, the C-in-C has ceased to interfere with Lord Wellington in such nominations.'[86] With detached disingenuousness, Secretary of State for War Lord Bathurst would provide political support for Wellington at home in a manner which did not waver.

> Great as were Lord Wellington's military talents, how unwilling he was to risk the lives of his soldiers; how careful he was of the means of his country; and how unwilling to sacrifice even what must be most dear to a soldier – an opportunity of obtaining personal renown – if that opportunity must be purchased with too great a loss of men.[87]

Notably in May 1813, George Murray agreed to return to Portugal as Quartermaster General, and upon arrival immediately made indispensible efforts to ensure preparation and mapping for forthcoming British operations.[88] He sent officers to examine all roads crossing the northern Portuguese border as well as examining the Duero valley and other river crossings to confirm potential routes of march. Cassini's maps dated 1798–1812 were also considered for the geography to be encountered across the French border. Most importantly Wellington now knew that he had the time and the resources, unavailable to the French, to formulate a vision for the execution of what would be a decisive campaign. Prime Minister Lord Liverpool wrote to Wellington: 'The only efficient French army [. . .] is that under Soult: and whatever it may cost Bonaparte to abandon Spain, I think he will prefer that alternative to the loss of Germany'.[89] There was an expectation that the French armies in Spain were now a spent force. The year had already seen Napoleon withdraw further major formations to bolster his German armies, and the French within Spain were certainly at bay. Napoleon's best advice to King Joseph was that Madrid be abandoned pre-emptively, with the French headquarters relocated to Valladolid, 120 miles further north.

Generals Graham and Picton now also returned to the army; Wellington specifically asked that Graham wave his claim to be second-in-command to enable Beresford to remain in-post.[90] Wellington's plans for the new campaign were kept so secret that they would come as a surprise to many senior officers. For the forthcoming campaign, the army was now in fine condition: 'we are equipped in a very superior style', observed Lieutenant Colonel George Bingham.[91] The port of Santander in northern Spain had previously been liberated on 3 August 1812 by the actions of the Spanish in conjunction with ships of the Royal Navy, led by Commodore Sir Home Popham, RN. Santander would duly be established as a new supply base, so that a line of communication for the Peninsular Army potentially existed over a notably shorter route into Spain than that used to date from Lisbon. By late 1813, as the war moved towards the French border, supply for the army would be overwhelmingly directed from Santander. A notional total of 265 transport ships was routinely necessary to keep Wellington's army supplied.[92] The move wholly into Spain however somewhat strained relations with Portugal; they complained about the lack of recognition from Britain for all their past privations, and felt used and now cast aside by Wellington personally. Visits to both Cádiz and Lisbon in early 1813, for talks with government, were necessary for Wellington and which in addition now at this late stage granted him control of the Spanish armies. Wellington's diplomacy had not however improved since 1809, and it has been observed that: 'It is impossible to pretend that Wellington's command of the Spanish army was the greatest success of his career. Not only was he unable to extract much profit from his appointment in the military sense, but he presided over a dramatic deterioration in Anglo-Spanish relations.'[93] Nonetheless, in spring 1813, Wellington was finally vested with sole control of all military operations in the Peninsula by the Allied governments. In the drive for ultimate victory, this was power that enabled him to make use of his forces far more efficiently than his French opponents.

Once again Wellington employed diversionary tactics. It was Commodore Popham, RN, who with Allied marines again raided along the northern Spanish coast from June to August 1813; their aim, to inhibit any movement by the *Armée du Nord*. Lieutenant General Sir John Murray, with 10,000 Anglo-Sicilian troops in cooperation with 8,000 Spaniards, was made available and directed to assault Tarragona on the Spanish east coast, to thereby ensure that the French forces of Marshal Louis Suchet remained fully occupied. Wellington in typical fashion produced a Memorandum of Operations running to twenty-nine points by way of orders and instructions for Murray. However, the subsequent sequence of events would unfold in not quite the idealized manner for General Murray. Despite an initial victory over Suchet at the Battle of Castalla on 13 April 1813, Murray is accused of generating only muddle at Tarragona in June, before re-embarking aboard ship without his siege train. Back in England, though delayed until 1815, at Wellington's recommendation he was duly brought before a court martial for neglect of duty and 'disobedience of [Wellington's] express written orders', as well as the loss of those eighteen guns.[94] His defence intriguingly included the detail that Wellington's most specific direction had stated that he would 'forgive anything, excepting that one of the corps should be beaten or dispersed'.[95] Fear of Wellington's ire coupled with the provision of rigid instructions certainly appears once again as at least a partial factor in the trepidation shown by another subordinate general. Indeed, Napier considers that just as Wellington was deceived by the enemy's fortified strength at Salamanca, Burgos and elsewhere, so he was deceived with regards to Tarragona.[96] Certainly, Murray's successor Lieutenant General Lord William Bentinck found it equally difficult to prevail against the most capable Suchet, for whom the initial capture of Tarragona in 1811 had prompted his promotion to the marshalate. Murray's own failure has of course been roundly disparaged, but should be recognized nonetheless as preventing even a single soldier from Suchet's forces moving west in support of King Joseph. The outcome of Murray's court martial should similarly be recognized as an acquittal of all charges, save for an admonishment for the abandonment of his siege guns. Even this rebuke was immediately set aside by Prince George, the Prince Regent, who viewed Murray's fault as no more than a 'mere error of judgement'.[97]

General Pedro Girón's Spanish Army of Galicia, with some 25,500 effectives, would directly co-ordinate its movement with Wellington in the offensive of 1813. The Anglo-Portuguese army itself had now grown to exceed 81,000 men, and Wellington was compelled by this size to delegate his army within three 'columns', led by Beresford in the centre, with Graham to the left and Hill's column to the right. Beresford, accompanied by Wellington, thereafter routinely led the 3rd, 7th, 4th and Light Divisions; Graham the 1st and 5th; Hill the 6th, 2nd and Portuguese Division. Forces may still be seen to adhere to the symmetrical principles of seniority present from the array of 1808, though reversed; Hill from his days in Extremadura customarily held the army's right wing. With the enlarged army, in June 1813 the pool of senior staff officers was expanded when a brevet created new major generals from senior colonels. This patronage they owed to Wellington: 'they place such confidence in their Hero, that no-one questions his conduct'.[98]

A pontoon bridge was an important new component, assembled for the army's advance by Fletcher, the Commander of the RE. It was subsequently given priority over the artillery for road movement, since it was likely that two, if not three major rivers needed to be crossed before catching the French: the Duero, the Pisuerga and the Ebro. Wellington tersely commented: 'our confounded bridge has delayed us many days'.[99] Wellington had now also ensured the organization of a further siege train to await onboard ship at Coruña, pending events; Burgos could not be discounted for a second time. During May the army advanced back along the route through Salamanca. Meanwhile, the columns of General Graham and Spanish General Girón were directed through the wilds of northern Portugal to outflank potential enemy defensive positions; Wellington dictated the movement of all columns. To general relief, the French abandoned Burgos as they retreated; Wellington stating: 'I consider the evacuation of Burgos a very important event.'[100] While on the march, 9 June was remembered by QMG George Murray as the sole occasion he ever dared to offer advice to Wellington; it was not accepted.[101] Wellington personally assumed command of the Light Division to skirmish with the French at San Millán on 18 June, and the same day took control of Graham's 1st Division to contend again at the village of Osman. Yet, the French under King Joseph avoided battle until the remnants of three armies, now only 66,000 men, finally stood beyond the Ebro, behind a tributary, the River Zadorra at Vitoria. Their intention was to buy time while their huge baggage train escaped over the French frontier. Of the battle on 21 June, it could be said that it was lost by the French as much as won by Wellington; manoeuvre and attrition had already wrecked French morale.[102]

Wellington initially had Hill attack the heights dominating the French left and the route of the main road. Thereafter, Picton's 3rd Division attacked the French right, over unguarded river bridges, duly supported by the Light Division and Dalhousie's late-arriving 7th Division. That they were unguarded speaks volumes about French preparedness and proficiency; the capable General Jean-Baptiste Jourdan, chief-of-staff to Joseph, had been incapacitated with fever before battle. The fact that Picton pre-empted the attack by Dalhousie that Wellington had planned has been called insubordination, but can otherwise be seen as positive initiative.[103] Indeed, after the battle Picton declared, 'the 3rd Division had the principal share in the brilliant achievement', and was mortified that it went unrecognized, indeed snubbed by Wellington.[104] Dalhousie is among several generals, rather than Wellington himself, blamed for 'the imperfect consequences of the victory': in his case for being 'fussy and disobedient', as well as late.[105] The fact that Dalhousie at the least could not strictly adhere to a dictated timetable when marching across country might reasonably have been foreseen. The fact that Wellington was happy to split his army into several attacking columns in the face of the enemy shows that he anticipated no vigorous French response. The battle incorporated the largest artillery duel of the Peninsular War: seventy-five guns per side were at one stage exchanging fire in the centre. As battle raged, the French defensive position was, thereafter, further outflanked by Graham's left-most column. Though also marching across country, he had Wellington's orders not to attack until 2:00pm and then to advance against the French extreme right flank and rear, aiming to block the main road to Bayonne.[106] That Graham did not attack earlier or advance further has again been repeatedly criticized by historians.[107] However, it was not viewed in this way by participants: 'The left column was not in the main attack, but was, in my opinion, the cause of the very hasty retreat of the enemy.'[108] It has also been suggested that in case of mishap Wellington wished to ensure that Graham's force remained intact; a defeat might well have entailed a retreat in the direction of Bilbao.[109] Graham understandably followed Wellington's orders to the letter.

The eventual French rout left Vitoria and the surrounding area covered with supplies and loot that the Allied troops fell upon. Both sides had lost some 5,000 men killed and wounded, but the French had additionally lost some 3,000 prisoners, 150 guns and a horde of materiel. Pursuit of the enemy was derisory, though there was only one road remaining open for escape towards France. Of the large cavalry presence, only Colonel John Colquhoun Grant's brigade of hussars was significantly engaged from a British cavalry force which at 6,000 troopers was the equal of that at Waterloo. In addition, there were present 1,300 KGL and 900 Portuguese cavalry to oppose 10,000 French cavalry. The ground was reportedly too rough for mounted troops to act effectively.[110] Yet, this appears overstated; the cavalry should have played a greater role than sitting immobile, 'often under fire from enemy artillery'.[111] The movement of the cavalry was fully controlled by Wellington, notably since he had stationed his cavalry commander, Major General von Bock, remotely with General Graham. Bock was ostensibly in charge as Cotton was still absent from the army. Nonetheless, the envelopment of the French right in battle did produce a great and decisive victory, to ensure that the outnumbered and discouraged French were pushed out of north-west Spain. Wellington had been operationally brilliant, but tactical troop co-ordination at Vitoria showed many flaws. Oman believes that if the French had been destroyed then no subsequent campaign in the Pyrenees would have been necessary.[112] This is debatable, but manifestly Wellington's tight command and control at Vitoria prevented his subordinates from showing the initiative required to produce the best outcome: 'the results of the day were very far from satisfactory'.[113]

After the battle it required QMG Murray's intervention to ensure that Graham was permitted to follow the beaten French, until wet weather intervened. Graham was finally stopped at Tolosa, 55 miles distant and halfway to San Sebastian, by the troops of General Maximilien Foy.[114] Meanwhile, Wellington's focus was upon berating his own army: 'The 18th [Hussars, of Grant's brigade] are a disgrace to the name of a soldier', and in general, 'We have in the service the scum of the earth as common soldiers.'[115] It has been suggested that, 'a cavalry commander of exceptional ability was missing', but no commander would move without Wellington's direction.[116] 'Lord Wellington may not like to entrust officers with detachments to act according to circumstances,' wrote a cavalry officer, 'and I am not quite clear if he approves of much success, excepting under his own immediate eye.'[117] There are also indications that the British army had outrun its supplies at Vitoria, which both affected morale and was a most strong inducement to the undisciplined looting that took place; not counting the sheer value and quantity of the abandoned goods.[118]

Two days after the battle, on 23 June, Captain Norman Ramsey, RHA, a hero of the cavalry's celebrated defence at Fuentes de Oñoro, was arrested for supposedly disobeying the aggrieved Wellington's verbal order by moving his troop of Royal Horse Artillery (RHA) guns. Horse artillery, fielding light 6-pounder guns in direct support of the cavalry, had been a feature of Wellington's army since the summer of 1809. The events surrounding Ramsey's arrest were what virtually all contemporaries viewed as a misunderstanding, as Ramsey was otherwise in possession of a written order from QMG Murray to rejoin Major General George Anson's Brigade of dragoons. Fitzroy Somerset, Dickson and Graham all appealed in vain: 'Wellington would listen to no reason or explanation, and [. . .] raved like a madman [. . .] applying to Ramsay every ungentlemanly and vile epithet'.[119] Many gunners now considered Wellington's actions 'beyond the pale', for after this argument with Wellington Ramsey's career was broken.[120] Several other artillery captains felt sufficiently marginalized after Vitoria to complain to Wellington of being rudely overlooked: 'his Lordship must be either grossly ignorant of the matter in which his artillery are directed and disposed in the field, or he must be wantonly unjust to those who earned the credit, as they would (assuredly) have received the blame, had anything gone wrong'.[121] It is perhaps a reflection of the sheer exasperation and disaffection felt with Wellington by many individuals that malicious rumours at the time report that Wellington, 'has not overexposed himself to danger'.[122]

During the weeks following Vitoria, Wellington consolidated the gains achieved, advancing the army as far as the Pyrenees Mountains, where Spanish cavalry were deployed to watch the French border. He would appear to have discounted any thought of following hard upon the defeated, disorganized and thoroughly demoralized enemy; a route that possibly could have been taken, unopposed as far as the French city of Bayonne. He rather dispersed the army over a forty-five mile frontage to defend the gains made, maintaining the existing format of three corps-size columns. Possibly there was some small necessity to screen the army's right flank against any potential march by Marshal Suchet's forces, still intact 250 miles away on the Spanish east coast, but a major opportunity to push straight on into France would appear to have fully gone begging. Even some admirers of Wellington have speculated that an immediate march upon Bayonne would likely have turned the defensive Pyrenees line.[123] The French command was in thorough disarray as Napoleon now relieved the incompetent Joseph and the luckless Jourdan, while recalling Marshal Soult to command what was now titled the *Armée d'Espagne*. The subsequent six months would thus see more fighting and greater losses than in any comparable period of the war, as Wellington largely stood on the defensive and allowed Soult's forces to reconsolidate. The net results when the Allies did counter-attack were insignificant: the front line moved forward just 30 miles in those six months. The tenacity of the French was certainly one factor, Wellington's studied hesitancy and irresolution another: 'when I knew that the armistice [in Germany] had been renewed [. . .] I did not deem it expedient to attack the enemy'.[124] His decision to proceed cautiously resulted in increased human attrition, despite the French army's near collapse. Wellington's reluctance to advance with more celerity – 'I feel a great disinclination to enter the French territory' – could be interpreted by Britain's allies as not only unnecessarily cautious, but selfish.[125] His political outlook paralleled his attitude to army command: he arguably paid disproportionate attention to how events might have impact upon his personal prestige. Caution maintained his winning pre-eminence. Yet, the news that Wellington's concentrated army was advancing into Gascony could have demoralized the French in Germany, encouraged Napoleon's opponents and resulted in an earlier end to war. The similar example of Wellington's diplomacy with Spain to this date has been described as, 'an exemplar in lack of all tact and consideration'.[126] Wellington's personality certainly had a parallel impact upon his political effectiveness just as it affected the command and control of his army: the references made by some historians to political problems being merely 'superficial tensions' are not wholly convincing.

No time pressure now appeared to apply to the reduction of the French-occupied Spanish fortress cities of San Sebastian and Pamplona, which sat behind the new Allied lines. Wellington in effect spent the next four months reducing these fortifications; time spent by the French in reorganizing their forces and constructing new lines of defence in the Pyrenees. For San Sebastian, Spanish forces had initially and quickly sealed off the 3,170 defenders led by General Louis Rey. Wellington however ruled against continued blockade, since being a port any investment risked being imperfect. Almost predictably, Wellington complained and subsequently fell out with the Royal Navy regarding the effectiveness of their naval blockade. Viscount Melville, the First Lord of the Admiralty, wrote: 'I will take your opinion in preference to any other person's as to the most effectual mode of beating a French army, but I have no confidence in your seamanship or nautical skill.'[127] Heavy guns were nonetheless readily available and were duly brought from ship, with active siege work directed by Dickson, RA and Fletcher, RE. Also at the siege for the first time was a contingent of 100 men from the Royal Sappers and Miners, configured only from April 1812; by the end of the year 300 designated sappers would be with the army. Analysis of the siege has shown that due to the swift resurgence of French activity in the Pyrenees at the end of July, Wellington now felt suddenly hastened to strike and he once again cut corners.[128] A first assault on 25 July 1813 duly failed, and Major General John Oswald, temporarily commanding the 5th Division, was blamed by Wellington, despite having expressed dislike for the plan of attack. Most unfortunately, the long-serving and suffering Lieutenant Colonel Fletcher was killed during the assault; one of 25 engineer officers killed during the Peninsula War, out of just

102 who served overall. Ammunition shortages and the French counter-attacks in the Pyrenees led to the siege being suspended thereafter. Wellington wrote to Hill: 'The truth is, that having two objects in hand [San Sebastian and Pamplona] we are not strong on any point as we ought to be.'[129] In August the siege would be resumed and the town assaulted again on 31 August. Too late Soult launched that same day an unsuccessful counter-offensive against Spanish defenders at San Marcial and Vera, deployed behind the Bidasoa River. Soult of course hoped to further prolong events or even effect relief. Wellington uniquely called for volunteers from all divisions to lead the final assault upon San Sebastian, seen at the time by the rank and file as a slur upon the 5th Division. Nonetheless, Lieutenant General James Leith returned to command the 5th and lead the assault, though wounded in the effort.[130] Innovative close-supporting artillery fire was instrumental in the eventual success by the attackers, for which General Graham is credited.[131] The appetite of Wellington's troops for siege work would appear to have diminished with every such event in which they became involved, so that by San Sebastian they were only vaguely motivated. They fully expected heavy losses for little personal gain. Wellington lost some 3,000 men at San Sebastian, and some observers have considered that he was again fortunate to have avoided 'an unmitigated catastrophe'.[132] The repeated difficulties shown in siege operations by Wellington certainly emphasize a shortage of engineering resources and experience, but also Wellington's over-riding impatience, and tendency to always look for short cuts, almost regardless of the human cost. To add insult to injury the near total destruction of San Sebastian caused huge ill-feeling from the Spanish government, who felt Wellington's efforts were wanton and disproportionate. Losses at the corresponding, straightforward blockade of Pamplona would prove to be negligible. It may reasonably be questioned whether Spanish troops might also have been used to blockade and reduce San Sebastian within a parallel timescale. At Pamplona, initially General Hill on 26 June was responsible for establishing picquets to prevent crops being harvested in the surrounding areas and he also severed the aqueduct that brought water to the city. Thereafter the blockade was formed by the 6th and 7th Divisions of Major Generals Sir Charles Colville and Lord George Dalhousie, before in July Spanish forces under General Enrique O'Donnell concluded the blockade. Pamplona would surrender on 31 October; too long and vexing a timescale for Wellington. Though not carried out, he indeed suggested to the Spanish that they should shoot the officers and decimate the French garrison of over 3,800 men under General Louis Cassan for their temerity.[133] Wellington himself later said that the stratagem to subdue both San Sebastian and Pamplona in concert was, 'one of the greatest faults he ever committed in war'.[134] For Wellington it had meant the dispersion of the army with an associated unwelcome delegation of authority, in conjunction with the frustration of further siege operations.

The immediate border region with France, dominated by the Pyrenees Mountains, had at its western end upon the coastal plain the main lateral roads suitable for wheeled traffic. One additional road, 20 miles to the east through the Maya pass, was also suitable for vehicles. A further easternmost route from Roncesvalles to St Jean-de-Port was primarily a precipitous track of secondary importance. This was an area termed the Pyrenees Quadrilateral: lying between San Sebastian and Pamplona in Spain, Bayonne and St Jean-de-Port in France. Wellington's defensive dispositions within the mountains covered all these routes that crossed the frontier, but operational responsibility lay now by necessity with local commanders. On 25 July, with the Allies concentrating upon San Sebastian and Pamplona, Soult attacked the Maya and Roncesvalles passes, en route to Pamplona. Wellington's caution and inaction had allowed Soult to reorganize and seize the initiative. Soult also thoroughly deluded Wellington as to his intentions; this could have been avoided. Three French divisions exceeding 20,000 men under General Count Jean-Baptiste D'Erlon attacked the brigades of Colonel John Cameron and Major General William Pringle, of Stewart's 2nd Division, as well as the brigade of Major General Edward Barnes of the 7th Division at Maya, and General Hill readily agreed their retreat. General Stewart reported to Hill: 'A very spirited charge by Major General Barnes [. . .] enabled us to close an inauspicious day in a manner that imposed upon our enemy [and] if succour had arrived, we might this day have regained that ground, the loss of which I have been detailing with much pain to my feelings'.[135] General Lowry Cole's 4th Division, as well as newly promoted Major General Sir John Byng's Brigade of the 2nd Division, defended the Roncesvalles pass, and these units retreated when threatened with envelopment by further large French forces, totalling 34,000 men directly under Marshal Soult. The French attacked out of dense fog, while attempting outflanking movements that could have readily trapped the defenders. Byng's Brigade alone defended without support for 9 hours before retreating; the Duke of York was correct when he had described Byng as 'an intelligent and excellent officer'.[136] Picton's supporting 3rd Division joined the retreat, over the next two days, eventually to Sorauren, just 4 miles in front of Pamplona. The out of touch Wellington had, meanwhile, ordered Picton to stop Soult's advance at Zubiri, halfway between Roncesvalles and Pamplona, but Picton declined as he felt that all such positions could readily be outflanked. These withdrawals have been severely criticized by historians for both giving up the passes against Wellington's wishes, and failing to communicate events.[137] Stewart specifically fell afoul of Wellington for the loss of four guns at Maya: 'they are the only guns that have ever been lost by troops acting under my command'.[138] This was not strictly a true statement, as guns had been abandoned by Wellington at Burgos within the previous year. Stewart was unreasonably branded by Wellington as, 'unsuitable to command a division [. . .] he cannot obey an order'.[139] Yet, overall the defenders were hugely outnumbered and Wellington's own directions, similar again to those provided to Sir John Murray at Tarragona earlier in the year, stated the need to defend 'without committing the troops against a force so superior that the advantage of the ground would not compensate it'.[140] It is impossible here to agree with some commentators that Wellington was 'shamefully served by his subordinate generals'.[141] At Maya, Stewart lost 1,500 of the involved 6,000 men and was himself wounded, so the defence was hardly desultory. Otherwise, Cole has correctly, but atypically received insightful praise for his interpretation of instructions and thereby saving his force from destruction; his losses were in the order of 350 men.[142] Wellington also loudly expressed his irritation with Cole: '[he] never informed me exactly how far he found it necessary to give way, or let me know by what a superior force he was pressed and that he intended giving way'.[143] As for failing to communicate, Picton wrote to Wellington: 'the country offering no post between this place and Pamplona [. . .] I agreed with [. . .] Cole that it was advisable to retire [to] a position at as short a distance as practicable from Pamplona. If I had known your Lordship's intention sooner I [. . .] would have endeavoured to give effect to your Lordship's wishes.[144] Cole himself wrote, 'I did not receive your letter of the 24th until nine o'clock yesterday [the 26 July]'.[145] These messages make clear that communication was stretched: Cole's courier got his message to Wellington, 'more by luck than design'.[146] Communication between the troops originally at Maya and Roncesvalles was undertaken by Brigadier General Robert Long's 9th and 13th LD; he markedly took the precaution of making copy of all orders to pass on to Hill. General Hill otherwise appears oddly dispassionate about the dramatic events unfolding; while forces retreated he has been described as busy, 'sorting out his impedimenta' of supply vehicles, baggage and wounded.[147] While the whole of the Maya to Roncesvalles line was under attack, Fortescue confirms that Hill was inactive.[148] Stretched communication restricted Wellington's usual control, while perversely his close proximity neutered Hill's responsibility.

Retrograde movement allowed the still intact formations of Generals Cole, Stewart and Picton to collectively stand at Sorauren; a position as 'formidable as Buçaco'.[149] The location also notably allowed Wellington and the 6th Division, temporarily commanded in Clinton's absence by Major General Dennis Pack, to combine as reinforcement before battle. The generals had used their initiative, though their absent commander was intrinsically disinclined to be happy with the outcome. Nevertheless, upon reaching their chosen battlefield, Wellington's only change to Cole's dispositions was to move just one regiment of reserve. Units were otherwise located on reverse slopes in approved Wellington fashion. Wellington successfully defended the position on 28 July, before counter-attacking on 30 July. Soult's French troops had now out-run their supply, were over-stretched and they were readily pushed back over the mountains. They had suffered some 4,000 casualties, while the Allies lost a total of 2,650 men. The blockade of Pamplona remained intact. For the British, the entire defensive scenario had resulted from a notable misjudgement, as days before the attack Wellington was provided with intelligence that Soult's army had concentrated at St Jean-de-Port.[150] Wellington nonetheless had decided that any French counter-attack must aim to relieve San Sebastian. He ignored intelligence because he felt he knew better. He admitted: 'I had then no notion that with an army so lately beaten he [Soult] had serious thoughts [. . .] of driving us beyond the Ebro'.[151] With the front re-stabilized by 2 August, he merely resumed the defensive: 'It is a great disadvantage when the Officer Commanding-in-Chief must be absent, and probably at a distance. For this reason there is nothing I dislike so much as these extended operations, which I cannot direct myself.'[152]

Wellington gave no plaudits for the ultimately successful Pyrenean defence, despite the difficulties of operating in the mountains, and where artillery and cavalry support was limited by necessity. The important contribution of the two artillery brigades available at Sorauren was once again ignored by Wellington in his after-battle report. These were 9-pounders, which contributed greatly to British success since the French had been able to drag just two 4-pound guns over the mountains. Dickson, the CRA, would subsequently organize captured French light cannon as the nucleus of a new mountain gun troop: 'I think that either party would labour under a disadvantage were they without.'[153] The mountain troop would be commanded by Lieutenant William L. Robe, the son of Lieutenant Colonel William Robe, RA. The Pyrenean terrain certainly rendered the cavalry for the most part defunct: 'cavalry are not of much use in the country we are in'.[154] The few light cavalry regiments present, beyond delivering post, were retained merely for piquet and intelligence work.

After the death of Fletcher at San Sebastian, his deputy Lieutenant Colonel John Fox Burgoyne was expected to be confirmed as the next CRE. He was the experienced individual to hand, and promotion by Wellington was anticipated to parallel Dickson's rise within the RA. However, Burgoyne now immediately fell out with Wellington regarding the pontoon train. Wellington complained that he 'is really too bad'; for Burgoyne supposedly being too slow in reorganizing the train, and that the entire army's progress had been 'delayed by a mistake made by the officer of engineers'.[155] Harsh criticism since high river levels had already deferred Wellington's next planned advance into October and he himself again referred to a 'great disinclination to enter the French territory'.[156] As so often, the reality of the situation was a somewhat more uncertain picture, than has been painted by many historians: 'Due to the incompetence of the engineering officer attack across the River Bidassoa had to be postponed until 7 October 1813.'[157] Lieutenant Colonel Howard Elphinstone would subsequently assume command of the engineers. Due to the ambiguity of the situation, he would only dare quit his post at Lisbon to take up his new position with the field army in October, after first writing to Wellington to request clarification.

Wellington had been promoted to Field Marshal by a grateful British government after the success of Vitoria, and this had opened the way for the previously ineligible Lieutenant General John Hope to join him. Hope had been Moore's second-in-command in Spain and despite being a former critic of Wellington, now brought great experience and ability to the army. He should not be confused with his namesake, a major general who commanded the 7th Division temporarily in 1812, notably at Salamanca. It is a sad reflection that to date not one published work exists in dedication to the life and accomplishments of (either) General Hope. As General Hill, his modesty would subsequently downplay his own contribution to events: 'progress in this country of not much more than twenty miles, will hardly appear to deserve the honour so well as the labours of those that have gone through the war'.[158] Hope arrived to replace General Graham in command of the left flank as this column began to ford the Bidasoa River into France on 7 October. While Wellington was now aged 44 years old and Hope 48, Graham had reached the age of 65 and continued to have health problems: 'I have been suffering again a good deal from my eyes and stomach.'[159] Picton, Leith and Dalhousie were other prominent generals who went absent during the autumn of 1813 due to illness or injury. The opposed crossing of the Bidasoa River commenced at 7:25am and was fully secured by 9:00am. General Alten's Light Division, supported by Spanish troops, 3 miles to the right of the Bidasoa battle front, led the attack that captured the dominant La Rhune massif by the following day. QMG Murray's Bidasoa orders have been described as 'one of the most comprehensive movement orders for a set-piece operation ever issued by a staff officer'.[160] Such detailed orders reflect both Murray's capability, but also Wellington's degree of inflexible control that allowed no leeway for divisional commanders. In addition, Soult had had to place great reliance upon fixed defences due to the dubious morale of his troops, but this inflexibility only played to Wellington's strengths: 'I can pour a greater force on certain points than they can concentrate to resist me.'[161] Bidasoa was the first of three river battles that now occupied the Allies in pushing into France; all were limited assaults seeking specific geographic objectives rather than decisiveness. Wellington was still 'very doubtful indeed about the advantage of going any further here at present'.[162] But the crossing of the Bidasoa brought Hill's right wing down from the mountains before winter, and to rejoin with Wellington before the River Nivelle within France. Losses to both sides were in the order of 1,600–1,700 men. Again, no attempt was made to exploit the advantage achieved, which might have also taken the British across the Nivelle. Wellington's 80,000 troops would continue a methodical advance against the enemy's entrenched linear defences, in a progress likened to the western front battles of the First World War.

The Nivelle River line was similarly defended by 60,000 dejected French troops again reliant upon fixed defences. After the battle, Lieutenant George Hennell observed: 'Had they fought as French troops have fought [. . .] we should have lost a great number if not have been repulsed'.[163] Others were now equally confident: 'there is no doubt that we can do which we please, for the spirit of the French army is too low to give us a hope at its committing itself'.[164] On 10 November, as Hope's troops demonstrated near the coast, Generals Beresford and Hill, as well as major Spanish formations, attacked the upper Nivelle. Atypically, Dickson's artillery received praise from Wellington after the set-piece action, as his predecessors never had.[165] The day again ended with a French retreat: 'The Imperial soldiers made only half-hearted efforts.'[166] Yet, Soult, despite losses of 4,300 men to the 3,400 of the Allies, was easily able to retire into Bayonne, and even with 3 British cavalry brigades being readily available for pursuit. He expressed surprise at Wellington's lethargy. The Battle of the Nivelle again showed a marked British supremacy in numbers, morale and capability over a demoralized French adversary who hoped to offset his disadvantages by the use of fixed defences. Wellington inflicted heavy casualties and forced the enemy to retreat when breaking through their centre, but without any thought of greater strategic gain.

Lord Henry Bathurst, Secretary for War, now felt the need to urge Wellington onwards, as the Continental Powers were preparing to invade France: 'it should not be understood you have concluded your operations, knowing the prejudicial effect it will have upon our Allies'.[167] Wellington's response: 'I think that I ought, and I will, bend a little to the views of the Allies.'[168] Logistical concerns and the threat of provoking French unrest encouraged Wellington to leave most of the Spanish troops to the rear; it is telling that he here actually expressed preference for a small army that he felt would obey orders, rather than a larger 'disobedient' army. 'I have found, upon inquiry and from experience, the instances of misbehaviour of the Spanish troops to be so numerous, and those of their good behaviour so few, that I must conclude that they are troops by no means to be depended upon.'[169] The advantage for him was that a smaller army, while still adequate for the task, could be better controlled. This reduced force of 64,000 men was now opposed by just 54,000 dispirited Frenchmen. On 9 December, Hope's column recommenced the slow advance upon Bayonne; his orders dictated caution.[170] Hill in parallel moved eastwards, to cross the River Nive as ordered. The tenacious Soult would nonetheless ceaselessly work to rehabilitate his forces, and considered that Wellington had, 'lost his numerical advantage by extending himself in this manner, and I intend to attack him in the false position he has adopted'.[171] On 10 December Soult's entire command attacked General Hope to the west of the Nive, and was close to encircling the 5th Division before support from the 1st and Beresford's divisions could intercede; Wellington spent the day with Hill. The French nonetheless captured some 500 British prisoners; more men than at any other Peninsular battle. The French attack was stopped, but after a total British loss approaching 2,000 men, among whom General Hope was wounded. Yet, it was Soult, upon suffering similar losses who found that he could not continue the attritional fight, as his own German troops now began to desert. Major troop defections threatened upon the circulation of news that Napoleon had been defeated at Leipzig in October 1813. Hope's deployment has been criticized, but S.P.G. Ward's fundamental analysis should not be forgotten:

> All troops were placed in their positions at the direction of Wellington himself [. . .] no troops were moved except at his command [. . .] It may be more convenient to write that General So-and-so disposed his brigades in such-and-such cantonments. But it is, strictly speaking, wrong. General So-and-so put his brigades where he was told to.[172]

Having ascertained that most British forces were now positioned to the west of the Nive, on 13 December Soult attacked General Hill to the east, at St Pierre d'Irube. Wellington had pre-warning, if only from the sounds of French guns rattling through nearby Bayonne, but no reinforcement was made. Indeed, the pontoon bridge over the Nive inconveniently collapsed, so Hill with 14,000 men fought alone for 4 hours, during which General Stewart won acclaim for a crucial defence of the hardest pressed centre. Reinforcements proved unnecessary for Hill's ultimately successful defence, despite losses which included three generals: Brigadier General Charles Ashworth and Major Generals Edward Barnes and the Portuguese Carlos Lecor. They were among 1,800 Allied casualties compared with 2,400 for the French. Colonel John Colborne felt that Wellington had 'committed a great error' leaving Hill isolated east of the River Nive.[173] Most notably, the intensity of the battle uniquely led Hill to exhibit annoyance with Wellington for the lack of subsequent credit: 'Hill, of course, wrote a dispatch [. . .] expecting to see it published [. . .] Wellington only used it to compile his own dispatch, in which he made very little mention of Hill's affair.'[174] Others have subsequently quibbled regarding the veracity or importance of this snub, but it is certainly hard to see that Wellington exerted himself in the least to give praise or credit.

The need existed to avoid any further surprise French counter-attacks, for what was now a static Allied position outside Bayonne. In order to ensure effective communication, therefore, Wellington's besieging forces established another extensive semaphore system.[175] General Hope would subsequently extend this facility with blue lights for improved visibility both at night and in bad weather. Major General Sir Charles Colville received Wellington's ire when suggesting a particular officer for the control of a telegraph station: 'when I call upon a General Officer to recommend an officer to fill a station [. . .] I mean that he should recommend one fit to perform some duty and not one so stupid as to be unable to comprehend [. . .] who is recommended only because he is a favourite'.[176] Colville would likely decline to make recommendation another time. The telegraph facility allowed Wellington to place a large part of the army in cantonment during the ensuing weeks of winter. Battle at St Pierre otherwise brought operations to a conclusion for 1813 as the weather deteriorated. Wellington spoke truthfully with regard to the Nive battles when he said: 'I will tell you the difference between Soult and me: when he gets into a difficulty, his troops don't get him out of it; mine always do.'[177] Wellington's own words here contradict those spoken by certain adherents, such as Oman, who states, 'Against bad luck and the mistakes of lieutenants even the best of generals is not immune [. . .] Wellington was not served by all his lieutenants during those five days.'[178] Contrariwise, Hope and Hill both performed effectively within their imposed confines. The lack of credit for either general certainly does not otherwise imply that Wellington was giving them free rein, as has further been suggested.[179] By this stage of the war some have considered that Wellington was exhausted; he was with neither general when the Nive battles unfolded. Napier, whose brother served in the campaign, accordingly and tellingly observes that after 'a long course of victory [he] was somewhat negligent of his own security'.[180] It is quite probable that after the weak showing by the French at both the Bidasoa and the Nivelle, Wellington again underestimated their capacity for resurgence. However, the unique indignation expressed by General Hill in particular is a marked rebuttal to any criticism of the generals and was a notable 'contrast to the [concurrent] adulation emanating from other quarters' for Wellington's successes.[181] General Stewart was outraged enough to still write privately to Wellington as late as 30 April 1815, to complain about their treatment outside Bayonne. Wellington passed this letter on to Hill, with the typically dismissive and condescending comment that it 'appears to have been written in the anguish of mind [he] does not do justice to himself or his troops, and I did not send it home or communicate it, I believe to anybody'.[182]

Wellington might ignore his subordinates, but he could not ignore the city of Bayonne, located at the confluence of the Nive and Adour Rivers; it was a major obstacle on the route into France. Hope's column was thus delegated to blockade it, while the main army marched eastward. Such blockade of a port was of course a tactic deemed inappropriate just months earlier with San Sebastian. Another newly arrived rocket troop, led by Captain Henry Lane, was made use of by Hope as his troops now crossed the River Adour, below the city in February 1814. They duly sank one of three deployed defensive French gunboats as a crossing was affected. Hope's major developing siege works entailed judicious co-operation with Spanish forces, and also with Rear Admiral Charles Penrose, RN, who provided naval support on the Adour river estuary during bridge-building operations. Once completed, the bridge allowed the city to be fully invested from both river banks, in an operation of great complexity. An attack by Hope north of the Adour was needed on 27 February 1814 to finally close the siege. Yet, Bayonne was defended by 12,000 Frenchmen; a frustration for Hope whose Allied force of 20,000 men within the 1st and 5th Divisions, as well as three independent Portuguese brigades and two Spanish divisions, had no realistic hope of assaulting the city.[183] When Hope queried the availability of additional resources, Wellington stated that he needed all other forces with him; at this stage of events he evidently did not relish another siege.[184] Just as for General Hill: 'There were those [. . .] who performed superbly, but because of their humility, their lives and careers were overlooked by history [. . .] Hope is unquestionably one of these soldiers.'[185]

Wellington, with the 43,000 troops of Beresford's and Hill's columns, commenced his major eastward movement on 12 February 1814. Hill, still leading the right of the army, was able to outflank Soult's defences on both the Bidouze and Saison river lines, before all forces converged upon Orthez, north of the River Gave de Pau. Wellington initially aimed to attack late on 26 February, but would leisurely defer until 27 February, even though it was considered that the French might slip away.[186] However, Soult's army of 36,000 men did stand: 'The enemy behaved much better than I have seen them do for a great length of time, which was the less expected as we have been so much accustomed to drive them before us.'[187] Though they did commit to battle, the careworn French forces, with fewer men and guns, were capable only of passively defending a line between the villages of St Boès and Orthez that supported either flank. Wellington manoeuvred to bring localized superiority principally against their right, but it was the attacks of Picton's 3rd Division and Clinton's 6th Division in the centre that initially caused the enemy to give way. The French army was subsequently driven into headlong retreat, with losses of 4,000 men that far exceeded the 2,200 Allied losses. At Orthez Wellington was hit by a spent bullet, which temporarily incapacitated him for the only time in the war. While the attack was certainly victorious, if the main objective was finally to vanquish the French, it failed. Organizing an effective pursuit might have concluded events as the French army continued to evaporate. After prior examples, it is impossible to credit that: 'Error [by others] and ill-luck again prevented him [Wellington] from organizing a comparable pursuit', or 'Lack of initiative on the part of [Wellington's] senior officers' precluded pursuit.[188] In an echo of the Colonel Bevan affair, staff officer Lieutenant Colonel Henry Sturgeon was, 'very severely reprimanded by his Lordship in presence of a number of officers'. This was apparently for not having Guides readily to hand to enable Wellington to send a message to General Hope. Thereafter a remorseful Sturgeon is said to have purposefully and fatally exposed himself to enemy fire.[189] Implausible say some, but the very telling of the story is indicative of the way the Peninsular Army perceived their commander. A similar damning story also exists with regards to the suicide of a Major Alexander Todd of the Royal Staff Corps, who was publicly rebuked by Wellington for the collapse of a bridge during the winter of 1813–14. Wellington reputedly finished a typical tirade by asking sardonically whether post-war: 'Are you going to take up your father's trade?' Todd's father was a butler, and Major Todd had otherwise proudly risen in society.[190] True or false, these stories speak volumes.

Despite Marshal Suchet still having 17,000 troops on the south-eastern Pyrenean border within Spain, Wellington knew that he had virtual free rein with the French and felt fully able to disperse his forces. General Hope had already had the freedom to be able to reconnoitre towards Bordeaux, and now Beresford with the 4th and 7th Divisions was dispatched to take the city. He duly entered Bordeaux unopposed on 12 March 1814. Meanwhile, Wellington and Hill advanced upon the depot city of Toulouse, the army screened now by 8,000 Allied cavalry. Soult aimed to draw them away by a feint movement back towards the Pyrenees, but Wellington was confident enough to merely ignore this. With Bordeaux having declared for the Bourbon monarchy, the 7th Division under General Dalhousie would remain there; Beresford and the 4th Division rejoined Wellington. Marshal Soult had separated from Wellington's pursuit after a skirmish at Tarbes on 20 March and reached Toulouse on 24 March. He now had the materiel available here and enough time, such that he could again reinvigorate an army of 42,000 men. Wellington's true, but elusive objective yet remained the final defeat of Soult's forces, not geographic locations. Swollen rivers caused major problems for the approaching British army of 49,000 troops and on 27 March their pontoon train was found to be inadequate for a crossing of the Garonne River south of Toulouse at Portet. Yet again Wellington was furious with his engineers, but he had refused to believe Elphinstone's specific report that he had insufficient pontoons.[191] A second abortive crossing was to follow on 30 March: Hill would actually cross the Garonne, but could find no passable road to Toulouse through countryside water-logged from recent rain. Wellington was apparently relaxed and confident enough to have failed both to implement adequate reconnaissance, or then to ensure adequate information about local conditions, despite the sizable available cavalry forces. He still insisted upon keeping them close to hand. Nevertheless, a suitable crossing of the river was finally made on 4 April, at a narrower point north of the city, rather than on the direct route from the south. However, while Beresford with the 19,000 men of the 3rd, 4th and 6th Divisions crossed the river, further bad weather and a rising river level meant that the pontoons could not be used for a subsequent three-day period. During this time Beresford's troops were sat isolated and vulnerable in front of the enemy. That their French opponent was too disorganized and exhausted to implement a counter-attack was a saving grace from the potentially ruinous situation that could easily have unfolded. Wellington was altogether too overly relaxed, if not neglectful in his actions.

Wellington's entire army, save for General Hill's column, would eventually cross over the Garonne here, at Seilh. On 10 April, while Hill demonstrated against the western Toulouse suburb of St Cyprien, Wellington attacked and duly bested the French army stationed immediately outside the city to the east of the Garonne. Colonel John Colborne's describes Wellington's attack as, 'the worst arranged battle that could be, nothing but mistakes [. . .] I think the Duke most deserved to have been beaten'.[192] Indeed, overall the French defenders were attacked at three points and at two of these Wellington's forces were routed. The battle, just as during the period leading up to it, was typified by a lack of reconnaissance, care and co-ordination; Wellington was now impatient to end matters, yet surprisingly over-confident, if not sloppy in the face of repeated French resurgence. The division of Spanish General Manuel Freire firstly attacked the northern-most French redoubts upon Mount Rave to the east of Toulouse, before Beresford attacked the east and south end of the ridge. Picton has then been accused of over-exuberance, or even 'criminal disobedience' when also attacking in the north in order to relieve the pressure being felt by Beresford's main attack.[193] Yet, it is hard to imagine that Wellington had not provided him with instructions, or direction at the very least; Picton would not otherwise have been aware of events on Beresford's front at a distance. These attacks were uncoordinated and haphazard, lacking Wellington's usual over-arching care and circumspection in command, though Beresford would eventually prevail. As seen in former years, French General Eloi Taupin was, 'carried away by his ardour and the hope of a brilliant success [. . .] advanced with his whole force still in column. The English [. . .] commenced a vigorous fire [. . .] the brigade recoiled and the English advanced'.[194] For a final time in the Peninsular War the British line repulsed a French column, before the ridge that was the key to Toulouse was captured. Losses reflect the uncoordinated nature of Wellington's battle; some 4,600 Allied troops killed and wounded, to 3,200 Frenchmen. Thereafter, Soult was easily able to evacuate Toulouse to avoid entrapment via the only road left open. This led to the south and Carcassonne where junction with Suchet might be accomplished. Yet, on 12 April news finally arrived of Napoleon's abdication, after the troops of Austria, Prussia and Russia had entered Paris on 30 March. Combat nonetheless still occurred at Bayonne on 14 April; when desperate Imperial zealots launched an unexpected counter-attack upon learning of the abdication. The siege at Bayonne had previously been quiet for months, with genial French and British soldiers reported to be fraternizing and exchanging goods and letters.[195] General Hope was ambushed in the sortie, wounded and captured, while Major General Andrew Hay of the 5th Division was killed; but all to no avail. On 17 April 1814 Marshal Soult formally conceded defeat, after receipt of an official dispatch from the Imperial Chief of Staff, Marshal Louis-Alexandre Berthier. This confirmed the Emperor Napoleon's downfall. Bayonne subsequently surrendered on 26 April; the Peninsular War was at an end.

Despite Wellington's unchanging observations upon the inadequacies of his troops, the war was won because of Britain's ability to provide a well-trained and well-equipped army, coupled with the indispensable assistance of the Iberian armies and their respective guerrillas. These attributes can be most clearly seen in the later war years against a bankrupt opponent. Such statements from Wellington as: 'The man who enlists in the British army is [. . .] the most drunken and probably the worst man of the [. . .] town in which he lives', are wrong and misleading.[196]

Wellington's personal contribution has been deemed to include his systematic focus upon a strategy for achieving Britain's long-term objectives, and his ability to fight set-piece battles. Wellington's 'military system' has thus received much credit, but this examination of his practical command style would provide qualification. It is posited here that over the war years of 1812–14 his authoritarianism and micro-management negated the initiative and spontaneity of subordinates, if not, for some individuals inducing perplexity and dismay of his command. It must, at the least, have impacted upon the morale and enthusiasm of individuals, to engender some of the very inattention and indiscipline of which Wellington routinely complained.

Wellington's own perceived key challenge over the final two years of war was how to retain personal command of a much larger army, which was dispersed over a large operational area. In parallel, some of Wellington's essential strategic decisions have also been reviewed here and questioned. The fact that his army became during the 1813 campaign more of a 'manoeuvring army' than had been the case previously was not down to Wellington alone, but rather because his subordinate generals understood an altered reality.[197] Remotely located generals needed to employ their initiative, while managing Wellington's presuppositions; and it is a credit to the likes of senior Generals Graham, Hope and Hill that they and others met the challenge. They dispassionately exhibited greater practical capability than subordinates such as Generals Beresford and Cotton, whom Wellington valued for slavishly following his orders. Yet, admirers of Wellington, from his contemporaries up until today often see only his strength of personality: 'there is scarcely a general officer in this army of any talent [. . .] and I suppose no commander ever had so few clever men on his staff, almost all of them being cox comical and old women'.[198] Horse Guards ostensibly dictated appointments, but by 1813 Wellington had his own way amid a headquarters steeped in patronage. His ego always knew better than others. He was jealously disdainful of any sign of competence among his subordinates lest it should tarnish his own star, and he was as a result unwilling to delegate. The command chain was imperilled by such an attitude just as much as by Wellington's wounding at Orthez. Wellington was routinely critical of any general who showed initiative, but disregarded independent actions that were both necessary and crucial that occurred during the period: Le Marchant at Villagarcia, Stewart and Cole in the Pyrenees and Hill at St Pierre. Even today these actions are obscure and controversial, but that is principally thanks to Wellington's partisan reportage. Such an unwillingness to sanction initiative and give praise where it was due was bound to curtail the effectiveness of Wellington's immediate subordinates, and by undermining their morale and limiting unit cohesion, the effectiveness of the army overall was impacted.

During the years 1812–14, Wellington continued to ignore intelligence that did not agree with his preconceived notions: Soult's counter-attack in the Pyrenees and events before Bayonne would prove to be significant examples. Previous indecisiveness by Wellington at Burgos wasted lives and resources, though his ability to put a spin on the entire 1812 campaign was sufficient to ward off any criticism of his generalship. His exaggerated caution at the French border is partially understandable in light of political events, but the balance between caution and risk-taking likely involved not only the interests of Great Britain, but was intertwined also with his personal prestige and self-interest. As had happened to Moore in 1809, the reality may have further included a degree of apprehension that by advancing resolutely into France, he might without due intelligence find the Emperor Napoleon with overwhelming forces across a battlefield. Wellington himself in 1831 acknowledged that: 'at the head of a French army there never was anything like him. [. . .] I used to say of him that his presence on the field made the difference of forty thousand men.'[199] Otherwise the loss of a few guns at Maya had disproportionate importance to Wellington's self regard and formulated public persona. Even with successful operations, Wellington routinely failed to exploit them at a time when his opponent's morale and will to resist were without doubt fragile. This was a failing which only assisted the French, whose ability, given breathing space to recover from multiple setbacks, was commendable and underestimated. After Salamanca, though he demonstrated highly studied organizational and operational prowess to orchestrate the Vitoria battlefield, Wellington's regulated control meant tactical misapplication and defensiveness. The war might readily have been terminated long before it actually was. The leadership that Wellington displayed during this period frankly did not minimize casualties while maximizing strategic gains.

Reference has been made to the activities of the infantry, artillery and cavalry throughout these years and it is difficult to find fault with them. Wellington continued to give the artillery little praise or encouragement, refused to accept any commander not of his own coterie, but yet it always performed professionally. With experience the British cavalry became increasingly dominant on the battlefield. Wellington concurrently stated: 'Our cavalry never gained a battle yet [. . .] they never yet beat the French'.[200] This is incorrect: successes have been ignored, while the rare peripheral setback at Maguila has been given a disproportionate importance. His on-going restraint of independent cavalry action is abstruse, beyond a possible wish to avoid any perceived setback which might reflect upon him. Wellington's cautious micro-management of his army made it hard to achieve combined arms benefits and gain truly decisive results; attritional combat prevailed. In the Peninsula overall, only the battles of Vimeiro, Salamanca and Vitoria may claim decisiveness, though two of these battles were won against severely outmatched opposition. Only at Salamanca in 1812 did Wellington generate decisive victory through the organization of all combat arms, and for which, in a rare moment of freedom, the elan brought by Le Marchant's brigade of dragoons was crucial. Hence, in the employment of his forces in battle, and specifically with regard to siege works, Wellington can be seen on occasion to be 'a ruthless gambler with his men's lives', and if the gamble did not come off he relied upon his mastery of spin.[201] This potentially included the creation of scapegoats; showing disrespect for both individuals and indeed whole regiments.

By 1814 Britain had an unbeaten commander of huge stature, with an experienced army and experienced generals. This had come about, almost in spite of Wellington's methods of command and control: the flaws of 1809–12 endured. Above all else Wellington had shown boundless resolve and staying power in the overall war of attrition; only towards the end did this somewhat languish. The Spanish field armies and the Spanish guerrillas gave Wellington an indispensable strategic asset, principally in the prevention of the concentration of French forces. The routine intelligence that was provided to the Anglo-Portuguese in Spain was similarly critical, while the diminished provision of intelligence within France is reflected by Wellington's actions of 1814. The Peninsular War proved a huge morale boost for Britain, while for the French, rather a huge drain upon resources ideally required elsewhere. Napoleon himself stated, 'That miserable Spanish affair turned opinion against me and rehabilitated England. It enabled them to continue the war [and] is what killed me.'[202] By 1814 Wellington's experienced subordinates contrarily contained both acolytes who greatly admired his strength of will, but also detractors who rather perceived hubris and selfishness. It is Napier who records that post-war, Wellington's 'remembrance of the veterans' service' was swiftly forgotten, though his self-absorption remained.[203] Even more pointedly, Lieutenant William Grattan observed that while Wellington was one of the greatest men of the age, he 'neglected the interests and feelings of his Peninsular Army [. . .] Were he in his grave tomorrow, hundreds of voices, that are now silent, would echo what I write.'[204] Only in 1848 would even a medal, the Military General Service Award, be minted for veterans of the Peninsula, given to those few still alive. To the disgust of many who had served in the Peninsula, the jubilation after Waterloo had in contrast meant the immediate instigation of an appropriate medal of commemoration. It would be at Waterloo in 1815 that Wellington's star was firmly established for posterity, and with a brightness that has impacted upon the Peninsular War years. Prophetically in 1814, Captain Arthur Kennedy of the 18th LD had presentiment of the troubles ahead when he heard returning French prisoners of war crying, '*Vive Napoléon*'.[205]

Chapter 6

Wellington's Command Endures, 1815

'Now, I think I may say I am the most successful Genl. alive.'[1]

The preceding examination of Wellington's leadership shows that despite his victory in the Peninsular War, his divisive micro-management and overly autocratic and unyielding approach to command must surely have negatively impacted upon the effectiveness of both individuals and his forces overall. Wellington's army otherwise had many markedly commendable attributes among both its officers and men, which as a result of Wellington's own comments are regularly discounted by commentators. During the Peninsular War Wellington's initiative most often alone controlled the pace of operations, limited only by available resource and potentially the actions of his allies. As the war progressed his influence over all extraneous criteria would markedly increase; Wellington's command became ubiquitous. It has been reasoned that it was in fact the elements of ineffectuality within Wellington's own system of command that generated certain consequential limitations for the Peninsular Army, such as its failure to fully exploit its own successes. Such shortcomings have otherwise been alluded to, but generally left unresolved by historians, thanks largely to the magnitude of his victory at Waterloo in 1815. The Waterloo campaign, though in fact only weeks long, is a worthwhile finale to this study, to corroborate the imperfections inherent in Wellington's method of command and control. Wellington vigorously objected to any subsequent attempts to study his campaigns; firstly, because in his view no individual present could faultlessly recollect such tumultuous events, and, secondly, because any study would expose fault as well as distinction. It is not unreasonable to infer that his intention could only be to safeguard his personal reputation by looking to ensure that all other accounts were of secondary importance to his own. The Peninsular War years did not necessarily prepare Wellington for the reality of directly opposing the French Emperor Napoleon. The scale, speed and intensity of the conflict in 1815 were unexpected, and the initiative for the campaign lay firmly with Napoleon. Wellington had neither the freedom for punctiliously spent hours of administration, nor did he enjoy the quantitative and qualitative supremacy to which he had become accustomed. Furthermore, working cooperatively with allies had been seen repeatedly to be a weak area for Wellington. For these reasons, Wellington's leadership and operational command ability would come under the closest scrutiny in 1815.

Napoleon had waged a brilliant defensive campaign in France 1814, but ultimate defeat against insuperable odds had led to his abdication and exile to the tiny island of Elba off the coast of Italy. His return to France was nothing less than tumultuous. Quitting Elba on 26 February 1815, with only the 1,100 men permitted as his personal guard, he landed upon the French mainland, near Cannes on 1 March. Upon hearing this news, the out-of-touch Wellington declared: 'It is my opinion that Buonaparte has acted upon false or no information, and that the King [Louis XVIII of France] will destroy him without difficulty, and in a short time.'[2] Yet, Napoleon's subsequent progress to Paris soon became a triumphal march as he was inundated by popular support, and within a month he was reinstalled as Emperor of France. The military campaign that followed resulted from the pledges of the Great Powers who had been the instruments of his 1814 defeat – Prussia, Russia, Austria and Britain – to once and for all rid Europe of 'the ogre'. In congress at Vienna Wellington stated: 'Here we are all zeal, and [. . .] anxious to take the field'.[3] The pledge was to assemble 4 armies of 200,000 men each, twice what France could muster. The Austrians and Russians, once prepared, would advance on Paris from east of the Rhine. Meanwhile, in the north would assemble the combined forces of Britain and the Netherlands at Brussels, and Field Marshal Gebhard von Blücher's Prussian army would muster about Namur. Napoleon himself would, in due course, organize 128,165 men within his *Armée du Nord*, to anticipate any Allied invasion; most of these soldiers were veterans of at least one or two campaigns: 'Never had Napoleon under his hand an instrument of war so redoubtable nor so fragile.'[4] It may be considered that the morale of the energized French army was undermined only by the troop's perception of their own senior officers, who had largely changed sides twice during the preceding year. The most obvious initial threat to their idolized Emperor's rule came from the two armies assembling in Belgium. Wellington here observed: 'There is no doubt that for [Napoleon] it would be most important to force back the troops we have before Brussels [. . .] This would be a terrible blow to public opinion here and in France.'[5]

At the Congress of Vienna Wellington was appointed to command the notional Anglo-Dutch army assembling in Belgium; just 36 per cent of the army would eventually however be British, 19 per cent Dutch-Belgian, while 45 per cent of the army would speak German as a first language.[6] Travelling directly from Vienna, Wellington arrived in Brussels on 5 April 1815. Belgium had previously been under French control since 1795, and only in March 1815 had the Congress of Vienna forced its unification with the Netherlands upon word of Napoleon's return. Any consolidation of the respective military units of the Netherlands and Belgium was intrinsically fragile, while many of these troops had previously fought for Napoleon. Concerns would likewise abound regarding the efficacy of the assembling German-speaking troops from Nassau and Brunswick. Indeed, the Prussians had wanted these soldiers within their own forces and it took some wrangling at the Congress to ensure they joined with Wellington; he had argued that his army would be impossibly short of men if Britain could only rely upon its traditional Hanoverian allies. Wellington would only formally take control of these mustering battalions of the Anglo–Allied army on 11 April, and it may be considered that Wellington's singular strength of personality was in fact necessary to ensure their integration. Previously in charge of the assembling troops was his regal former ADC of 1811–12, the Dutch Prince William of Orange. The Prince was now nominally a full general in rank within the British army, though still only 22 years of age. Lieutenant General, now Lord Rowland Hill had arrived in Brussels on 1 April and was asked to 'hold the prince's hand' until Wellington himself arrived. Wellington had been required to await his own appointment as a Field Marshal in the service of the Netherlands before he could formally take overall command. This would appear to have taken some little time as King William I of the Netherlands is recorded as disliking Wellington's peremptory proposal to mix the Dutch–Belgian troops with other nationalities. Wellington in turn would exhibit marked distrust of Napoleon's former allies, and which was patently ill-received; his diplomatic skills were once again found to be questionable. The Prince of Orange has otherwise been described as 'a very amiable, deserving youth [. . .] liked by everyone', or alternatively one whose 'great failings are excessive vanity and obstinacy'.[7] From the actuality of the events of 1815 and within many subsequent histories the 22-year-old Prince has been accused of an assortment of military crimes, just as have his Dutch–Belgian troops; indeed, far too many for them all to be reasonably possible, especially when overseen by Hill and Wellington. The distrust and deprecation concerning the contribution of foreign arms in 1815 has more recently and deservedly been accounted for as a prime example of the wish to aggrandize Britain's own success. If events had gone badly for the Allies in 1815, it is easy to see who would have received the lion's share of condemnation.

Due to the speed of events in April 1815 deficiencies within the assembling army were readily acknowledged by Horse Guards in London: it initially contained, 'inefficient second battalions as [. . .] sent to Holland upon a sudden emergency'.[8] Wellington nonetheless now repeatedly and loudly complained: 'I have got an infamous army, very weak and ill-equipped, and a very inexperienced staff.'[9] He complained of lethargy among the British authorities, and of troop shortages: 'You have not called out the militia [. . .] by which measure your troops [. . .] elsewhere might become disposable'.[10] Despite some initial justification which had been acknowledged, such copious complaints were disproportionate; they indeed caused the British government to send representatives to Brussels in order to placate him. These were Tory governmental Cabinet Ministers Lord Harrowby and William Wellesley-Pole, Wellington's brother; accompanied by Major General Henry Torrens, who continued as MS to the Commander-in-Chief, Horse Guards in 1815. The trepidation and misrepresentation on display must have reflected

Wellington's own perceived lack of full sway over the processes surrounding the assembling army. Wellington's leadership style, based upon absolute personal control, had worked well with a small force, but was both less appropriate and harder to achieve the larger the army grew. His outlook when meeting King William also again shows Wellington's inherent mistrust when it came to both political negotiations with foreign allies and the very troops he now commanded. In marked contrast the Prussian leader, Blücher, had a most competent chief-of-staff, Major General August von Gneisenau, who handled political issues for him, as well as the Prussian army's logistics and tactical details. Gneisenau is another who has been dismissed in British sources as a 'hidebound staff officer', for displaying suspicion of the Duke, but this has rather reversed their roles: he distrusted what he saw as arrogance and selfishness in the reactionary Wellington: 'So accustomed himself to duplicity that he had at last become such a master of the art as even to outwit the Nabobs [of India] themselves.'[11] Yet, as Wellington assumed command of the Anglo-Allied army, Gneisenau had already reluctantly yielded to his proposals for the overall deployment of both armies within Belgium, and which was duly implemented, rather than the initial Prussian wish to combine both armies at Tirlemont, east of Brussels. The British plan for deployment emphasized their own communication and logistical links back to the Channel ports, rather than prioritizing Antwerp.* Events would show that the initial Prussian scheme would have been the safer and likely the better plan. After concentrating the French forces as secretly as possible, Napoleon's own strategic choice would duly and typically be to firmly grasp the initiative by making a swift descent in great strength upon the Belgian city of Charleroi. From here he would drive between the disconnected British and Prussian armies, forcing them back upon their respective lines of communication before defeating each in turn.

In Brussels Wellington's initial vexation found focus with officer appointments: in the headiness of the initial crisis and with Wellington at Vienna, Horse Guards had understandably acted without consulting him. Yet, the wealth of Peninsular War experience is readily to be seen in these appointments. British cavalry Major Generals, Lord Edward Somerset of the 1st Cavalry Brigade, Sir William Ponsonby, 2nd, Sir John Vandeleur, 4th, Sir John Colquhoun Grant, 5th, Sir Hussey Vivian, 6th, as well as Colonel Sir Frederick Arentschildt of the 7th Brigade were all veterans of the Peninsular Army; only the German Wilhelm von Dörnberg of the largely KGL 3rd Brigade was not. Wellington would find Lieutenant Generals Lord Rowland Hill, II Corps, as well as Sir Henry Clinton of the 2nd Division already in Belgium, and other infantry Lieutenant Generals, Sir Carl von Alten,

---

*See Map 3, for the key centres and communication routes within northern France and Belgium.

3rd Division, and Sir Charles Colville of the 4th Division, soon joined. Lieutenant General Sir Galbraith Lowry Cole, 6th Division only missed the campaign as he was on his honeymoon, and was replaced by his experienced deputy Major General Sir John Lambert. Only Major General George Cooke of the 1st Division, from among the appointed divisional commanders, had not directly experienced Wellington's Peninsula leadership: he had rather spent the war years commanding British troops stationed at Cádiz. Lieutenant General Sir Thomas Picton of the 5th Division would be a late arrival, only getting to Brussels on 15 June as the first confused reports of clashes emerged. Picton was initially 'not much pleased with his interview', and he is recorded as resenting Wellington's 'peremptory personal instructions'.[12] Wellington otherwise has been recorded as thinking that, despite their years together, Picton was on the whole 'too familiar' with him.[13] Wellington's stark welcome for his officers underwhelmed rather than galvanized his subordinates. George Murray was one notable absentee, being in Canada, but he was replaced as QMG by the experienced Colonel Sir William De Lancey. As Edward Pakenham had been killed in early 1815 fighting the Americans at New Orleans, Major General Sir Edward Barnes was appointed AG. He had formerly led a brigade from Vitoria to the end of the Peninsular War, so was well known to Wellington. Of thirty-three headquarters' staff, thirty-one had Peninsula experience: 'Although there was undoubtedly some friction in the matter of appointments to the staff [. . .] Wellington had his own way and had no right to complain that his staff was without experience'.[14] Indeed, overall: 'Few British generals have opened a campaign with so much proven experience at their command.'[15] The Duke's staff in 1815 was said, by the renewed MS and now Lieutenant Colonel Lord Fitzroy Somerset, to have, 'executed its duties with the regularity of a machine'.[16] It was never possible to reassemble fully the Peninsular Army; Wellington's copious complaints ignored both practicalities and realities.

For the cavalry, Wellington acquiesced when insistence from the Prince Regent had Torrens write: 'There appears to be a very general wish [. . .] that Lord Uxbridge should be appointed' to overall command; though Wellington would doubtless have preferred Cotton.[17] Uxbridge had led Sir John Moore's cavalry in December 1808, notably defeating the opposition French cavalry in action at Sahagún, as well as at Mayorga and Benavente. The fact that the defeated French at Benavente included elements of the Imperial Guard cavalry in itself offers a further perspective upon the quality of the British cavalry forces in the Peninsula. Captain Charles Jones of the 15th Hussars recognized Uxbridge's ability, yet found it hard to define the inherent faculty that he had: 'He is not the cleverest cavalry officer in the British Empire, but unfortunately he is almost the only one with a cavalry genius.'[18] For Wellington the nobility and connections of Uxbridge now over-rode other possible objections; of which the fact that Uxbridge had absconded with his brother, Henry Wellesley's wife in 1809 must be one that came to mind. Discounting the Prince of Orange, who would be kept under Wellington's personal wing, the seniority of Uxbridge also qualified him as the army's second-in-command. The only other candidate that Wellington might have preferred as second was of course Sir William Beresford. However, he remained in Portugal as commander-in-chief of their army, and de facto ruler while awaiting the return of the Portuguese royal family from Brazil. Equally vexatious for Wellington was again the artillery command, which fell to Colonel George Wood. He had been passed over by Wellington in 1813 for supposedly being 'too fat, depend on it', but was now already in Belgium.[19] He had nonetheless served here with distinction, initially under Lieutenant General Sir Thomas Graham, who had been persuaded to manage the minor Flanders campaign of 1814. Yet, to Wellington: '[He] knows no more of his business than a child, and I am obliged to do it for him.'[20] Wellington's first choice for CRA would again doubtless have been Lieutenant Colonel Alexander Dickson, but he was another away in America. Dickson did yet return to Europe just in time to participate in battle as a troop commander of RHA. Nevertheless, both Wood and the appointed Commander of the RHA, Lieutenant Colonel Sir Augustus Frazer (CRHA), would both prove competent in 1815. Frazer's demeanour and immediate discernible energy in re-equipping three RHA troops with heavier 9-pound cannon impressed and predisposed Wellington towards him. Having also served under Wellington in the Peninsula, Frazer would have the greater influence in artillery matters; Wood who had not served directly would rather receive Wellington's hostility. Earl Henry Mulgrave, the Master General of Ordnance had previously expressed eagerness to meet all of Wellington's stated artillery requirements; though the ultimate provision of 191 guns would be less than the 296 guns of the Prussian army, and the 370 guns deployed by the French.[21] Captain Edward Whinyates would arrive at the front in May with another rocket troop; Wellington allowed these to remain only on the condition that the gunners would also crew artillery guns. Wood nonetheless wrote home, 'I do believe there never was in the world such a proportion of Artillery so well equipped.'[22] Wellington made complaint regardless of the actuality, and continued his enduring antipathy to the RA: when reviewing Clinton's 2nd Division in April, he found fault only with the attached artillery component led by Lieutenant Colonel Charles Gold.[23]

For the Waterloo campaign, Wellington notionally created formal corps for the first time. These were to be led by the Prince of Orange, I Corps, General Hill, II Corps and himself leading a Reserve Corps; in addition a segregated cavalry force led by General Lord Uxbridge. It was Napoleon, who had fully established the corps system, but his rationale was to devolve tactical freedom to each commanding general, he would direct only their strategic movement. For Wellington's leadership, however, the corps command structure was once again for administrative and political purposes only, and remained fully constrained by Wellington's individual authority. As was his custom, in battle, command for Wellington still firmly meant hands-on control of every possible formation. With noise, confusion and general lack of visibility from gunpowder smoke it is easy to understand why Wellington's command preferred a battlefield of constricted dimensions.

Wellington's light cavalry would guard the French frontier in early 1815, and the limitations imposed upon them by Wellington echo those of the earlier Iberian campaigns. Uxbridge and the main force of cavalry were bivouacked immediately west of Brussels, while at the capital itself were based Wellington and the Reserve. Hill's corps had its headquarters furthest west of Brussels at Ath, to specifically guard the army's line of communication to Ostend, while the Prince of Orange was located south of Brussels at Braine le Comte, closest to where Napoleon would actually strike. Each corps had two Anglo–Hanoverian divisions as well as another foreign contingent: Dutch–Belgians with the Prince of Orange and Hill, while Wellington's Reserve Corps had the Brunswick and Nassau troops: 'The Hanoverian levies are much superior to what I expected. The Duke means to mix them, as well as the Dutch, with our troops, according [. . .] to the arrangements adopted with the Portuguese.'[24] These troops in reality were not to be discounted: 'The Nassau troops are excellent; and the Dutch military are a very good body of men.'[25] It was principally the Brunswick contingent that may be claimed to contain a goodly proportion of inexperienced recruits, but this would not undermine their commitment. Among the British troops twenty-three battalions were veterans of the Peninsular War and were, as might be expected, the best troops in Wellington's eyes. Veterans accounted for a predominant 60 per cent of British troops overall. By the middle of June Wellington's field army was up to strength and contained over 110,000 men; he was now confident: 'almost complacent'.[26] Nonetheless, it cannot be claimed that the army intrinsically matched the cohesive unit that had marched from Spain and into France in 1814. Yet, neither was it as poor as many have asserted when, for example, declaring that the army was certainly 'much inferior' to that of 1814. That such a historian as Oman should indeed accuse the Dutch–Belgians of being cowardly, ineffectual and even traitorously sympathetic to Napoleon is both mischievous and emphatically wrong.[27]

On 3 May Wellington and Blücher met together at Tirlemont, east of Brussels to discuss strategy. Though co-operation between both armies was reaffirmed, they were still unsure or could not reach agreement regarding the timing of any combined advance into France. When any such advance did commence, it was agreed that Wellington would do so from the direction of Mons towards Cambrai while the Prussians would move from Charleroi and Mauberge. All commanders in 1815 would doubtless rely upon the maps of Belgium published in 1777–8 by Joseph Comte de Ferraris, which were much superior to those that Wellington had initially needed to rely upon in Spain. Little cognizance as to whether Napoleon himself might advance against the Allies, or upon which line any such advance might occur was evident. It did not help, though it is little surprise, that there was 'a distinct personality clash between Gneisenau and Wellington'.[28] The circumspect Wellington in fact positively vetoed any advance into France before 1 July, when the Austrian army would be ready to strike westwards across the Rhine. Blücher still wrote dismissively: 'Napoleon does not attack us. For that we could wait another year.'[29] Wellington stated: 'We have reports of Buonaparte joining the army and attacking us [. . .] I judge [. . .] that his departure [is] not likely to be immediate. I think we are now too strong for him here.'[30] Wellington personally considered that no conceivable French attack could occur before July and then the only logical target could be against the British supply links. Lord Henry Bathurst, Secretary for War buttressed Wellington's concerns when writing to him in May: 'Your Grace is well aware of the importance [. . .] attached to the possession of Antwerp and Ostend, not only as a means of providing for our communications with the army, but as securing a retreat in case of mischance'.[31] More than ever before Wellington relied upon his own intuition and judgment over the available intelligence. Contrarily, the subsequent potent French moves owed their surprising rapidity to the effective delegated leadership of Napoleon's corps commanders; anathema as a principle to Wellington. His reactions have been described as, 'less alert and appropriate than those into which Gneisenau and the emerging Prussian professionals helped steer Blücher'.[32] Bluntly, if both Allies had reacted immediately and concentrated together, they would have been too strong for Napoleon.

Wellington's appraisal of his enemy's intensions would prove to be deficient, indeed a marked error of underestimation, just as he had in the past. In early April Wellington considered that, 'it would not be advisable to enter France before the arrival of the Russians'.[33] Yet, shortly after, based upon fresh reports of internal French opposition to Napoleon, he wrote that, 'no time should be lost in commencing our offensive operations'.[34] Wellington indeed has rather been said to have 'basked in complacency' in the almost carnival atmosphere of Brussels to which British society had flocked.[35] Complacency bred indecision and political prevarication both for Britain and Prussia, as the Allied offensive was repeatedly postponed, tentatively awaiting progress from the Austrians and Russians.[36] Meanwhile, the engineers commanded by Lieutenant Colonel James Carmichael-Smyth destroyed no bridges, because the Allies thought of attack, not defence. The combined Allied front within Belgium stretched for some 90 miles and Wellington believed it was impossible for Napoleon to approach without warning. Wellington's staff could distribute orders for the whole army within 6 hours, and 48 hours would theoretically see Wellington's forces concentrated. But Napoleon's capacity for resurgence and obfuscation was certainly underestimated. The British army was reliant upon its thin screen of cavalry through which three major approach roads – through Lille, Mons and Charleroi – invited penetration. Nonetheless, Wellington incessantly worried regarding his line of communication to the coast and ensured that all existing fortifications, principally at Mons, Ath and Antwerp, were fully secure. Furthermore, he certainly made plans for an emergency re-embarkation from Ostend and Antwerp if it proved to be a necessity.[37] Napoleon actually allowed the British to perceive French troops opposite Mons to encourage misinformation; any pull of forces to the west could only help to separate the Anglo–Allied and Prussian armies. Wellington defended geographical locations, while Napoleon considered the destruction of armies.

Wellington was without the intelligence resources he was accustomed to receive while in Spain: he relied upon travellers and deserters as much as tractable spies within the French capital. Based close to the frontier, the unfamiliar KGL General Dörnberg of the 3rd Cavalry Brigade was a key intelligence operative for Wellington, being the only senior British officer who spoke French, German and English; Wellington was grudgingly obliged to place reliance upon him. Wellington also had available at headquarters the services of the code-breaker AQMG Sir George Scovell, who had served him well in the Peninsula. The liaison officer for the Prussian staff, Major General Baron Karl von Müffling, stated: 'The Duke of Wellington informed by me that Prince Blücher's espionage was badly organised, was very certain of his [own]'.[38] Yet, communication between the frontier and Allied headquarters was a weak link, compounded by Wellington's personalized interpretation of all received intelligence. In the days before combat commenced, Wellington had perfectly good intelligence regarding Napoleon's advance, but simply did not believe it. General Dörnberg would subsequently tell General Henry Clinton on 14 June: 'I believe it now, but the Duke, despite being very well informed, doesn't believe it.'[39]

Previously, on 9 June Lieutenant General Hans von Ziethen, who commanded the Prussian I Corps, closest to Wellington's own forces, became cognizant of the startling news that major French formations were on the move adjacent to the frontier. Further west, General Dörnberg with Wellington's light cavalry at the border also saw increased activity. There were clashes between Allied outposts and the French from 10 June. Subsequently, on both 12 June and the 13 June Dörnberg transmitted information to headquarters on perceived French activity and warned that a major attack appeared imminent. On 14 June the Prussians were ordered to concentrate, yet Wellington did nothing, despite Dörnberg's warnings; wariness of an unfamiliar officer who had once fought for Napoleon may have played its part. As late as 15 June Wellington stated to a Dutch government minister that he did not expect to be attacked.[40] He in fact ordered the Dutch QMG Jean-Victor Constant-Rebecque, attached to the Anglo–Allied I Corps nearest the Prussian positions, to stand down his attentive troops.[41] However, advised by Rebecque, the inexperienced Prince of Orange obtained 'a clearer perception of what was going on than did his commanding officer [Wellington]'.[42] Early on 15 June the French attacked the Prussians at the frontier in earnest and pushed through the Belgian city of Charleroi, where the main road crossed the River Sambre. Still Wellington prevaricated, noting later: 'I did not hear of these events till the evening of the 15th.'[43] Most historians have taken Wellington's words at face value and duly record this as an accurate statement of events. However, in more recent years this has been strongly contradicted by others who highlight an earlier letter that Prussian General Ziethen apparently sent to Wellington regarding the French attack; a message that should conceivably have been received in the morning of 15 June.[44] Wellington's idiosyncratic modus operandi has raised the suspicion that, although later claiming that word was not received until late in the day, the possibility exists that he received Ziethen's message, but did not initially take it seriously until further confirmation was forthcoming. This endorsement would have been that which Marshal Blücher himself assuredly wrote to Wellington during the afternoon of 15 June, advising him of the overall Prussian situation.[45] Wellington personally adjudged all intelligence, though with regard to the communications of this day the arguments are likely to continue. Nevertheless, whatever the hour on 15 June that Wellington was finally in possession of the information regarding French offensive action, he should have ordered his army to concentrate at once; but he still did not. Rather, preparation was yet further delayed that day as he did no more than write to the Tsar of Russia stating that he would take the offensive at the end of June or early July in accordance with the agreed Allied plans.[46] One specific excuse for Wellington's slowness has been that he awaited direct intelligence from the noted intelligence officer Lieutenant Colonel Colquhoun Grant, who was actually in Paris, to corroborate the situation. In this connection General Dörnberg has been strongly condemned for not immediately identifying a letter that arrived on his desk from Grant regarding Napoleon's latest actions. Yet, this is stock criticism of a subordinate when Wellington had kept totally secret the details of Grant's intelligence activities in Paris, even, or especially, from Dörnberg. The specific importance that Wellington is claimed to have placed upon Grant's tidings was delayed briefly, one letter among a plethora of other reports. It would be harsh to designate any blame for such a subordinate as Dörnberg, when he was merely the conduit for a mishmash of conflicting intelligence reports that all required Wellington's final judgment. It is hard to see other than suspicion and intransigence from Wellington, when despite all the signals of 15 June he markedly shrank from trusting others. He personally felt certain that the French advance was a feint and that any conceivable threat to the Anglo–Allied Army must be aimed towards Mons and the supply ports. Wellington profoundly disbelieved the received intelligence and was inordinately slow to abandon these preconceptions. Meanwhile, on the evening of 15 June, Lieutenant General Henri-Georges Perponcher-Sedlnitzky, in command of the 2nd Netherlands Infantry Division, clashed with French-Polish lancers, under the direction of Marshal Michel Ney. The Anglo–Allied troops were driven back upon the crossroads of Quatre Bras, on the main road to Brussels. Major General Prince Bernhard of Saxe-Weimar informed Perponcher that his

2nd Brigade was, 'too weak to hold out here for long'.[47] Yet, when Wellington first became aware that this clash had occurred, he undeniably ordered Perponcher to withdraw a further 6 miles, westward to the town of Nivelles, which was located both further away from the Prussian Army and west of the main road that led from Charleroi to Brussels.

It was midnight on 15 June when Wellington finally accepted the truth: 'Napoleon has humbugged me [. . .] he has gained 24 hours march on me'.[48] Yet, apparently it still required the confirmation that was contained within Grant's intelligence for Wellington to fully believe the reports: he was asleep at 2:00am on 16 June when this was finally received, and Wellington 'shot up' in bed.[49] Before first light that day, Wellington ordered troops to Nivelles, though still screening Mons. He left Brussels himself at 7:30am with his staff, in the wake of the Reserve Corps under the direction of General Picton. That day Uxbridge was unfairly blamed by Wellington for the cavalry's slow journey eastwards. It was rather the case that Uxbridge had to specifically request orders from Wellington after a delay at Enghien, west of Hal where updated march orders were awaited.[50] The rush to provide orders to all units meant that QMG De Lancey did not have enough riders to transmit all orders promptly on the morning of 16 June.[51] Further confusion yet occurred: it was the Prince of Orange who noted that the autonomous Netherlands cavalry, attached to I Corps had been forgotten and ordered them to Nivelles. Two brigades of heavy, 18-pound guns located 6 miles north of Brussels were also notably overlooked; these would never make it to Waterloo, where their presence would have been invaluable. Wellington's leadership controlled all activity, yet his orders still contained a mistake to match Napoleon's aspirations: in looking to concentrate the army at Nivelles he allowed French access to the *Chausée de Charleroi*, the main road to Brussels which ran between and split the two Allied armies. It would seem to have been unclear, a necessity unforeseen, as to who should guard this most important of roadways. That Wellington should discount or misconceive the importance of his army's junction with the Prussians is extraordinary. The problem was solely addressed by the initiative of General Perponcher when he maintained his division at Quatre Bras. Only Perponcher's men, with no immediate prospect of reinforcement, were available to defend the vital crossroads; and they were there because their commander disobeyed Wellington's explicit order. The brigade of Major General Willem, Count Bijlandt was deployed west of the main road and the brigade of Major General Prince Bernhart of Saxe-Weimar to the east of the road. A stray detachment of fifty Silesian hussars of the Prussian cavalry, under Lieutenant Karl von Zehelin, who had also retreated before the French, agreed to remain with Perponcher as his sole cavalry support. Wellington would finally ride to Quatre Bras on the morning of 16 June after receiving the Prince's reports, and where he latterly approved Perponcher's deployment.[52] Nonetheless, Prince Bernhart was unsurprisingly left 'sullen and resentful' by Wellington's thankless attitude.[53] After the war Prussia would decorate Perponcher with the Order of the Red Eagle for ensuring the protection of the right flank of their army; certainly recognition that Wellington would never have instigated. Wellington was still a day behind the pace of the campaign. As the French cavalry before Quatre Bras now appeared quiescent, awaiting infantry reinforcement, Wellington next journeyed eastwards to the village of Brye, between the two Allied armies to meet and confer with Blücher; the Silesian hussars formed a guard for Wellington as he rode. At this meeting Wellington once again engendered controversy by giving the Prussians totally misleading information as to the location of the dispersed British forces, only set in motion within the last few hours.[54] Even those well-disposed historians have struggled to provide a plausible reason for Wellington's dissembling at Brye, but only one explanation appears creditable: Wellington knew that he had been wrong-footed by Napoleon and through prevarication sought to avoid reproach. It would otherwise be most hard to believe that Wellington was ignorant of the whereabouts of his own army. The Prussians were left with reason to expect that rather than passively defend, sufficient British forces would be in position to positively attack from Nivelles and Quatre Bras down the connecting Namur road and onto the flank of Napoleon's army that now faced them at Ligny. Outright loss of Quatre Bras would have exposed the Prussian army's right flank and been a disaster for them. As things stood it was indeed General Perponcher and not Wellington who had saved Blücher's army from immediate catastrophe. Napoleon's initiative caught Wellington by surprise, and disaster was only averted when General Perponcher disobeyed his orders on the night of 15 July. Perponcher was singularly not rebuked and the wisdom of his action was confirmed when Wellington subsequently amended the location for army concentration; an unspoken acknowledgment of an error that led to totally uncharacteristic, extemporized actions by Wellington.

In the afternoon of 16 June, Napoleon's 80,000-man *Armée du Nord* attacked and defeated the Prussian army at Ligny, while the corps of Marshal Ney indecisively screened Wellington at Quatre Bras. Marshal Nicolas Soult, now Napoleon's chief-of-staff, correctly observed, 'We've caught the enemy with his trousers down just as he's trying to combine with the English.'[55] In contesting open countryside, merely a road junction, Wellington's battle was uncharacteristically spontaneous and his personal role was 'curiously obscure'.[56] He presided over the necessary piecemeal reinforcement of the position; Major General George Cooke's 1st Division had to march to the sound of the guns without orders.[57] Wellington made no telling interjection; the engagement was far removed from his set-piece battles of the Peninsula. The French troops performed with a level of aggression not seen by Wellington since Talavera. The delayed and uncoordinated British were short of both cavalry and artillery, which has correctly been blamed for the subsequent high casualty figures.[58]

At the start of the battle, in the early afternoon, Wellington had just eight battalions of Dutch troops present, while the attached Allied artillery consisted of just sixteen guns, to ninety-two French guns. The 11th LD cavalry alone had arrived before the French attacked in earnest. The French would prove to be an effective combined arms force; even their skirmishers were reputedly superior.[59] Only the arrival of Picton's 5th Division at 3:30pm prevented collapse. Picton had been delayed south of Brussels, while Wellington yet decided whether or not to order him to Nivelles.[60] Wellington nonetheless typically micro-managed the tactics of battle at Quatre Bras throughout, for example, instructing the 92nd Rifles of 5th Division: 'don't fire until I tell you'.[61] If, 'the very essence of war [. . .] consists in the combination of careful planning with rapid improvisation, in a fog of partial, late and inaccurate information', the French undoubtedly had the edge.[62] Amidst the fluctuating action, Wellington himself was nearly captured by charging French cavalry and had to jump his horse into a square of the 92nd Highlanders to escape. Anglo–Allied losses would eventually reach in the order of 5,000 men, as reported by AG Sir Edward Barnes, as well as 1,000 Dutch lost as prisoners, as opposed to 4,200 French casualties. The French never had above 25,000 men in combat while of Wellington's 95,000 troops, 62,000 failed to reach the battlefield. The mass of British cavalry arrived at twilight as combat subsided. Quatre Bras was otherwise a stalemate of a battle as both sides finished the day roughly in the positions in which they had started.

In the wake of what proved to be defeat at Ligny, the remaining 55,500 organized Prussian troops retreated due north to Wavre, not east to their own supply and communication centre at Namur. They had lost some 18,000 men, as well as another 10,000 conscripts who were suitably unnerved and fled eastwards overnight; French losses were 13,721. The Prussian path of retreat was the critical decision of the campaign, taken by Lieutenant General Gneisenau, in his role as chief-of-staff to the wounded Blücher. While annoyed and mistrustful of Wellington for failing to directly assist them, the Prussians yet promised their own support: 'Wellington had promised to strike the enemy in the rear; he didn't come [. . .] because his army, heavens knows why, couldn't concentrate in time'.[63] In ignorance of the Prussian's defeat, at 9:00pm on 16 June Wellington told MS Fitzroy Somerset that the next day the combined Allied armies should counter-attack.[64] Gneisenau would in fact dispatch Major Graf Winterfeld to bring news to Wellington of the Prussian defeat and their future intentions, but he was waylaid by the French, shot and wounded. A repeat dispatch was only received by Wellington during the night, though uncertainty regarding the scale of the Prussian defeat still meant that Wellington considered the options for taking offensive action the next day. Wellington's army now unwittingly stood alone before 100,000 Frenchmen. It was only on the morning of 17 June that the compelling need to retreat was revealed, when Blücher confirmed that his army would not be in a fit state for renewed action until 18 June. The Anglo–Allied infantry retreated first, followed by the cavalry at 2:00pm, just as the French advanced. Wellington ensured that the troops still at Nivelles moved in parallel, north to Mont St Jean. Uxbridge's cavalry would capably screen the infantry's withdrawal, while of course Wellington's ability to micro-manage all units was invaluable in the retreat. Nonetheless, the Dutch artillery park, which transported their reserve ammunition, fled unchecked all the way to Brussels, thereby missing battle at Waterloo. Major Whinyates' rockets certainly played a part in the retreat when they demolished a French gun deployed to lay harassing fire upon the screening cavalry. Wellington would now make another questionable decision, when he diverted fully 17,000 troops from Hill's II Corps westwards to the town of Hal, fearful that Napoleon might yet sidestep his army. Had defeat ensued at Waterloo, he would have struggled to explain the unavailability of these troops, located 3 hours march away. Justification for this action has again been posited by those historians who question the quality of the delegated Dutch–Belgian elements. Yet, it should not be overlooked or discounted that the main contingent was in fact the entire 4th British Division of 6,000 men, led by Lieutenant General Sir Charles Colville. While Wellington's proponents have stated that he only sent these troops to Hal in full knowledge of substantial Prussian support the next day, this cannot have been fully clear at this juncture. The Prussians needed to revitalize their forces, while concurrently retreating before the French pursuit led by Marshal Emmanuel de Grouchy at the head of over 30,000 troops.

By the early hours of 18 June, Wellington had arrived at his preferred defensive location between Mont St Jean and Waterloo, south of Brussels, and from messages received was now convinced of Prussian support. Indeed, he hoped soon to see the arrival of three Prussian corps rather than the one originally solicited. Nevertheless, even on the battlefield Wellington's dispositions remained notably weighted to the right, favouring his army's communications, and justifiable solely by the expectation of Prussian support. Perversely, it may be suspected that he actually yet doubted the Prussians and wished primarily still to ensure his own army's path of retreat. The Anglo–Allied army at Mont St Jean was duly deployed in dense line of battle at approximately 20,000 infantry per mile of frontage, which compares, for example, with 8,000 per mile, as deployed at Salamanca. Mont St Jean was part of a location previously surveyed by the RE, only 2½ miles in length, and offering the reverse slopes that Wellington desired.[65] In this self-same area, on 7 July 1794, fighting between the forces of French General Jean-Baptiste Jourdan and Austrian Marshal Friedrich Sachsen-Coburg had occurred during the Revolutionary War. Here, in the aftermath of the major battle of Fleurus on 26 June 1794, Coburg fought a rearguard action, as the defeated Allies fled; a young AG Soult was with General Jourdan. Fitzroy Somerset reports that

Wellington had originally considered making use of the La Belle Alliance ridge upon which the French would themselves subsequently deploy, but this was ultimately rejected as being overly elongated for the size of Wellington's army. Anglo-Allied infantry at Mont St Jean would be uniquely deployed four-men deep, which reflects and emphasizes the cramped conditions. Wellington forbade any entrenchment which he felt might encourage Napoleon to yet manoeuvre to his right and threaten the lines of communication.[66] Wellington's strategy for the climactic battle to come was the familiar reliance upon his personal management of manpower, means and materiel, to wear down the enemy's energy and outlast him in a prolonged contest of defensive attrition. This was his forte and his safest option, but it hardly makes him the 'greatest improviser in the history of war', as has been claimed.[67] Wellington's subsequent orders, as expected, show both his attention to detail, but also his willingness to bypass the chain of command. The farmsteads of Hougoumont, La Haye Sainte and Papelotte alone were to be fortified, though La Haye Sainte would prove to have defensive short-comings for which Wellington's sketchily communicated directions for Colonel Smyth, RE have been blamed.[68] The solidly constructed, main timber gates to the farmyard here had been unwittingly used as fuel by wet and hungry troops, over night. Most artillery guns were deployed at Wellington's order as individual companies in support of the infantry divisions, which themselves were largely hidden from the French behind their reverse hill slopes. Captain George Barlow reports that the army was 'perfectly concealed from the enemy who could by no means get a sight of its force or disposition'.[69] The troops of the horse artillery, by majority, had been allocated in support of Uxbridge's 13,350 total cavalry. Yet, at the height of the action, Wellington still directly controlled and duly relocated most elements of these artillery units elsewhere for the defence. Napoleon's own thoughts however were manifestly more aggressive. With his own army in position on the morning of 18 June, he would in due course seek decisiveness upon the centre and the weaker left flank of the Anglo-Allied army, as he strove for outright victory.

Wellington, once again, unmistakably cut across army organization to ensure his own individual control at the Battle of Waterloo; he would separate the components of more than one infantry division so that he could handle battalions personally. General Hill's notional II Corps held the right wing, Wellington was initially in the centre with the I Corps of the Prince of Orange, while General Picton now commanded the Reserve Corps situated on the left flank. Here the terrain offered less opportunity for cover and Picton would condemn the position as 'one of the worst ever chosen'.[70] Wellington's battlefield entourage consisted of some forty individuals, his staff officers and eight ADC, as well as artillery and engineer assistants. Wellington's outlook: 'I assembled my officers and laid down my plan, and it was carried into effect without any more words.' His orders as ever were 'all short, quick, clear and to the purpose'.[71] However, Wellington's numerous battlefield movements and personalized commands would subsequently lead to the wholesale depletion of his aides; towards the end of the battle he had astonishingly to make use of a fortuitously located Birmingham button salesman to deliver orders.[72]

Wellington's army of 72,000 men with157 guns – one-third British, the rest German and Dutch-Belgian – stood solidly upon the defensive as 74,500 French troops with 246 guns attacked at 11:30am. The extreme disquietude generated by the ferocity of the French assaults meant that he would merely react to events for most of the day, but Wellington doubtless knew his own strengths and advantages. Still, certain historians have considered, possibly unfairly in light of his enemy's elan, that he was both 'perplexed and unsettled' by the tactics of the French throughout the battle, and that his command duly sustained heavy casualties as a result of being too overly passive.[73] An initial French bombardment was followed by the assault of Marshal Honoré Reille's II Corps, led by Prince Jérôme Bonaparte's 6th Division, against the west of centre Hougoumont chateau. The French would suffer here through limited knowledge of the defensive positions they encountered, and while Hougoumont would be assailed throughout the day, it would not fall. Wellington's control was evident from this first assault as he disregarded the chain of command. He assumed full personal oversight when it might have been far better to delegate control, for example, to the adjacent General Cooke of the 1st Division, if rational trust had been in evidence. Indeed, his over-arching presence intimidated others in the chain of command who might on occasion have acted in a timelier manner. When the French sneaked along the east flank of Hougoumont's orchard their presence was pointed out to the Prince of Orange, but he refused to order any counter-action, since he felt sure that Wellington would take care of it. When the French finally broke into Hougoumont's farm compound, crisis resulted because Wellington was then too far distant to see and immediately react to events. He yet sent messages directly to Lieutenant Colonel James Macdonell, who commanded the Coldstream Guards deployed within the burning Hougoumont buildings: 'after they [the roofs] will have fallen in occupy the ruined walls'.[74] Hougoumont was finally held, but required continued reinforcement of its over-small initial garrison. Wellington would eventually be forced to deploy over 4,500 troops here, of whom 2,500 became casualties. Yet, through the day, the French would actually feed into the attack some 12,700 men, 23 per cent of Napoleon's entire army, and of whom nearly half became casualties. Nonetheless, as Napoleon desired, the initial violent attacks upon Hougoumont forced Wellington to focus his attention here. Wellington was also compelled to reinforce with the supporting fire of five additional artillery companies, despite the perceived formation of a French *Grande Batterie* of artillery further to the east. At this juncture Wellington still had plenty of reserves to call upon; the narrowness of the front meant that he defended in depth.

As fighting raged at Hougoumont, the fire from the eighty guns of the *Grande Batterie* continuously targeted the centre and left wing of Wellington's front. Here from 1:30pm Count Jean-Baptiste d'Erlon's entire I Corps advanced in a crucial assault against the Allied forces deployed between La Haye Sainte and Papelotte. However, the French were firstly disrupted by the fire from the chateaux, and ultimately repulsed by the combined arms of the Allied infantry, their supporting artillery, and finally by Uxbridge's heavy cavalry. This intense fighting has indeed been described as the crisis of the entire battle, and though d'Erlon's attack was repulsed and defeated, his four infantry divisions within I Corps were not wholly shattered, as is so often stated. General Picton, who was already suffering from broken ribs sustained at Quatre Bras, died here at about 2:00pm, at the head of his 5th Division; Major General James Kempt replaced him in command. The eastern defensive frontage beyond La Haye Sainte had been founded upon just two complete infantry divisions, Perponcher's 2nd Netherland, and Picton's 5th Division, combining elements of the 6th; and with Uxbridge's heavy cavalry formations their main reserve. For every infantryman, cavalryman and gun deployed to this frontage by Wellington it may be noted that two were positioned to the west of La Haye Sainte. It has been suggested that it was tactical complacency by Wellington that neglectfully assumed that his infantry, here led by the proficient Picton, would always prevail whenever standing upon the defence.[75] Here they would however falter under the enormous pressure of numbers, and the subsequent charge made by Uxbridge's massed heavy cavalry was a necessity to finally repulse d'Erlon's assault; it swept through the French ranks with abandon. The cavalry captured two enemy eagles in short order, while only two had previously been taken in the whole of the Peninsular War. Uxbridge ensured the safety of Picton's position, but the absence of light cavalry support for the charging heavies was a mistake: Major Generals Richard Hussey Vivian and John Vandeleur of the 6th and 4th Light Brigades would not move without a direct order from Wellington.[76] Indeed, Karl von Müffling records Wellington as stating that if they had attacked without orders, 'I must have brought them to a court-martial'.[77] The only support came from the Netherlands 1st Light Cavalry Brigade, initially held in reserve, but led forward by Major General Charles de Ghigny on his own initiative. Not for the first time in the campaign, the individual enterprise shown by a Dutch formation would be significant, despite ignoring Wellington's standing orders. Meanwhile, rockets fired by Major Whinyates aided both the cavalry assault and helped survivors retreat back to the British lines, after they in turn had been decimated by a French cavalry counter-attack. Uxbridge subsequently would graciously praise Wellington's 'coolness and decision in action', while chivalrously accepting responsibility for the losses incurred by the heavy cavalry from the charge.[78] Uxbridge has been oft criticized for the ruination of the heavies, partially as a result of his own self-deprecating words, but the necessity for the charge was of Wellington's making. Elsewhere it has more accurately been observed that: 'Uxbridge blamed himself, unnecessarily'.[79]

At 3:30pm Marshal Ney launched forward the French cavalry in the centre with continued ferocity, as elements of the VI Corps of General Georges Mouton, Count Lobau now attacked Wellington's easternmost farmstead bastions of Frichermon, Papelotte and La Haye, as well as the hamlet of Smohain. However, also to the east, Prussian General Freidrich von Bülow's IV Corps was beginning to arrive, and at approximately 4:30pm the Prussian vanguard commenced its co-ordinated attack upon the French right flank. In his post-battle report Wellington wrote that, 'about seven in the evening [. . .] the march of General Bülow's corps [. . .] had begun to take effect'.[80] Despite the tumultuous events of the day, considering the actual time of the Prussians' arrival, Wellington's statement potentially dissembles. Direct communication with the Prussians had been re-established at 10:00am that morning, and it is claimed that Wellington himself observed the Prussians advancing in the direction of Chapelle St Lambert at about 3:00pm. Wellington was further aware that the Prussians had commenced skirmishing in the direction of Plancenoit village before 4:00pm. It has, as a result, been claimed that: 'Wellington misled his superiors as much as he misled his allies. His report cannot be taken as an accurate account of the events of the day in question.'[81] Although sent after the defeated Prussians on 16 June, Marshal Grouchy's detached right wing containing the substantial French III and IV Corps had failed to prevent Prussian intervention. As early in the day as 11:25am Grouchy's subordinate, General Maurice-Etienne Gérard, leading the IV Corps, had advised him to march to the sound of the guns at Waterloo, but was ignored. Their route would have been undefended, and events would prove this failure to have been a mistake that eclipsed any made by the Allies. Nevertheless, the Anglo-Allied central bulwark of La Haye Sainte fell after repeated French attacks at about 6:00pm; Wellington stated that it fell 'about 2 o'clock', and blamed it on the neglect of the officer commanding.[82] Wellington would subsequently concede that its loss caused: 'much of the injury done to the British Army', while at least one historian has described Wellington's actions as 'negligent'.[83] The whole of the British line was in crisis. AQMG James Shaw reported that a half-mile gap existed in the heart of the left flank, with Wellington in 'a state of despair' as his army 'fled around him'.[84] At 7:00pm General Kempt, now commanding the 5th Division, was reported as saying: 'My Lord, if I am charged again by the enemy, I am not able to stand, for my division is cut-up to a skeleton.'[85] Yet, an hour earlier the Prussians already had 29,000 men and 64 guns to oppose Lobau's 9,000 troops on the French right wing. This figure would rise to an unstoppable 49,000 Prussian soldiers with 134 guns engaged at Waterloo.

At 7:30pm eight battalions of French Imperial Guard, the leading five from the Middle Guard, the other three being Old Guard, were thrown at Wellington's centre; Napoleon's last intact formations. They would be supported by elements of the depleted forces of d'Erlon and Reille, though ten other Guard battalions were already fighting the Prussians to the east. The climactic French attack was met by the British Guards of General Cooke's 1st Division. They were supported by Major General Frederick Adam's Brigade of Clinton's 2nd Division on their right; Hill was here with the 52nd Regiment that flanked the French as they attacked.[86] The disregarded Brunswick and Nassauer troops still stood to the left of the Guards, as well as whatever reserves Wellington could personally marshal. Beyond the infantry fire, a concentration of thirteen Allied batteries, feasibly seventy-five guns firing, notably pounded the French attack, despite ammunition shortages.[87] The Imperial Guard firstly wavered and was then sent into climactic retreat. Major General August von Kruse, who led the Nassauer Infantry Brigade, stated: 'In less than half-an-hour a brilliant victory had been won over an enemy who had believed they were the victors, and that with good reason.'[88] Wellington himself described the implosion of the French forces as 'one of the most remarkable phenomena of sudden and total rout of a disciplined army he had ever seen'.[89] The Prince of Orange would soon write: 'It was my corps which principally gave battle and to which we owe the victory, but the affair was entirely decided by the attack which the Prussians made on the enemy's right.'[90]

But, Wellington did not like to share victory: 'I firmly believe, that if anything happened to me at Waterloo the battle was lost', and three months later he gave an account in which he unambiguously defeated the Imperial Guard prior to any intervention by the Prussians.[91] By September of 1815, even the patience of Marshal Blücher wavered in the face of this perceived affectation: 'Wellington's conduct was not always good.'[92] During Wellington's subsequent lifetime, any account of the great battle that contradicted his own predominance would receive short shrift; he would bemoan: 'But I am really too hard worked to [. . .] review these lying works called histories'.[93] Historian Peter Hofschröer, though a critic, nevertheless suggests that after the singularly intense campaign, Wellington's 'circumspection when dealing with his own errors is understandable', and 'no worse than [. . .] certain of his contemporaries'.[94] Yet, for Wellington to state that he won the battle without Prussian support is assuredly wrong. His centralized leadership style did work at its very best upon the restricted battlefield of Waterloo. It was a brilliant defensive battle for Wellington and his Anglo-Allied forces, but the decisive counter-attack was Prussian led. Major General Sir Hussy Vivian succinctly records: 'We were greatly indebted to the Prussians, and it was their coming on the right and rear of Napoleon that gave us the victory at Waterloo.'[95]

The French *Armée du Nord* was not entirely destroyed at Waterloo, but its morale was broken. Recent non-partisan research suggests that battlefield casualty figures were actually lower within the French army than for the Allies.[96] Plausible figures for losses are likely 17,000 Anglo-Allied, 7,000 Prussian and a roughly equal 24,000–26,000 French, but this figure includes 6,000–7,000 prisoners taken at the end of the battle. For Wellington such losses exceeded three times that of any other of his prior battles. General Picton was killed, QMG De Lancey mortally wounded and most other senior officers were debilitated to varying degree; but no failures of command had occurred, despite Wellington's suspicion of the foreign contingents. Defensive artillery fire, as an adjunct to the stolid infantry, was certainly instrumental in achieving the victory, with the flexible use of guns repeatedly disrupting French manoeuvre. Yet, Wellington stated: 'I was not very well pleased with the artillery [. . .] they ran off the field [. . .] I should have had no artillery during the whole of the latter part of the action, if I had not kept a reserve.'[97] Analysis has otherwise found evidence for individuals within just three gun companies, from eighteen, leaving the field of battle, potentially to ensure re-supply before returning; it should be recalled that elements of the artillery park were missing.[98] Furthermore, the hapless Colonel Wood, CRA was severely reprimanded by Wellington after the battle and in front of the entire staff, for failing to speedily organize the capture of the French guns. This has recently been described as 'a cruel and ill-handled snub by Wellington to a man who, following his performance [. . .] merited more respect'.[99] The cavalry contribution was crucial at Waterloo: from Uxbridge's great charge, to the performance of the light cavalry during the afternoon, when both breaking up the massed French cavalry and plugging gaps in the British line. With the expected steadiness of the infantry line troops, including the disparate Allied units, all arms indeed performed with the utmost credit. Wellington's doubts regarding the capability of the Dutch-Belgian troops appears to have had as much to do with prejudice against Napoleon's former allies than to reality. Blücher met with Wellington post-battle at the farmstead of La Belle Alliance and the Prussians suggested that this highly appropriate title be used to name the battle. Wellington of course refused; preferring the Waterloo appellation, which reflected solely upon the British, and his own battlefield contribution. A year later Wellington would actually even deny that he had met Blücher at La Belle Alliance: 'It happened that the meeting took place after ten at night, at the village of Genappe.'[100] Again, Sir Hussey Vivian, whose 6th Cavalry Brigade was best placed to be aware of Prussian activity, located as he was on the extreme eastern flank of the army, stated: 'I care not what anyone may say to depreciate the importance of the Prussian aid [. . .] but for that aid our advance never would have taken place [. . .] it's not fair not to give it its due weight and the Prussians their due credit'.[101]

Wellington's complaints at the start of the campaign were now mirrored post-Waterloo: 'with the exception of my old Spanish infantry, I have not only got the worst troops, but the worst equipped army, with the worst staff, that was ever brought together in the shape of an Army'.[102] Ministers again sought to placate him, shipping reinforcements and sending conciliatory letters, while ignoring the obvious histrionics. The exasperated Torrens however was personally offended and wrote:

> It is really too bad that the Duke should complain of us [. . .] after all that
> has passed, and it does not dispose me to continue the exertions I have

used to [. . .] serve him in a thousand little details, for which I never get a word of thanks![103]

Wellington here most clearly showed his facility for alienating even those who were the most predisposed towards him.

Wellington's failure to give praise after such a climactic battle was unsurprising and was perhaps the product of his arrogance and insecurity, which had only increased over time: 'He feels he owes all to his own great abilities.'[104] More objective bystanders such as Lord Castlereagh were happy to state that, as well as the Dutch–Belgians, 'the Prussian army had the same claims on our gratitude'.[105] Although foreign contingents made up 64 per cent of his army in 1815, in his post-battle Waterloo dispatch Wellington merely found praise for Major General August von Kruse of the Nassau Brigade, Lieutenant General Albert Trip van Zoudtlandt of the Netherlands heavy cavalry and a non-existent General Vanhope.[106] It is merely guessed at, that this person could be Colonel Hendrik Detmers who commanded the 1st Netherlands Infantry Brigade that was involved with the repulse of Napoleon's Guard. With his command idiosyncrasies of autocracy, micro-management and distrust, more than ever Wellington personally felt he should bear no responsibility for any setbacks; be it the misdirecting of troops, or the critical loss of La Haye Sainte. Blame and the creation of scapegoats were integral to Wellington's command style. As ever he merely desired a staff of efficient field officers in whom he had enough faith to follow his orders implicitly; he wanted no initiative on show.

To be overcautious is doubtless better than to be critically deceived, yet during the short campaign of 1815 Wellington's leadership had certainly erred in both regards. At first he dispersed his army too widely across Belgium, always fearful for his communications, and thereafter as a result he was caught at a disadvantage by Napoleon's sudden surge across the frontier. His flat-footed reactions were compounded by not being with his troops at the front at the critical moment in time, but rather attending to social functions in Brussels. He was fortunate that the Dutch–Belgians were the least used to awaiting his every diktat. As strategic events critically unfolded, he knowingly and assuredly provided false information regarding his troop dispositions to the Prussians. After a tentative defensive showing at Quatre Bras he still continued with his obsessive regard for the army's line of communication when diverting valuable troops to remotely garrison Hal. Even on the battlefield of Waterloo, Wellington may be accused of an imperfect initial deployment of his forces; the charge again relating to an over-concern for his right wing, at the expense of his left. The entire 3rd Netherlands Division of Lieutenant General Baron David Chassé, of which Colonel Detmers' brigade formed part, spent much of the day inactive on the extreme western flank, at the town of Braine l'Alleud. Called into the battle only latterly, they suffered just 10 per cent casualties; the smallest percentage of any involved unit. In the crisis of battle, the loss of La Haye Sainte was a major setback for the Anglo-Allies, and Wellington's own faulty preparation or communication appears to have played its part. Finally, the failure to ensure the availability of such resources as the 18-pound cannon left at Brussels was a significant over-sight. The overall evidence of prevarication and ignored intelligence prior to Waterloo, as well as mistakes during the great battle itself, is compelling; Wellington obstinately relied solely upon his own instinctive capabilities, when the initiative and ability of others, most specifically in 1815 the leadership of the Dutch-Belgian generals, was clearly on show. Wellington's British officers were largely moulded to his modus operandi; it was his foreign contingents in 1815 that fortuitously were not.

Questions about Wellington's words and actions during the campaign were subsequently mooted and his conduct questioned by firstly the Prussian General Staff, and thereafter by renown German military theorist Carl von Clausewitz. He believed that Wellington's words from 1815 had misled English-speaking sources, and so it is regrettable that only recently has the work of Clausewitz been translated into English.[107] In a letter from 1842 Wellington described the Prussians as 'mine enemy'; he of course did not appreciate having his pronouncements discussed and dissected by those he doubtless believed guilty of their own partisanship.[108] In response to the increasingly chauvinistic British narrative, in 1868 historian Charles Chesney stated that: 'The popular English version of the great battle [. . .] is hardly less a romance than the Famous Waterloo chapter in Victor Hugo's *Les Miserables*'.[109] Thereafter, chauvinism only increased. It is to be hoped that the most recent studies of the battle of Waterloo have now rendered such an observation as outdated and frivolous. In 1815 Wellington had certainly both underestimated the French and reacted indecisively, in part the consequence of his habitual and unchanging inability to trust or work co-operatively with others. The Prussians were not alone in showing great forbearance for his conceit and mistrust; many individuals must again have felt slighted or sidelined by his command. Wellington's army would have not withstood Napoleon's attentions alone without the Prussians, and in standing at Waterloo the Anglo-Allied army had to quiescently absorb the heaviest of punishments, as they waited for that assistance. Yet, Wellington's leadership certainly gained and deserved the lasting veneration that he sought, when the great battle was won. The victory, then and now, resonates with the British public as the termination of a long war and the downfall of Napoleon. Wellington's command primarily displayed the strength of his personality and purpose, in holding his forces together through sheer individual hard work, while also again having the good fortune to be among the few unwounded senior officers. With negligible thanks for the quality of the military resources made available to his army, he demonstrated that his own indefatigable leadership upon a chosen defensive battlefield could secure victory. Waterloo perpetuated the unfortunate myth that this was an ideal formula, and that one such battle could settle a war.

Conclusion

Wellington's Mandate

'I learned how futile the waging of war becomes when the higher command refuses to [. . .] delegate command to chosen subordinates'.[1]

This reassessment of the Duke of Wellington's leadership began by questioning the traditional narrative offered by historians regarding his army command during the pivotal campaigns against the French from 1808 to 1815. Notwithstanding such reconsideration, Wellington's formidable and tangible achievements have of course been rightly praised. Historian Huw Davies, for example, is hardly alone in recording that Wellington's leadership embraced all the military virtues: the strategic, for the ability to translate political aims into military objectives; the operational, for the achievement of decisive outcomes in battle; the tactical, not least through the appreciation of terrain. Wellington's record of success is prodigious; though it may be acknowledged nonetheless that 'he was lucky', if not even 'among the luckiest generals in history'.[2] Indeed, even Wellington himself stated his belief that his virtually uninterrupted good health upon campaign reflected divine assistance: 'The finger of Providence was upon me, and I escaped unhurt.'[3] Most pertinent to this work, the heavy-handed severity with which he controlled his forces has invariably been recorded as a substantive imperative to that success. But can one agree that Wellington's military genius alone effectively moulded sub-standard subordinate leadership and all arms components into a winning team? It is otherwise affirmed here that such an appreciation is unreasonable; it is too much the product of Wellington's own bequeathed words as well as that of his early standard-bearers, encapsulated by the likes of Oman and Fortescue.

Some histories, as acknowledged, describe and criticize the personal contra-dictions within Wellington's character, but he is nonetheless routinely absolved, when not indeed praised for his forcefulness, even to today. In just one typical scholarly example it is stated that, 'the obedience he exacted from all ranks was required for the health and efficiency of the army'.[4] Contrariwise, the exaggerated nature of his command and control is as hard to accept now as it was for many of his documented officers. It may alternatively be considered that Wellington's concern regarding the health of his forces ran no further than to ensure that they, by and large, remained physically active in the field, while the efficiency of the army was wholly subservient to his most rigorous jurisdiction. While Wellington battled on behalf of Great Britain, it is difficult not to conclude that he also never failed to consider how his actions might be favourably judged by both his superiors and the public at home, in 1815 just as in 1808. Indeed, the self-confidence and mental well-being of many of Wellington's subordinates could only have been eroded by his single-minded application of command. Some of the resultant negative implications have been highlighted here, but his success has otherwise negated criticism. Other perceptible elements of ineffectiveness, that have to some degree gone unacknowledged, have been rationalized in the preceding chapters when considering the idiosyncrasies surrounding Wellington's command. These same traits have in parallel and to a notable extent also negatively impacted upon the perceptions of both troops and generals, whose endeavours have been routinely diminished. Yet, examples have also been recorded here of the positive attributes displayed by Wellington's forces and despite the criticisms they received. It may be hoped therefore that this generalized reassessment has provided a more subjective view of the inter-relationships within the component parts of Wellington's army and their contributions to success. This is not to undermine the achievements of Wellington, but to provide ideally a more inclusive and credible, if nuanced perspective.

The very appointment of Wellington in 1808 marked progress on the path to ensuring that personal ability transcended less tangible attributes, such as patrimony when choosing an individual for command. Yet, Wellington proved himself to be an anachronism. He was conservative in the extreme, and to an extent that is barely comprehensible today. Despite an introverted personality – French diplomat Charles Maurice de Talleyrand would describe him as the most complex man he had ever met – he nonetheless displayed an extraordinary level of ambition from first joining the army. His snobbish esteem for nobility meant that he always exhibited an aloof and anti-intellectual streak; for Wellington this meant that in practice an individual's lineage overrode the mere actuality of any education and the very concept of professional development. He otherwise always relied ultimately and solely upon his own intuition and ostensible common sense. Even such staunch supporters as Oman, after long study, ultimately found his over-bearing manner and sarcasm towards his contemporaries distasteful. Former subordinates Grattan and Napier both considered, with evident understatement that: 'He did not make the hard-working military crowd feel that their honest, unobtrusive exertions were appreciated.'[5] Such an attitude can only have impacted upon his generalship, and with the ramifications that have been affirmed here. The future French prime minister Count Louis-Mathieu Molé met Wellington in 1815 and gave this impression of his personality:

> He possesses that imperturbable will which [. . .] wears down all resistance.
> No obstacle surprises him, no difficulty deters him. Never [. . .] blinded

by success, he is fond of praise, even undiscerningly so [. . .] Born under
a Government in which all men invested with power are answerable for
their actions and all glory subject to discussion, [Wellington] seems to live
in the constant expectation of seeing his own attacked.[6]

Wellington's steadfast command style was always one of cool and clear-headed,
yet very formal control, as has been described. He was both self-opinionated and
certainly jealous of his reputation. His ego could brook no opposition to his will,
even if he was misguided; this was indeed hubris. Both Wellington's desire and
sheer ability to keep the whole elaborate organization of his army in his own hands
was certainly singular. Many consenting accounts have indicated the necessity of
Wellington's need to effectively manage his army through a 'fanatical insistence
on orders', rather than to inspire it.[7] Yet, this is fitting the facts to match the
outcome – what may be termed 'confirmation bias' – alternatives did exist for
success. While other leaders might appeal to the emotions of their officers, the
stark formality and cynical outlook of Wellington was totally incapable of making
any such appeal. In depending less upon his subordinates than other commanders,
he made purely personal choices and rejected the benefits of delegation. He
would always command rather than lead. With due consideration of Wellington's
temperament, the wholesale censure of his subordinates is unjust. To both inspire
and command is patently a more attractive outcome, as was certainly displayed by
Wellington's contemporaries, Napoleon and Lord Nelson. The relationship that
these great commanders had with their subordinates was integral to the generation
of *esprit de corps* and their very success; such a relationship of mutual trust was
always anathema to Wellington. Or, as Lord Roberts observed in 1895: 'the more
we go into the actions and his writings [. . .] the less do we like him as a man'.[8]

It has been described how Wellington's senior officers all had backgrounds
with a degree of privilege; despite the Duke of York's reforms they were not
fully the products of merit or professionalism. Their abilities were reliant upon
the vagaries of self-education and experience, and war was dangerous. Including
Wellington, eighty-five British generals served in the Peninsula and at Waterloo.
Of these, sixteen were either killed in action or otherwise died, while twenty-nine
were captured or wounded. Beyond their raw courage and patriotism, most if not
all senior commanders also displayed loyalty, commitment and equanimity. Any
comparison to the egalitarian French system of officer appointment shows little
practical difference in outcomes: generals such as Hope and Hill were certainly not
outclassed by the skill of their experienced French opponents. Even Beresford, who
seemingly lacked equanimity in battle, was ultimately successful at Albuera; thanks
to the fine qualities of the attendant British troops. Wellington's officers under
command were certainly the equal in quality of their French opponents and indeed
were an integral part of Wellington's success, not an adjunct. Despite Wellington's

ceaseless complaints, Horse Guards did its best to address his wishes with regard to both appointments and re-supply, and it is little wonder that Henry Torrens became incensed by 1815. Wellington himself was an exceptional individual, but overall it may be interpreted that the subordinate commanders also displayed excellent qualities, despite the insensitivity emanating from headquarters. It is hard to reconcile Wellington's criticism of them when one fully appreciates the very extreme restrictions their leader imposed. 'He was constitutionally cold and impassable, stern in the execution of duty, careless in the reward of merit, the end his mighty object, the means a matter of indifference.'[9]

The senior generals Hill, Graham and Hope displayed estimable qualities; their composure and grace meant that they were largely able to work effectively both under Wellington's control or independent of him. Wellington awarded them the most respect: not normally for them the observation that his visitors often left his presence 'boiling with rage'.[10] Hill, for example, undertook the crucial independent Almaraz expedition of May 1812, and Graham won independent battle at Barrosa in March 1811; both with great adroitness. Hope at Bayonne in early 1814 notably co-ordinated a most difficult combined arms operation that involved not only Portuguese and Spanish troops, but the Royal Navy. The fidelity shown by these generals to Wellington, or was it rather to Great Britain's best interests, is typified by the conjectured fighting of a duel by Hope in Paris, upon Wellington's behalf in 1823. King George IV, it is reputed, asked Hope to fight the son of a French marshal so as not to compromise Wellington's position within government.[11] The always combative Hope was wounded in the duel, and the fever that led to his death in August that same year has been suggested to have been a result.

With regard to other prominent subordinate generals, Cole, Picton and Clinton similarly gave most commendable service under trying circumstances; reference to their successes has been recorded here. Beyond forbearance, they and other senior officers must have learnt how to manage the expectations that Wellington routinely demanded. For example, when asked as to the number of rounds of ammunition the particular allotted artillery held, one unnamed general immediately replied 'four hundred and twenty'. He subsequently confided to a fellow officer that the real, but unknown figure could always be adjusted later. The lack of instant response otherwise earned AQMG Sir Hudson Lowe the rebuke from Wellington: 'D—d old fool!'[12] Some most promising generals, such as Generals John Mackenzie and notably Robert Craufurd, had their well-founded commands cut short by untimely death, in 1809 and 1812 respectively. In life Craufurd appears to have endeared himself to Wellington principally from the standpoint of being a similarly harsh disciplinarian; his disparaging comments upon Craufurd after his death were patently callous. General Erskine is an individual who has been perennially denigrated, since his career was tarnished by the recurrence of mental illness,

---

which led to his suicide in 1813. Yet, he had met Wellington's rigorous expectations in 1812, and was positively praised by him for 'prudence and circumspection'.[13] Discernment has been lacking from the historical record, based in this case upon Wellington's ultimate discharge of Erskine, once beset by illness. Charles Stewart, William Stewart, Sherbrooke and Spencer are also commonly dismissed by historians as being at best ineffectual, but all displayed competence if one looks beyond the hyperbole: conflict with Wellington's ego dominates their record. The Fuentes de Oñoro, Pyrenean and Nive battles all showed that the generals could perform with effect when able to use their initiative. Finally, in 1815, the limited timescale of the campaign precluded any great effort by Wellington to inculcate his will upon Uxbridge and the foreign generals. Lieutenant General Perponcher notably saved the campaign for Wellington, and it may have helped that he had not previously been subject to Wellington's jurisdiction. Even Oman acknowledges at one point in his lengthy history, that intelligent co-operation is better than blind obedience.[14]

Both Beresford and Cotton were firm favourites with Wellington throughout the war, and flourished thanks to their administrative abilities rather than for their initiative or their ability in combat. Lady Combermere states of her husband: 'The Duke of Wellington thought most highly of his qualities as a cavalry general, and often was heard to remark that, when he gave an order to Sir Stapleton Cotton, he felt sure it would be obeyed, not only with zeal but with discretion.'[15] Beresford of course was hugely effective in his reorganization of the Portuguese forces, but was markedly less effective as a field commander. His successful reorganization of the Portuguese forces was indeed absolutely critical to ensuring adequate Allied manpower throughout the war. Criticism is due for Beresford's poor handling of the Battle of Albuera, yet Wellington must, as recorded, certainly take his share of the responsibility. The successes these officers did display clearly demonstrate that effective commanders must possess several different attributes. Beresford for one was certainly a better administrator and innovator, than tactician. Yet, the vast majority of senior officers under Wellington's command were never given the opportunity to display any independent leadership potential.

Wellington's own personal leadership relied heavily upon his administrative organization of control under strict discipline. As the war and strategic situation progressed, army size and the required dispersion of forces did the most to undermine this standpoint. With time, familiarity, success, and possibly sheer weariness during the long Peninsular War, Wellington's command and control appears to have marginally relaxed; no one can be fully certain of his movements during the Nive battles, for example. QMG George Murray, by 1814, felt Wellington's strictures soften towards him more than most; the support that he provided best exemplifies what Wellington might have gained from other talented individuals. The more individualistic support given to Sir John Moore by such subordinates as Generals Baird, Hope and notably Henry Paget during his short campaign of 1808–9 should not be forgotten. Understandably for the campaign of 1815, Wellington tried his best to recreate his Peninsular Army as far as possible. However, despite a headquarters full of veteran officers, Wellington was forced to do without Murray as the QMG and, as a result, reverted to his most authoritarian of outlooks. This would only exacerbate his strategic misconceptions. Whereas the Prussian army learnt the benefits of having an effective chief-of-staff in Gneisenau, Wellington's personalized command and control would provide the template for a different, but a misconceived organization.

Wellington was routinely mistrustful of the Allied foreign contingents encountered between 1808 and 1815, and he was doubtless not alone in exhibiting xenophobic attitudes. With the opprobrium heaped upon the Iberian forces, initially British officers required a promotion equivalent to two levels to induce them to transfer into Portuguese service. Many of the British troops would otherwise record that they felt more in common with the enemy French than their merciless Spanish allies. Wellington routinely criticized the capabilities of firstly the Portuguese and subsequently the Spanish soldiers throughout the Peninsular War, as he would also the Dutch-Belgian and German contingents in 1815. Yet, even Wellington would subsequently acknowledge that the availability and performance of the Portuguese troops ultimately decided the Peninsula campaign.[16] Nevertheless, from the ponderous political results that he achieved in the Peninsula, it is hard to see that Wellington was other than an indifferent diplomat and an even less impressive politician. Even with regards to his subsequent career, at least one author lists him among the ten worst British prime ministers: 'as far from a conciliator as you could begin to imagine, alienating friends and opponents alike.'.[17] General John Hamilton, who successfully led the Portuguese Division until his health failed in 1813, would seem to have been treated as a peripheral, if idiosyncratic figure. Wellington had observed on one occasion, when affairs did not progress as he desired: 'I cannot be answerable for a madman'.[18] Hamilton was not a madman; his obituary within the *Gentleman's Magazine* of 1836 speaks of the 'energy and zeal' which attended his command of the Portuguese 'under difficulties of no ordinary nature'. Indeed, in 1815, Wellington requested that Portuguese troops should join his reassembling army, and had again to acknowledge their good qualities.[19] He rightly gauged them, once trained, as a match for their excellent British counterparts: 'The Portuguese troops are very nearly as good as the British.'[20]

The British troops that Wellington referred to were of course the reviled men of whom Wellington dismissively said: 'It all depends upon that article whether we do the business or not.'[21] Yet, any tactical difficulties that Wellington encountered upon the battlefield were routinely addressed by his infantry; despite being otherwise characterized as the 'scum of the earth', they were always most highly effective.[22] They proved themselves to be routinely stalwart, with an indomitable spirit which can only reflect equally well upon the officers who led them. The British regimental system generated a group dynamic unmatched by most Continental armies. Yet, the soldiers' oft-times strained relationship with Wellington is candidly reported by Oman: 'It is seldom that the veterans who have served under a great commander have failed to idolize as well as to respect him.'[23] It has been pronounced that Napoleon's soldiers fought, 'in bright fields, where every helmet caught some beams of glory, but the British soldier conquered under the cold shade of aristocracy [. . .] his life of danger and hardship was unchequered by hope, his death unnoticed'.[24]

It was the British government that restricted the provision of cavalry, artillery and engineers on the basis of cost; it should not be forgotten that the Royal Navy was still the 'senior service'. Training for these arms overall was good, but practical experience was initially understandably limited, notably for those cavalry upon vedette duty. A question mark has sat predominantly against cavalry officer appointments, due to their voguish popularity at the time. Yet, the copious criticism of, for example, Generals Long and Slade has never included any consideration of them as dilettantes. Despite the occasional setback, most of the criticism of the cavalry is hard to substantiate. Taking into consideration the nature of their patrolling duties, it would not be reasonable to expect unbroken success throughout the whole six years of war in the Peninsula. General Long's reputation, in particular, has been unjustly tarnished, as has been recorded, and creditably that is as a result of his open and enduring criticism of his own superiors. Beresford's complaints of him were largely spurious and otherwise appear to be a sop to Wellington's known prejudices. Le Marchant's untimely death in 1812 removed one of the most talented British cavalrymen of the war, but, once again, other leaders were never given the opportunity to shine: Hanoverian General von Bock's unique achievement at Garcia Herrnandez was not to be repeated. Yet the battles of Vitoria and Orthez in 1813 and 1814 respectively are hardly unique examples of victorious battles that were not pressed by Wellington's cavalry. He rather excused himself by casting doubt both upon the discipline and the tactical skill of his cavalry officers, even after the years they had spent in the field. Indeed, the only examples of effective British cavalry manoeuvres in a major action were at Fuentes de Oñoro, Salamanca and Waterloo. But this limitation was largely due to the restrictions that Wellington himself imposed; away from him any problems usually disappeared. One has only to consider the successes gained by the British cavalry during Moore's short campaign. Despite Wellington's copious criticisms, the only two occasions where French cavalry achieved anything like tactical success in the Peninsula are with their flank attack at Fuentes de Oñoro and similarly at Albuera. Despite the criticism, the French were never able to gain dominance over their British cavalry counterparts in battle. Wellington's restrictive attitudes were a self-fulfilling prophecy.

The segregated command of the artillery and engineers was a complication not of Wellington's making. However, percipient, positive leadership was needed to achieve the best outcome and this was never forthcoming. Instead, Wellington displayed a marked antipathy towards a succession of artillery commanders that had limited substantive justification. Captain Cairnes, RA was hardly alone in observing Wellington's 'abominable intemperance and disregard of all consideration of all feeling'.[25] Dickson became the artillery commander that Wellington demanded: doubtless a talented gunner, but six predecessors infer that Wellington's focus was upon personal attributes as much as professional effectiveness. Colonel Wood performed capably in charge of the Waterloo artillery, despite having been specifically passed-over by Wellington in 1813. Wellington had dismissively considered Wood to be too fat. Technically, British artillery achievements have been understated. New weapon systems, notably shrapnel shell, made a very big difference in battle, just as Wellington's use of the defensive reverse slope reduced the effectiveness of the enemy's guns. The officers and men of the artillery showed nothing but professionalism. The equally professional Royal Engineers, more than any other service, suffered throughout the period from personnel shortages. Because of this Wellington's control rode roughshod over them and gambled with men's lives spectacularly during consecutive siege operations. This presumption by Wellington, of his own infallibility would be a factor in the deaths of a quarter of the engineer officers who served in the Peninsula overall.

In 1808 Britain faced a modern French army which had defeated the *ancien régimes* of Continental Europe. That the British army was able to survive, develop and ultimately defeat Napoleon's forces is testament not only to Wellington, but to the developing systems that provided the officers and men. Systems that to Wellington's chagrin included governmental checks and balances to inhibit the absolutism he would appear to have desired. Wellington was autocratic, yet initially in 1808 he was respectful of colleagues and led without rancour. He did not fully share his intentions, but the compact army in-being suited his leadership style: it enabled him to keep personal control over most aspects of manoeuvre and battle. He was cautious, but was certainly effective with his new command when continuing the 'light and quick' campaigning style which he was familiar with from India.

Wellington's strategic leadership transformed to a more attritional affair after the lessons and losses of Talavera; difficulties which derived partly from the larger forces engaged and partly from Spanish allies who matched Wellington's intransigence of outlook. Wellington's 'habitually haughty and intolerant behaviour may have been acceptable in his dealings with his own army, but it was unsuited to the conduct of relations with an allied power', be it Portugal, Spain or Prussia.[26] The concurrent problematic events of May to October 1809 and beyond, regarding rank within the British and Portuguese armies only served to fuel and exacerbate his mistrust and resentment for his officers. Wellington could not deal with emotive issues and his leadership became evidently more autocratic at this precise juncture. His revised army organizational structure paralleled a tougher approach to command, seemingly adopted in response to perceived insubordination as much as army size and French pressures. Wellington set standards for subordinates that he never necessarily met himself, and despite his aspirations disrespect for his own superiors was perennial. Personal pressure might explain, but cannot excuse, the similar unjust opprobrium that he heaped upon those unfortunate subordinates Colonel Bevan and Captain Ramsey. Such events probably had a dismal effect upon army morale. Nonetheless, the capability of Wellington's French opponents waned conspicuously through the pressure of ceaseless attritional warfare, and most specifically and fortuitously by the troop withdrawals necessitated by Napoleon's invasion of Russia in June 1812.

Over the final two years of his campaign in the Peninsula and France, Wellington's approach was measured, if not still outright cautious; even at Vitoria he opened the battle knowing that his advantages over the enemy were pronounced. He had subsequently to disperse his army to cover the expanded operational area, and proved markedly critical and even more dismissive of the achievements of his independent commanders. The events in the Pyrenees and beyond and the associated contributions of Wellington's subordinates are the least considered of Peninsular War campaigns. As Lord Bathurst had previously observed, Wellington did indeed display a great care for the resources of Great Britain, but towards the end of the war this now appears exaggerated, if not pernickety. Beyond any measure usually applied to a senior commander, his punctiliousness surely contains a concern for his personal reputation and his place in history; he could not, for example, bear the thought of losing a single gun in case it might tarnish his reputation. Wellington's final stuttering offensive operations repeatedly failed to suppress a French opponent who was largely bankrupt, well before the defeats of 1814. Thereafter, in 1815, Wellington complained the loudest about not being able to reconstitute the Peninsular Army. All grievances ultimately appear spurious: he largely got his own way. Wellington's strategic concerns when facing Napoleon were judicious, but were excessive. He ignored intelligence, even at great risk to his Prussian allies, of whom he was typically disdainful. Wellington's hubris had an impact upon all his decisions; his preoccupation that he and Great Britain alone should claim victory at Waterloo is a culminating arrogance. 'You now desire that I should point out to you where you could receive information on this event, on the truth of which you could rely. In answer to this desire I can refer you only to my despatches.'[27]

The Peninsular War was fought without the sweeping displays of strategic genius associated with Napoleon's campaigns; rather a measured process of attrition, due both to the quantitative limitations of British land power and Wellington's approach to command. Wellington's control excelled principally with a compact and centralized army organization. He proved a highly capable general, but it is hard to disagree with the more dispassionate view presented by American author Russell Weigley when pronouncing that Wellington triumphed 'not because his strategic and operational designs were inspired, but because he was resolute'.[28] He was markedly purposeful, if inconsistent in all administrative matters, including logistics and in the employment of the indispensable British infantry bequeathed by Sir John Moore. The huge problems faced by the French should in addition certainly never be underestimated or forgotten: Napoleon's campaigns away from Spain shaped events in the Peninsula immeasurably. Wellington overall had the intuitive skill to maximize his advantages and keep his army in play. The combat tactics that Wellington dictated in battle were predominantly effective, but of course always subject to his personal control. The Battle of Fuentes de Oñoro in 1811 has been flagged as a particular instance of questionable tactics, when the unusually elongated British defensive position here stretched Wellington's usual control of the infantry line regiments. Wellington's use of artillery always worked positively as an adjunct to the effectiveness of the outstanding British infantry; it is hard to fully rationalize the rancour that existed for the gunners. Otherwise the lack of use or misuse, both operationally and tactically, of his cavalry resources shows the least facility from Wellington for this arm of his army. These very internal and enduring antipathies must have reduced those advantages that his army might otherwise have enjoyed in battle from effective combined arms co-operation and flexibility.

Wellington's character is specifically praised for its attributes within Norman Dixon's unique analytical work, *On the Psychology of Military Incompetence*. Yet, it is impossible to agree with the key positive assessments that he makes: rather, Wellington was *not* routinely open to new ideas; he could and did underestimate his enemy; and he was arguably xenophobic. Dixon's statement that Wellington's 'warm humanity' earned him the lasting affection and loyalty of his men is unwarranted and can only be gauged as unsupportable.[29] Wellington was palpably not an incompetent military commander, but neither was he infallible. It has otherwise been demonstrated here that Wellington in actuality displayed sundry characteristics associated with 'incompetent' command and control, as defined in the main by Dixon.[30]

- Overall, Wellington was autocratic and conservative. His ideal subordinate was a competent, gentleman officer of 'fortune and character'.[31] His endorsement of the outworn tradition of patronage was reflected in his appointed personal aides, who were predominantly the sons of dukes; talent alone was insufficient. Such haughtiness in turn generated an undisguised contempt for the perceived lower classes; he was regularly scathing about the rank and file. Coupled with an addiction to discipline in all its forms, the reality is that Wellington cuts an unattractive personal figure.

- He consistently micro-managed his army and thereby reduced his generals to ciphers; he pre-supposed ineffectiveness. Wellington's demand for total personal control generated problems and divisiveness. He displayed a basic lack of trust, as well as conceit with regard to his personal abilities. Examples have thus been provided of subordinates' responsibilities being overridden, and with morale and unit cohesion undermined accordingly.
- Wellington wholly failed to develop the skills of his subordinate generals. Those who found favour with Wellington could thus be exposed to failure by his excessive demands, when events required independent initiative. Beresford's southern command of 1811 is an obvious example, and of course any such occurrence again perversely only fuelled Wellington's self-perception of indispensability. Unsanctioned initiative was otherwise condemned or crushed.
- Insularity and propriety bred inconsistency for Wellington's autocratic command, and could thus beget irresolution and trepidation, brilliance or recklessness, as historian Huw Davies records; the Salamanca campaign alone displayed all such traits. Indeed, when bypassing his officers and obstinately persisting with tasks, he could verge upon the fixated; as, for example, to ensure he ultimately retook the lost Badajoz fortress.
- His communication of command was always detailed, but could still be fallible, as with the dispersion of blockading forces about Almeida in 1811. His impatience and perceptible irritation with those outside his immediate control applied most obviously with his artillerymen and engineers. Wellington's furious siege operations, involving both technical arms, habitually wasted lives. He clearly felt that he knew better than his professionally trained experts, and success alone reinforced his sense of rightness.
- There was certainly, at the very least, ambivalence to Wellington's political skills just as with his command and control; effective co-operation with allies proved hard to achieve. At Talavera specifically his control suffered due to the distraction of the idiosyncratic Spanish forces and the problems he found in cooperating effectively. Events at Lisbon in 1810 otherwise displayed indifference for the well-being of the civilian population, reminiscent of episodes in India. As doubtless other commanders have, he manipulated news of events for home consumption, as at Albuera. Yet, army morale was founded upon success alone; Wellington otherwise failed to inspire through positive communication. As most markedly after Waterloo, his own version of events had always to take precedence.
- Wellington repeatedly ignored strategic intelligence; overwhelmingly so in 1815 and such that the presumption, once again, has to be that he felt he alone knew best. He could indeed sometime fail to reconnoitre effectively; as both before and after battle at Talavera, and also at Toulouse. Wellington

always knew better than subordinates or mistrusted allies. He could thus underestimate his enemy, and almost to his detriment, for example, at Santarém, when an unwise attack was only latterly cancelled. While intelligence-gathering was excellently organized, its misuse was purely down to Wellington.

- He failed to exploit the disarray of his opponents through his conspicuous control; both Soult's and Masséna's successful retreats from Portugal would not be unique events. Positive outcomes from battle went unexploited by pursuit; he was seemingly concerned that any troops might venture beyond his personal control. The 1813–14 campaign similarly shows a repeated underestimation of the recuperative powers inherent to the French. Wellington's sluggishness provided a final opportunity for Soult to reconstruct his army at Toulouse, just as he had done more than once beforehand.
- Wellington's readiness to find scapegoats is exemplified in the cases of Colonel Bevan's suicide, or the actions of the 13th LD cavalry at Campo Mayor. Such events were unpleasant and likely affected both army morale and unit cohesion. His inability to accept any personal recrimination both shows hubris and an ego unable to learn from mistakes.

It is harder to rationalize the generals' contribution against such defined criteria, since the individuals were always firmly within Wellington's shadow. None of course were faultless, and no claim is made here that any of Wellington's subordinates might have acted with his effectuality. Yet, Wellington's own stark command and control ensured that the responsibility for his generals' shortcomings lay ultimately with him; his micro-management was inherently de-motivating. When faced with any sort of query from a subordinate his response was likely to be: 'I will get upon my horse and take a look and then tell you.'[32]

What might Wellington have gained from a more enlightened approach to command and control? Permitting greater initiative from his senior officers would have prompted their greater attention to the detail of tasks, and inspired more positive support for both him and each other. There would be less chance of personal overload for Wellington, and the possibly of operational benefits, for which conjecture can now only be problematic. In any situation of emergency, a more fully conversant subordinate would have been to hand. It may be stressed that command delegation need not degrade control; initiative and flexibility within Wellington's combat arms would purely have provided enhanced capability. Such subsequent great generals as the iconic Confederate General Robert E. Lee, the very antithesis of Wellington, would have been 'irked that he had needed to take so much charge [. . .] into his own hands', rather than leave to capable subordinates.[33] Certainly a more positive economy of effort from Wellington would have better motivated his officers; unit cohesion, combined arms benefits and improved army morale would have all likely resulted. Wellington indirectly introduced a real vulnerability into his army through his severely individualistic style of command and control.

Intriguingly, the military theorist T.N. Dupuy has analytically modelled the Battle of Waterloo in his work *Numbers, Predictions & War*. Starting from the historical outcome he works backwards to generate a factored command ability for Napoleon which he demonstrates as being one-third better than for Wellington. This work has similarly rationalized the components of effective command relative to control, initiative and combat ability, and has observed the difficulty for any individual to equally excel at all three. Wellington, it may be believed, had better personal initiative and combat skills than the optimum effective command and control within his army. Wellington was a great commander, but he was not a great leader of men. His otherwise excellent and resourceful management of systems was inherently compromised; a viewpoint not routinely recognized. This study has certainly deduced that the undue recorded criticism of subordinates resulted in a lack of command reciprocity within the army and the enforced inability of officers to fully employ their own skills. Likewise, the individual arms of the army would struggle to generate combined arms benefits; restrictions and resentments were endemic within Wellington's administration. The inescapable conclusion is that by his divisive insistence upon absolute control Wellington's command did engender a dilution in the potential effectiveness of the forces he commanded between 1808 and 1815. This may have been by only a relatively small factor, but had an impact nonetheless. The largely capable subordinate generals could have contributed more to army effectiveness if allowed to use reasonable initiative, but they were not permitted to do so. Even on the battlefield itself, local commanders were routinely sidelined as tactical dispositions were subject to Wellington's micro-management. It may be surmised that on occasion a general could be unsure as to the orders for a regiment that he was ostensibly in control of. All subordinates customarily displayed professionalism, but poor inter-personal relationships within the army undermined effectiveness: fear of Wellington soured co-operation. The existing historiography has largely downplayed or ignored any such a perspective upon events.

From the immediate aftermath of Waterloo, Wellington has been routinely lauded for his stringent control of supposed ineffectual forces, on his way to achieving ultimate victory over the French. Oman comments that, 'His frigid formalism was regarded with respect and even admiration [. . .] praised as signs of Spartan virtue', and any episodes that did not fit with this picture have thereafter been deliberately down played.[34] Yet, that very success for Wellington's command subsequently motivated a perverse culture of austere resolve that permeated Queen Victoria's armies; to ape Wellington's 'Spartan virtue' was generally an aspiration for British army officers.[35] Senior leaders sought to duplicate Wellington's accomplishments by closely replicating his manner of command and control. This desire unsurprisingly provoked difficulties: most notably for the command of Fitzroy Somerset – later Lord Raglan – in the Crimean War of 1854–6, where he is described as 'Wellington's disciple'.[36] It has been said that Raglan and his officers still 'revelled in the afterglow of Waterloo', forty years on.[37] Wellington's very success as a commander, which others found impossible to reproduce, stagnated British military thinking for decades after his last glorious battle.

Appendix A

Wellington's Battle Record Against the French, 1808–15

Date	Battle	Location	Outcome
17 Aug. 1808	Battle of Roliça	Portugal	Indecisive
21 Aug. 1808	Battle of Vimeiro	Portugal	Decisive victory
12 May 1809	Battle of Oporto	Portugal	Victory
27–8 Jul. 1809	Battle of Talavera	Spain	Victory
27 Sep. 1810	Battle of Buçaco	Portugal	Victory
3–5 May 1811	Battle of Fuentes de Oñoro	Portugal	Indecisive
5 May–16 Jun. 1811	2nd Siege of Badajoz	Spain	Defeat
7–20 Jan. 1812	Siege of Ciudad Rodrigo	Spain	Victory
16 Mar.– 6 Apr. 1812	3rd Siege of Badajoz	Spain	Victory
17–27 Jun. 1812	Siege of Salamanca Forts	Spain	Victory
22 Jul. 1812	Battle of Salamanca	Spain	Decisive victory
19 Sep.–21 Oct. 1812	Siege of Burgos	Spain	Defeat
21 Jun. 1813	Battle of Vitoria	Spain	Decisive victory
7–25 Jul. 1813	1st Siege of San Sebastian	Spain	Defeat
24 Aug.–8 Sep. 1813	2nd Siege of San Sebastian	Spain	Victory
26–8 Jul. 1813	1st Battle of Sorauren	Spain	Victory
28–30 Jul. 1813	2nd Battle of Sorauren	Spain	Victory
7 Oct. 1813	Battle of the Bidassoa	France	Victory
10 Nov. 1813	Battle of the Nivelle	France	Victory
9–12 Dec. 1813	Battle of the Nive	France	Victory
27 Feb. 1814	Battle of Orthez	France	Victory
20 Mar. 1814	Battle of Tarbes	France	Victory
10 Apr. 1814	Battle of Toulouse	France	Indecisive
16 Jun. 1815	Battle of Quatre Bras	Belgium	Indecisive
18 Jun. 1815	Battle of Waterloo	Belgium	Decisive victory

Appendix B

Principles of 'Mission Command'

Wellington's command and control was some distance from what today is seen as the ideal. Army Doctrine Publication, 'Command', Army Code No. 71584, 1995, chapter 2, 0210, states:

> The modern British Army's philosophy of command has three tenets: timely decision-making, the understanding of a superior commander's intention, and a responsibility to fulfil that intention. Together, this requires a style of leadership which promotes decentralised command, freedom and speed of action, and initiative.

Mission Command has the following key elements:

- A commander gives his orders in a manner that ensures that his subordinates understand his intentions, their own missions and the context of those missions.
- Subordinates are told what effect they are to achieve and the reason why it needs to be achieved.
- Subordinates are allocated the appropriate resources to carry out their missions.
- A commander uses a minimum of control measures so as not to limit unnecessarily the freedom of action of his subordinates.
- Subordinates then decide within their delegated freedom of action how best to achieve their missions.

Historically, this approach has proved to be the most appropriate to contend with the demands, uncertainties, and frictions of command in war. It requires the development of trust and mutual understanding between commanders and subordinates throughout the chain of command, and timely and effective decision-making, together with initiative (a quality of a commander) at all levels.

Appendix C

Combat Variables

Dupuy, p. 33, lists the criteria below as combat variables. The chart is condensed here for items A–J. From studies undertaken by the US Department of Defence and the British Defence Operational Analysis Establishment.

	Combat Effect Factor	Calculable	Incalculable
A.	Weapon effects:		
B.	Terrain factors: *defence*	1.0–1.55	
C.	Weather factors: *attack*	0.6–1.0	
D.	Season factors: *attack*	1.0–1.1	
E.	N/a (air superiority)		
F.	Posture factors: *attack & defence*	1.0–1.6	
G.	Mobility effects:		
H.	Vulnerability factors:		
I.	N/a (tactical air effects)		
J.	Other combat processes: *mobility, surprise, fatigue, casualties, disruption*		
K.	Intangible factors: *qualitative*		
	63 Combat effectiveness	Z	
	64 Leadership	X	
	65 Training and experience	Z	
	66 Morale		Z
	67 Logistics		
	68 Time		
	69 Space		
	70 Momentum		
	71 Intelligence		Z
	72 Technology		Z
	73 Initiative	Y	

(continued)

The elements that Dupuy lists under 'K: Intangible Factors' approximate to the referenced key criteria for effectiveness, namely:

X	Leadership/control	
Y	Initiative	
		{ Combat effectiveness of troops
		{ Training and experience
Z	Combat ability —	{ Troop morale
		{ Intelligence
		{ Technological advantage/weapons effects

Appendix D

Chronological Unit Leadership

All general officers unless otherwise noted. The listing is simplified to omit temporary commands caused by leader absence.

Order of Battle, 1808

General officer commanding	Wellington
Second–in–Command	Spencer
Adjutant General	Lt Col. Tucker
Quartermaster General	Lt Col. Bathurst
Military Secretary	Lt Col. Torrens
Infantry	
1st Brigade	Hill
2nd Brigade	Ferguson
3rd Brigade	Nightingall
4th Brigade	Bowes
5th Brigade	J.C. Craufurd
6th (Light) Brigade	Fane
Cavalry	
20th Light Dragoon Regiment	Lt Col. Taylor
Artillery	Lt Col. Robe
Engineers	Capt Elphinstone
22 August Dalrymple arrived and assumed command	
7th Brigade	Anstruther
8th Brigade	Acland

Order of Battle, 1809

British garrison in Lisbon

General officer commanding	Cradock
Second-in-Command	Sherbrooke
Brigades	H. Campbell/Hill/Mackenzie/Tilson/ Sontag/A. Campbell/R. Stewart/ Cameron/J. Murray
Cavalry	Cotton

April amendments

General officer commanding	Wellington
Second-in-Command	Sherbrooke
Adjutant General	C. Stewart
Quartermaster General	Col. G. Murray
Military Secretary	Lt Col. Bathurst

Infantry

Brigades (Guards + 1–7)	H. Campbell/Hill/Mackenzie/Tilson/ Sontag/A. Campbell/R. Stewart/Cameron
KGL	J. Murray/Langwerth/Drieberg

Portuguese Army — Beresford

Portuguese Brigades	Blunt/Bacellar/Sousa/Silveira/Wilson/ Mousinho/W. Campbell/Lecor
Cavalry	Lusignano

Cavalry

	Cotton
	Fane

Artillery — Howorth

Engineers — Lt Col. Fletcher

June amendments

Infantry

1st Division	Sherbrooke
2nd Division	Hill
3rd Division	Mackenzie > R. Craufurd
4th Division	A. Campbell > Cole

Cavalry

	Payne
A Brigade	Fane
B Brigade	Cotton
C Brigade	Anson

Order of Battle, 1810

General officer commanding	Wellington
Second-in-Command	Sherbrooke > Spencer
Adjutant General	C. Stewart
Quartermaster General	Col. G. Murray
Military Secretary	Lt Col. Bathurst > Capt Fitzroy Somerset

Infantry

1st Division	Sherbrooke > Cotton > Spencer
2nd Division	Hill
3rd Division	R. Craufurd > Picton
4th Division	Cole
Light Division	R. Craufurd

Cavalry

Cavalry	Payne
A Brigade	Fane
B Brigade	Slade
C Brigade	Anson

Artillery	Howorth
Engineers	Lt Col. Fletcher

April–May amendments

Cavalry	Cotton
Attached to Hill's Division	Fane
A Brigade	Col. De Grey

November amendments

Infantry

5th Division	Leith
6th Division	A. Campbell
Portuguese Division	Hamilton

Order of Battle, 1811

General officer commanding	Wellington
Second-in-Command	Spencer > Graham
Adjutant General	C. Stewart
Quartermaster General	Col. G. Murray
Military Secretary	Maj. Fitzroy Somerset

Infantry

1st Division	Spencer > Graham
2nd Division	W. Stewart > Hill
3rd Division	Picton
4th Division	Cole
5th Division	Leith > Dunlop
6th Division	A. Campbell
7th Division	Houston > Sontag > C. Alten
Light Division	R. Craufurd >Erskine
Portuguese Division	Hamilton
Portuguese Brigades	Pack/McMahon

Cavalry

A Brigade	Cotton
A Brigade	Col. De Grey
B Brigade	Slade
C Brigade	Anson
D Brigade	Long

Artillery — Howorth > Lt Col. Framingham

Engineers — Lt Col. Fletcher

June–August amendments
Cavalry

1st Cavalry Division	Cotton
B Brigade	Slade
C Brigade	Anson
E Brigade	V. Alten
Portuguese Brigade	Madden
2nd Cavalry Division	Erskine
A Brigade	Col. De Grey
D Brigade	Long
F Brigade	Le Marchant

Order of Battle, 1812

General officer commanding	Wellington
Second-in-Command	Graham > Beresford
Adjutant General	C. Stewart
Quartermaster General	Cols G. Murray > Gordon
Military Secretary	Lt Col. Fitzroy Somerset

Infantry

1st Division	Graham > H. Campbell > W. Stewart
2nd Division	Hill > Tilson
3rd Division	Picton > Pakenham
4th Division	Colville > Cole
5th Division	Leith > Oswald
6th Division	A. Campbell > Clinton
7th Division	C. Alten > J. Hope > Dalhousie
Light Division	R. Craufurd > C. Alten
Portuguese Division	Hamilton
Portuguese Brigades	Pack/Bradford
Spanish Division	España

Cavalry

1st Cavalry Division	Cotton > Bock
A Brigade	De Grey
C Brigade	Anson
E Brigade	V. Alten
F Brigade	Le Marchant > Ponsonby
G Brigade	Bock
2nd Cavalry Division	Erskine
B Brigade	Slade
D Brigade	Long

Artillery	Borthwick > Lt Cols Framingham > Waller
Engineers	Lt Cols Fletcher > Burgoyne

Order of Battle, 1813

General officer commanding	Wellington
Second–in–Command	Beresford > Hope
Adjutant General	Pakenham
Quartermaster General	G. Murray
Military Secretary	Lt Col. Fitzroy Somerset

Infantry

1st Division	W. Stewart > Howard > Graham > Hope
2nd Division	Hill > W. Stewart
3rd Division	Pakenham > Picton
4th Division	Cole
5th Division	Oswald > Leith > Hay
6th Division	Clinton >Pack
7th Division	Dalhousie > Walker
Light Division	C. Alten
Portuguese Division	Hamilton
Portuguese Brigades	Wilson/Bradford
Spanish Division	España

Cavalry

1st Cavalry Division	Bock > Cotton
C Brigade	Anson > Vandeleur
E Brigade	V. Alten
F Brigade	Ponsonby
G Brigade	Bock
H Brigade	Rebow > Rob. Hill > O'Loghlin
2nd Cavalry Division	Erskine
B Brigade	Slade > Fane
D Brigade	Long > Col. Grant > Vivian
I Brigade	Col. Grant > Somerset

Artillery	Lt Cols Fisher > Dickson
Engineers	Lt Cols Fletcher > Elphinstone

Order of Battle, 1814

General officer commanding	Wellington
Second–in–Command	Hope
Adjutant General	Pakenham
Quartermaster General	G. Murray
Military Secretary	Lt Col. Fitzroy Somerset
Infantry	
1st Division	Hope
2nd Division	W. Stewart
3rd Division	Picton
4th Division	Cole
5th Division	Colville
6th Division	Clinton
7th Division	Walker > Dalhousie
Light Division	C. Alten
Portuguese Division	Le Cor
Portuguese Brigades	Wilson/Bradford
Cavalry	Cotton
B Brigade	Fane
C Brigade	Vandeleur
D Brigade	Vivian > Fane
E Brigade	V. Alten >Vivian > Arentschildt
F Brigade	Ponsonby
G Brigade	Bock > Bülow
H Brigade	Somerset
I Brigade	O'Loghlin
Artillery	Lt Col. Dickson
Engineers	Lt Col. Elphinstone

Order of Battle, 1815

General officer commanding	Wellington
Second-in-Command	Uxbridge
Adjutant General	Barnes
Quartermaster General	Col. De Lancey
Military Secretary	Lt Col. Fitzroy-Somerset
Infantry	
1st Corps	Prince William
1st (Guards) Division	Cooke
3rd Division	Alten
2nd Netherlands Division	Perponcher
3rd Netherlands Division	Chassé
2nd Corps	Hill
2nd Division	Clinton
4th Brigade	Mitchell
Reserve Corps	
5th Division	Picton
6th Division	Lambert
Brunswick Division	Brunswick > Olfermann
Nassau Brigade	Von Kruse
3rd Corps	Prince Frederick
4th Division	Colville
1st Netherlands Division	Stedman
Cavalry	Uxbridge
Netherland Cavalry Division	Collaert
Heavy Brigade	Trip
1st Light Brigade	Ghigny
2nd Light Brigade	Merlen
1st (Household) Brigade	Somerset
2nd (Union) Brigade	Ponsonby
3rd Brigade	Dörnberg
4th Brigade	Vandeleur
5th Brigade	Grant
6th Brigade	Vivian
7th Brigade	Arenschildt
Hanoverian Brigade	Estorff
Artillery	Col. Wood
Horse Artillery	Lt Col. Frazer
Engineers	Lt Col. Smyth
Strategic Reserve	
7th Division	McKenzie
Hanoverian Reserve	Decken
French Royal Army	Duc de Berry

Appendix E

Administrative Offices of the Army

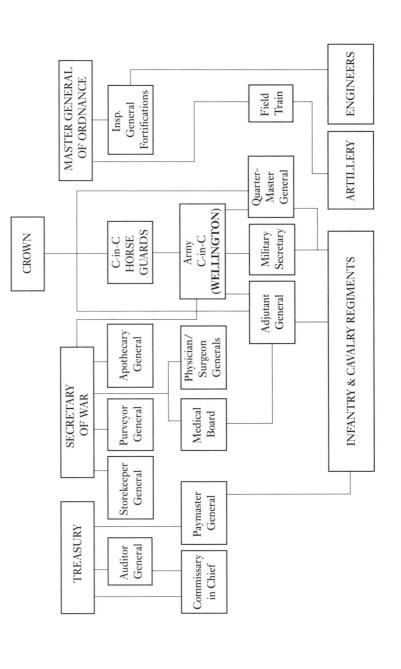

Appendix F

Wellington's Peninsular Army, 1808

Force organization demonstrating the practical impact of seniority.

British 'Disposable Force', Portugal, August 1808

General officer commanding		Lt Gen. Wellesley
Second-in-Command		Maj. Gen. Spencer
1st Brigade	5th/9th/38th Regs	Maj. Gen. Hill
2nd Brigade	36th/40th/71st Regs	Maj. Gen. Ferguson
3rd Brigade	29th/82nd Regs	Brig. Gen. Nightingall
4th Brigade	6th/32nd Regs	Brig. Gen. Bowes
5th Brigade	45th/50th/91st Regs	Brig. Gen. Crauford
6th Brigade (Light)	2/95th & 5/60th Batt.	Brig. Gen. Fane

Note: Brigade numbers reflect the seniority of the general. 'In all duties, whether with or without picquets or court martial, the tour of duty shall be from the oldest downwards': C. James, *A New & Enlarged Military Dictionary*, 2 vols (London: Egerton, 1802).

Notional Battle Array, Portugal, August 1808

[2]	[4]	[5]	[3]	[1]
2nd BRIGADE	4th BRIGADE	5th BRIGADE	3rd BRIGADE	1st BRIGADE
36th/71st/40th	32nd/**6th**	50th/91st/**45th**	82nd/**29th**	9th/38th /**5th**
6th Light				
BRIGADE				
5/**60th** & 2/95th				

The brigade order is noted [1] to [5] and the senior regiment is noted in **bold**.

(continued)

In battle, 'The eldest brigade takes the right of the first line [. . .] the youngest always possessing the centre': James, *Military Dictionary*. The same principle applies to the regiments within brigades; the right flank is the 'post of honour'. The left flanking brigade is the second 'post of honour' and here regiments would be reversed. The Light Brigade stood outside of the line of battle.

Appendix G

The French Commanders that Opposed Wellington

Omitting the French armies of Catalonia and Aragon, based in Eastern Spain.

1808

Armée du Portugal
August–September 1808: General Junot, Duke d'Abrantes.

1809

Armée du Portugal
September 1808–March 1810: Marshal Soult, Duke of Dalmatia.

Armée du Sud
September 1808–December 1809: Marshal Victor, Duke of Bellune.

Armée du Centre
August 1808–December 1812: King Joseph Bonaparte; Chief-of-Staff Marshal Jourdan.

1810–14

Armée du Portugal
May 1810–May 1811: Marshal Masséna, Prince of Essling.
May 1811–July 1812: Marshal Marmont, Duke of Ragusa.
July–September 1812: General Baron Clausel.
September–November 1812: General Souham.
November 1812–January 1813: General Drouet, Count D'Erlon.
January–July 1813: General Reille.

Armée du Sud
January 1810–March 1813: Marshal Soult, Duke of Dalmatia.
March–July 1813: General Gazan.

(continued)

Armée du Nord
January–July 1811: Marshal Bessières, Duke of Istria.
July 1811–May 1812: General Dorsenne.
May 1812–January 1813: General Caffarelli.
January–July 1813: General Baron Clausel.

Armée du Centre
January–July 1813: General Drouet, Count D'Erlon.

Armée d' Espagne
July 1813–April 1814: the four armies were merged under the command of Marshal Soult.

1815

Armée du Nord
March–July 1815: Emperor Napoleon Bonaparte.

Appendix H

Wellington's Peninsular Army, 1809–14

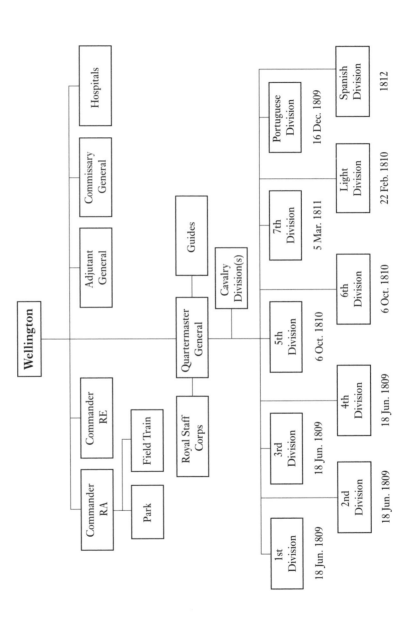

Appendix I

Peninsular War General Officers Commanding

Officers listed in order of Seniority; those with the rank of Major General or above who commanded divisions and higher formations under Wellington.

General	Final Command, 1808–15
• John Hope	Left column 1813–14
• Henry Paget, Earl of Uxbridge	Cavalry 1815
• Thomas Graham	Left column 1813
• John Sherbrooke	1st Division 1809–10
• William Payne	Cavalry 1809–10
• Edward Paget	1st Division 1813
• Brent Spencer	1st Division 1810–11
• Stapleton Cotton	Cavalry 1810–14
• Rowland Hill	II Corps 1815
• William Beresford	Centre column 1813–14
• George Ramsey, Earl of Dalhousie	7th Division 1812–14
• James Leith	5th Division 1810–13
• John Mackenzie	3rd Division 1809
• Thomas Picton	5th Division 1815
• Lowry Cole	4th Division 1809–14
• William Erskine	2nd Cavalry Division 1811–12
• William Stewart	1st Division 1812–14
• John Hamilton	Portuguese Division 1810–13
• William Houston	7th Division 1811
• John Slade	2nd Cavalry Division 1812
• Miles Nightingall	1st Division 1811
• Henry Clinton	2nd Division 1815

(continued)

- John Sontag   7th Division 1811
- James Dunlop   5th Division 1811
- Alexander Campbell   6th Division 1810–11
- Henry Campbell   1st Division 1812
- George, Baron von Bock   Cavalry 1812–13
- Carl, Count von Alten   3rd Division 1815
- John Hope   7th Division 1812
- Charles Colville   4th Division 1815
- Kenneth Howard   1st Division 1813–14
- John Oswald   5th Division 1812–13
- Robert Craufurd   Light Division 1810–12
- Andrew Hay   5th Division 1813
- Robert Burne   6th Division 1811–12
- George Cooke   1st Division 1815
- George Walker   7th Division 1814
- Edward Pakenham   6th Division 1813
- Denis Pack   6th Division 1813
- Edward Howorth   Royal Artillery 1811
- William Borthwick   Royal Artillery 1812

Notes

Introduction

1. *The Times*, 20 February 2016, quotes Saul David.
2. Charles J. Esdaile, *The Peninsular War* (London: Lane, 2002). p. 441, and Sir William F.P. Napier, *History of the War in the Peninsula and the South of France, from the Year 1807 to the Year 1814*, 6 vols (London: Warne, 1828–40), IV, p. 405.
3. Douglas H. Bell, *Wellington's Officers* (London: Collins, 1938), p. 111.

Chapter One

1. Francis Grose, *Advice to the Officers of the British Army* (London: Kearsly, 1782), p. 7.
2. Sir John Fortescue, *A History of the British Army*, 10 vols (London: Macmillan, 1899–1930), IX, pp. 255–6.
3. *Supplementary Dispatches, Correspondence, and Memoranda of Field Marshal Arthur Duke of Wellington, K.G.*, ed. Arthur Richard Wellesley, 2nd Duke of Wellington [*WSD*], 15 vols (London: John Murray, 1858–72), VI, p. 589, AW to Wellesley-Pole, 5 September 1810.
4. *The Croker Papers, 1808–1857*, 3 vols (London: John Murray, 1884), ed. Louis J. Jennings, II, p. 123, and Michael Glover, *Wellington's Army in the Peninsula 1808–1814* (Newton Abbot: David & Charles, 1977), p. 144.
5. Esdaile, *Peninsular War*, p. 85.
6. Michael Glover, *Wellington as Military Commander* (London: Batsford, 1968), p. 161, and Rory Muir, *Wellington*, 2 vols (London: Yale University Press, 2013–15), I, p. 412.
7. Robert Harvey, *The War of Wars: The Epic Struggle between Britain and France 1789–1815* (London: Constable, 2006), p. 599.
8. *The Life and Correspondence of Major-General Sir John Malcolm*, ed. Sir John W. Kaye, 2 vols (London: Smith, Elder, 1856), II, p. 102.
9. Francis S. Larpent, *The Private Journal of Judge Advocate Larpent attached to the Headquarters of Lord Wellington during the Peninsular War* (Staplehurst: Spellmount, 2000), p. 306.

10. *The Dispatches of Field Marshal the Duke of Wellington, during his Various Campaigns from 1799 to 1818,* ed. John Gurwood [*WD*], 13 vols (London: John Murray, 1837–9), VII, p. 412, AW to Beresford, 30 March 1811.
11. Royal Artillery Museum [RAM], George Jenkinson Letters, MD/212, 29 May 1811.
12. *WD*, XII, pp. 478–87 (p. 483), AW to Bathurst, 19 June 1815.
13. Lewis Butler, *Wellington's Operations in the Peninsula 1808–1814* (London: Unwin, 1904), p. 187.
14. Sir Charles Oman, *History of the Peninsular War*, 7 vols (London: Clarendon, 1902–30), II, p. 301.
15. Philip Haythornthwaite, *Wellington's Military Machine* (Tunbridge Wells: Spellmount, 1989), p. 87.
16. Gwent Archives [GA], Raglan Papers, MS A/34, AW to Wellesley-Pole, 5 September 1810.
17. Ruscombe E. Foster, *Wellington and Waterloo: The Duke, the Battle and Posterity* (Stroud: Spellmount, 2014), p. 20.
18. Rory Muir et al., *Inside Wellington's Peninsular Army 1808–1814* (Barnsley: Pen & Sword, 2006), pp. 275–303.
19. Chris Woolgar, 'Wellington's Dispatches and their Editor, Colonel Gurwood', *Wellington Studies I* (Southampton: Southampton University Press, 1996), 189–210 (p. 192).
20. Muir, *Wellington*, II, p. 477.
21. Peter Hofschröer, *1815: The Waterloo Campaign*, 2 vols (London: Greenhill, 1998–9), I, pp. 341–3.
22. W.F.P. Napier, *War in the Peninsula*, II, p. 114.
23. W.F.P. Napier, *War in the Peninsula*, I, p. 162 and IV, pp. 404–5.
24. M. Glover, *Wellington's Army*, p. 121, and Stephen G.P. Ward, *Wellington's Headquarters: A Study of the Administrative Problems in the Peninsula, 1809–1814* (London: Oxford University Press, 1957), p. 150.
25. Francis Egerton, 1st Earl of Ellesmere, *Personal Reminiscences of the Duke of Wellington* (London: John Murray, 1904), p. 192.
26. Kyle van Beurden, '"No Troops but the British": British National Identity and the Battle for Waterloo' (masters thesis, University of Queensland, 2015), p. 7.
27. John Fane, Lord Burghersh, *Memoir of the Early Campaigns of the Duke of Wellington in Portugal and Spain by an Officer Employed in His Army* (London: John Murray, 1820), p. 232.
28. Jasper Heinzen, *Making Prussians, Raising Germans, A Cultural History of Prussian State Building after Civil War, 1866–1935* (Cambridge: Cambridge University Press, 2017), p. 108.
29. Oman, *Peninsular War*, II, p. 310.

30. Oman, *Peninsular War*, II, pp. 304–13, and VII, p. 526.
31. *The Correspondence of Charles Arbuthnot*, ed. Arthur Aspinall, 9th Earl of Bessborough (London: Royal Historical Society, 1941), pp. 167–8, Arbuthnot to his son, 15 March 1833.
32. Oman, *Peninsular War*, III, p. 170, and II, p. 298.
33. Oman, *Peninsular War*, IV, p. 403.
34. Oman, *Peninsular War*, III, p. 266.
35. Oman, *Peninsular War*, II, p. 310n.
36. Oman, *Peninsular War*, II, p. 296.
37. Oman, *Peninsular War*, VII, p. 527.
38. Oman, *Peninsular War*, I, pp. 119–20.
39. Sir Charles Oman, *Wellington's Army 1809–1814* (London: Arnold, 1913), p. 104.
40. Oman, *Wellington's Army*, pp. 45–6, AW to McGrigor, Surgeon-General.
41. Elizabeth Longford, *Wellington: The Years of the Sword* (London: Weidenfeld & Nicolson, 1969), p. 357.
42. Fortescue, VII, pp. 413–14.
43. Fortescue, VII, p. 253.
44. Fortescue, X, p. 508.
45. Fortescue, VI, p. 212.
46. Fortescue, X, p. 217.
47. Foster, p. 203.
48. Francis L. Clarke, ed., *The Royal Military Chronicle* (London: Davis, 1810), I, pp. 1–17, and II, pp. 333–9.
49. Finlay C. Beatson, *With Wellington in the Pyrenees: Operations between the Allied Army and the French from July 25 to August 2, 1813* (London: Goschen, 1914), pp. 274–5.
50. Finlay C. Beatson, *Wellington: The Bidassoa and Nivelle* (London: Arnold, 1931), pp. 180–1.
51. Ward, *Wellington's Headquarters*, p. 65.
52. Ward, *Wellington's Headquarters*, p. 154.
53. John F.C. Fuller, *The Decisive Battles of the Western World*, 2 vols (London: Granada, 1970), II, pp. 164–5.
54. Fuller, II, p. 181.
55. Hofschröer, I, p. 217, and Tim Clayton, *Waterloo: Four Days that Changed Europe's Destiny* (London: Little, Brown, 2014), pp. 123–4.
56. David G. Chandler, *The Campaigns of Napoleon* (London: Weidenfeld & Nicolson, 1966), p. 1092.
57. Jac Weller, *Wellington in the Peninsula, 1808–1814* (London: Vane, 1962), p. 375.
58. Weller, *Wellington in the Peninsula*, p. 72.
59. Sir Henry Edward Bunbury, *Narrative of Some Passages in the Great War with France, 1799–1810* (London: Davies, 1927), p. 457.

60.   Jac Weller, *Wellington at Waterloo* (London: Longmans, 1967), p. 167.

61.   E. Longford, pp. 318–19.

62.   M. Glover, *Wellington's Army*, p. 144.

63.   James P. Lawford and Peter Young, *Wellington's Masterpiece: The Battle and Campaign of Salamanca* (London: Allen & Unwin, 1972), p. 207, and W. Copeland Trimble, *The Historical Record of the 27th Inniskilling Regiment* (London: Clowes, 1876), p. 81.

64.   Rory Muir, *Salamanca, 1812* (London: Yale University Press, 2001), p. 216.

65.   M. Glover, *Military Commander*, p. 123, and p. 237.

66.   Paddy Griffith et al., *Wellington Commander: The Iron Duke's Generalship* (Chichester: Bird, 1983), p. 17.

67.   David Gates, *The Spanish Ulcer* (London: Allen & Unwin, 1986), p. 375.

68.   Norman Gash et al., *Wellington: Studies in the Military and Political Career of the First Duke of Wellington* (Manchester: Manchester University Press, 1990), pp. 36–42.

69.   Esdaile, *Peninsular War,* p. 96, and p. 441.

70.   Huw J. Davies, *Wellington's Wars: The Making of a Military Genius* (London: Yale University Press, 2012), pp. 249–51.

71.   Haythornthwaite, *Wellington's Military Machine*, pp. 6–8.

72.   Philip Haythornthwaite, *Wellington: The Iron Duke* (Dulles, VA: Potomac, 2007), pp. 43–8.

73.   Muir, *Inside Wellington's Peninsular Army*, p. 30.

74.   Ian Fletcher, *Galloping at Everything: The British Cavalry in the Peninsular War and Waterloo, 1808–15: A Reappraisal* (Staplehurst: Spellmount, 1999), p. 280.

75.   Nick Lipscombe, *Wellington's Guns: The Untold Story of Wellington and his Artillery in the Peninsula and at Waterloo* (Oxford: Osprey, 2013), pp. 389–98.

76.   Frederick Myatt, *British Sieges of the Peninsular War* (Stroud: Spellmount, 1995), p. 44, and p. 143.

77.   Guy C. Dempsey, *Albuera 1811: The Bloodiest Battle of the Peninsular War* (Barnsley: Frontline, 2011), p. 248.

78.   Joanna Hill, *Wellington's Right Hand: Rowland Viscount Hill* (Stroud: Spellmount, 2011), p. 133.

79.   Mark Adkin, *The Waterloo Companion* (London: Aurum, 2001), pp. 93–4, and *One-Leg: The Life and Letters of Henry William Paget, First Marquess of Anglesey*, ed. George Paget, 7th Marquess of Anglesey (London: Jonathan Cape, 1961), p. 133.

80.   Rory Muir, 'Wellington', commentary 2/2, <http://www.lifeofwellington.co.uk/the-books/> [accessed 14 January 2016].

81.   Hofschröer, I, p. 336.

82.   Clayton, p. 351.

83. Clayton, p. 27.
84. Clayton, p. 144.
85. Muir, *Wellington*, I, pp. 511–13.
86. Muir, *Wellington*, II, p. 516, and *Letters and Journals of Field-Marshal Sir William Maynard Gomm from 1799 to Waterloo, 1815*, ed. Francis C. Carr-Gomm (London: John Murray, 1881), p. 373.
87. Muir, *Wellington*, I, p. 426.
88. Archie Hunter, *Wellington's Scapegoat: The Tragedy of Lieutenant-Colonel Charles Bevan* (Barnsley: Leo Cooper, 2003), p. 180.
89. *WSD*, VIII, p. 373, AW to Hill, 7 March 1833.
90. Lipscombe, *Wellington's Guns*, p. 15.
91. *Peninsular Portrait, Letters of Captain William Bragge*, ed. Simon A.C. Cassels (London: Oxford University Press, 1963), p. 89.
92. *Waterloo Archive*, ed. Gareth Glover, 6 vols (Barnsley: Frontline, 2010–14), I, p. 6, quotes Dr H. James.
93. M. Glover, *Military Commander*, p. 226.

Chapter Two

1. Grose, p. 9.
2. Joint Chief-of-Staff, US Department of Defense, *Dictionary of Military & Associated Terms*, JP1-02 (Honolulu, HI: University Press of the Pacific, 2002).
3. Norman Dixon, *On the Psychology of Military Incompetence* (London: Jonathan Cape, 1976), p. 28.
4. Joachim H. Stocqueler, *The Wellington Manual: Being a Compilation from the Dispatches of His Grace the Duke of Wellington* (Calcutta: Rushton, 1840), p. 73.
5. Baron Karl von Müffling, *Passages from my Life, together with Memoirs of the Campaign of 1813 and 1814*, trans. P. Yorke (London: Bentley, 1853), pp. 242–6.
6. Muir, *Wellington*, I, p. 73.
7. W.B. Howieson and H. Kahn, 'Leadership, Management and Command: The Officer's Trinity', <http://www.raf.mod.uk/pmdair/rafcms/mediafiles/225f3a4a_5056_a318_a8f33369f4c3b15f> [accessed 10 June 2016].
8. Trevor N. Dupuy, *Numbers, Predictions and War: Using History to Evaluate Combat Factors and Predict the Outcome of Battles* (London: Macdonald and Jane, 1979), pp. 32–9.
9. Dempsey, p. 177.
10. David G. Chandler, *The Oxford Illustrated History of the British Army* (Oxford: Oxford University Press, 1994), p. 145.
11. *Armies of the Napoleonic Wars*, ed. Gregory Fremont-Barnes (Barnsley: Pen & Sword, 2011), pp. 128–9.

12. *Croker Papers*, ed. Jennings, I, pp. 342–3.
13. Ward, *Wellington's Headquarters*, p. 159.
14. *WD*, XI, p. 143, AW to Bathurst, 25 September 1813.
15. National Records of Scotland [NRS], Melville Papers, Additional MS 1060 fol., p. 184, Hope to Dundas, 27 July 1810.
16. University of Southampton, Hartley Library [USL], Wellington Papers [WP], 1/337, Liverpool to AW, 8 August 1811.
17. USL, WP, 1/315, Torrens to AW, 19 September 1810.
18. M. Glover, *Wellington's Army*, p. 22, and p. 83.
19. [An Officer of Dragoons] 'The British Cavalry in the Peninsula', *United Services Journal and Naval and Military Magazine*, II (1883), 63–70 (p. 70).
20. Edward J. Coss, 'The Misadventures of Wellington's Cavalry, from the Peninsula to Waterloo', *Journal of the Waterloo Committee*, X (April 1988), 18–30 (p. 21).
21. Thomas Morris, *Recollections of Military Service: Including some details of the Battles of Quatre Bras and Waterloo* (London: Madden, 1845), p. 50.
22. Nick Mansfield, *Soldiers as Workers: Class, Employment, Conflict and the Nineteenth-Century Military* (Liverpool: Liverpool University Press, 2016), p. 55.
23. W.F.P. Napier, *War in the Peninsula*, II, p. 401.
24. Mark Urban, *Generals: Ten British Commanders Who Shaped the World* (London: Faber, 2005), p. 138.
25. *WD*, VII, p. 442, AW to Campbell, 15 March 1811.
26. *WD*, VII, p. 91, AW to Stuart, 31 December 1810.
27. *At Wellington's Right Hand: The Letters of Lieutenant-Colonel Sir Alexander Gordon, 1808–1815*, ed. Rory Muir (Stroud: Sutton, 2003), Gordon to Aberdeen, 27 November 1811.
28. Oman, *Peninsular War*, III, p. 233.
29. Richard Holmes, *Acts of War: the Behaviour of Men in Battle* (London: Jonathan Cape, 1985), p. 343.
30. Russell F. Weigley, *The Age of Battles: The Quest for Decisive Warfare from Breitenfeld to Waterloo* (London: Pimlico, 1993), p. 538.
31. S.L.A. Marshall, *Men Against Fire: The Problem of Battle Command* (New York: Morrow, 1947), p. 66, and Bruce I. Gudmundsson, *On Artillery* (Westport, CT: Praeger, 1993), pp. 43–68.
32. David G. Chandler, *Atlas of Military Strategy: The Art, Theory and Practice of War, 1618–1878* (London: Arms and Armour, 1980), p. 13.
33. M. Glover, *Wellington's Army*, p. 77.
34. John Mitchell, *Thoughts on Tactics and Military Organization* (London: Longman, 1838), p. 160.

35. William Scarth Moorsom, *History of the Fifty-Second Regiment, 1755–1816* (Felling, Tyne and Wear: Worley, 1996), p. 137.

36. Edward J. Coss, *All for the King's Shilling: An Analysis of the Campaign and Combat Experiences of the British Soldier in the Peninsular War, 1808–1814* (doctoral dissertation, Ohio State University, 2005; pub. Norman, OK: University of Oklahoma Press, 2010), pp. 233–325.

37. Philip Haythornthwaite, *Napoleon's Military Machine* (Tunbridge Wells: Spellmount, 1988), p. 37.

38. *WD*, VII, p. 421, 8 April 1811, AW to Captain Chapman, RA.

39. Esdaile, *Peninsular War*, p. 99.

40. Charles Esdaile, '"Hard pounding Gentlemen": The Tactics of Waterloo', public lecture at University of Nottingham, 8 July 2015.

41. James R. Arnold, 'A Reappraisal of Column versus Line in the Napoleonic Wars', *Journal of the Society for Army Historical Research*, LX, 244 (Winter 1982), 196–208 (p. 197).

42. *An Intelligence Officer in the Peninsula: the Letters and Diaries of Major the Hon. E. C. Cocks, 1786–1812*, ed. Julia V. Page (Staplehurst: Spellmount, 1976), p. 21.

43. Stuart Reid, *Wellington's Army in the Peninsula 1809–14* (Oxford: Osprey, 2004), p. 75.

44. Fletcher, *Galloping at Everything*, p. xvi.

45. E. Longford, p. 268.

46. *The Letters of Colonel Sir Augustus Simon Frazer, K. C. B., Commanding the Royal Horse Artillery in the Army under the Duke of Wellington*, ed. Sir Edward Sabine (Uckfield: Naval & Military Press, 2001), p. 550, and Mark T. Gerges, 'Command and Control in the Peninsula: The Role of the British Cavalry 1808–1814' (doctoral dissertation, Florida State University, 2005), p. 406.

47. Richard Glover, *Peninsular Preparation: The Reform of the British Army 1795–1809* (Cambridge: Cambridge University Press, 1963), pp. 68–80.

48. Nick Lipscombe, 'Shrapnel's Shell, A Force Multiplier', *British Army Review*, 161 (Autumn 2014), 100–7 (p. 104).

49. Royal Artillery Institution, *Minutes of Proceedings of the Royal Artillery Institution V* (Woolwich: RAI, 1870), p. 403.

50. Charles W. Vane, 3rd Marquis of Londonderry [formerly Charles Stewart], *Narrative of the Peninsular War from 1808 to 1813*, 2 vols (London: Colburn, 1829), I, p. 581.

51. T.W.J. Connolly, *History of the Corps of Royal Sappers and Miners*, 2 vols (London: Longman, 1855), I, p. 194.

52. Weigley, pp. 499–500.

53. M. Glover, *Wellington's Army*, p. 11.

54. Royal Engineers' Museum [REM], R.E. Burgoyne Letters, 4601–72, Burgoyne to Fletcher, 1812–17, fol. 13.

55. Londonderry, *Narrative*, I, p. 581.
56. David G. Chandler, *On the Napoleonic Wars* (London: Greenhill, 1994), p. 140.
57. Richard Holmes, *Redcoat* (London: HarperCollins, 2001), p. 135.
58. Coss, *All for the King's Shilling*, p. 293.
59. Stocqueler, pp. 36–7.
60. *WD*, X, p. 473, AW to Bathurst, 26 June 1813.
61. Roger N. Buckley, *The British Army in the West Indies, Society and the Military in the Revolutionary Age* (Tallahassee, FL: Florida University Press, 1998), p. 105.
62. Coss, *All for the King's Shilling*, p. 63, and p. 146.
63. Philip H., 5th Earl Stanhope, *Notes of Conversations with the Duke of Wellington, 1831–1851* (London: John Murray, 1888), p. 13.
64. Larpent, p. 93.
65. Coss, *All for the King's Shilling*, p. 328.
66. Dixon, p. 217.
67. George F.R. Henderson, *The Science of War: A Collection of Essays and Lectures, 1892–1903* (London: Longmans, Green, 1905), p. 1.
68. Larpent, p. 96.
69. Ward, *Wellington's Headquarters*, p. 144.
70. Fortescue, VII, p. 414.
71. Oman, *Wellington's Army*, p. 46.
72. Oman, *Peninsular War*, VII, p. 527.
73. M. Glover, *Wellington's Army*, p. 134.
74. *Memoirs and Correspondence of Viscount Combermere* [Stapleton Cotton], ed. Viscountess Mary W.G.C. Combermere, 2 vols (London: Hurst and Blackett, 1866), II, p. 201, Murray to Cotton, 9 June 1811.
75. National Library of Scotland [NLS]: Murray Papers, MS 48, fol. 81, Cotton to Murray, 8 March 1814.
76. Haythornthwaite, *Wellington's Military Machine*, pp. 64–5.
77. *WD*, XII, p. 336, AW to Torrens, 29 April 1815.

Chapter Three

1. *WSD*, V, pp. 66–7, AW to Castlereagh, 1 June 1807.
2. Richard Glover, *Britain at Bay: Defence against Bonaparte, 1803–14* (London: Allen & Unwin, 1973), p. 128.
3. Tom Reiss, *The Black Count, Napoleon's Rival and the Real Count of Monte Cristo – General Alexandre Dumas* (London: Vintage, 2013), p. 224n.
4. *WD*, I, p. 24, quotes diary of General Harris, 5 April 1799.
5. R. Bayly, *Diary of Colonel Bayly, 12th Regiment, 1796–1830* (London: Naval & Military Press, 1896), p. 89.

6. H.M. Vibart, *History of the Madras Engineers*, 2 vols (London, W.H. Allen, 1881), I, p. 300, quotes Ensign Rowley.

7. *Master Mariner: Being the Life and Adventures of Captain Robert W. Eastwick*, ed. Herbert Eastwick Compton (London: Fisher Unwin, 1891), p. 123.

8. Harvey, p. 605.

9. Charles C.F. Greville, *The Greville Memoirs*, 8 vols (London: Longman (1874–88), I, p. 64.

10. *WSD*, I, p. 433, AW to Sydenham, 16 January 1800.

11. *WD*, I, pp. 192–3, AW to Munro, 1 August 1800, and the *Chartist Circular*, 22 May 1841.

12. *WD*, I, pp. 616–17, AW to Sindia, 6 August 1803.

13. *WD*, I, p. 739, AW to Malcolm, 28 September 1803.

14. Davies, p. 54.

15. Stanhope, p. 130.

16. *WSD*, V, pp. 66–7, AW to Castlereagh, 1 June 1807.

17. The National Archives [TNA], WO1/228, Secretary for War to AW, 30 June 1808.

18. Oman, *Peninsular War*, IV, pp. 551–2n.

19. *Croker Papers*, ed. Jennings, I, p. 343, 25 May 1831.

20. Muir, *Wellington*, I, p. 235.

21. Sir George B. L'Estrange, *Recollections of Sir George B. L'Estrange: Late of the 31st Regiment, and afterwards in the Scots Fusilier Guards* (London: Low, Marston, 1874), p. 152.

22. J. Hill, p. 13.

23. British Library [BL], Hill's Papers, Additional MS 35/064, 23 June 1808.

24. Sir Richard D. Henegan, *Seven Years' Campaigning in the Peninsula and the Netherlands, from 1808 to 1815*, 2 vols (London: Colburn, 1846), I, p. 20, and M. Glover, *Wellington as Military Commander*, p. 195.

25. *WD*, V, pp. 523–4, AW to W. Stewart, 27 February 1810, and *Gentleman's Magazine*, October 1812, p. 404.

26. *WD*, VII, p. 14, AW to Liverpool, 30 November 1810.

27. M. Glover, *Wellington as Military Commander*, p. 218.

28. *WD*, IV, p. 71, AW to Robe, 8 August 1808.

29. University of Nottingham, Manuscripts and Special Collections [UNM], Mellish Letters, Me 4c1, 5 August 1808.

30. *WSD*, VI, p. 95, AW to Richmond, 1 August 1808.

31. Oman, *Peninsular War*, I, p. 232.

32. *WSD*, VI, pp. 107–9, GO, 9 August 1809.

33. *WD*, III, pp. 77–80, AW to Castlereagh, 16 August 1808.

34. Stanhope, p. 40.

35. Gash, pp. 21–2.

36. *WSD*, VI, p. 96, GO, 3 August 1808.
37. Georges Blond, *La Grand Armée*, trans. Marshall May (London: Arms and Armour, 1995), p. 169.
38. Laure Junot, Duchess de D'Abrantès, *Memoirs of Emperor Napoleon*, trans. S.M. Hamilton, 3 vols (London: Dunne, 1901), III, p. 113.
39. GA, Raglan Papers, MS A/4, AW to Wellesley-Pole, 19 August 1808, and *WD*, IV, p. 96, AW to Castlereagh, 17 August 1808.
40. GA, Raglan Papers, MS A/5, AW to Wellesley-Pole, 19 August 1808.
41. M. Glover, *Wellington's Army*, p. 99.
42. *WD*, IV, pp. 98–9, AW to Castlereagh, 17 August 1808.
43. Richard Partridge and Michael Oliver, *Battle Studies in the Peninsula, May 1808 – January 1809* (London: Constable, 1998), p. 145.
44. *WD*, IV, p. 99, AW to Castlereagh, 17 August 1808.
45. Emperor Napoleon I, *Maxims of War* (London: Kessinger, 2009), VI.
46. *The Life of John Colborne, Field-Marshal Lord Seaton*, ed. George C. Moore Smith (New York: Dutton, 1903), p. 84.
47. W.F.P. Napier, *War in the Peninsula*, I, p. 132.
48. Stephen P.G. Ward, ed. and J.M. Wynyard, 'Vimeiro to Corunna: An Eyewitness Account', *Journal of the Royal United Services Institute*, 114 (December 1969), 33–42 (p. 36).
49. Oman, *Peninsular War*, I, p. 248.
50. Count Maximilien S. Foy, *History of the War in the Peninsula under Napoleon*, 2 vols (London: Treuttel and Würtz, 1827), II, p. 521.
51. RAM, Robe Papers, MD/914, Robe to Shrapnel, 25 August 1808, and Allen C. Guelzo, *Gettysburg: The Last Invasion* (New York: Vintage, 2013), p. 382.
52. Gerges, 'Command and Control in the Peninsula', p. 36.
53. *Recollections of Rifleman Harris*, ed. Henry Curling (London: Hurst, 1848), pp. 53–4.
54. *WD*, IV, pp. 113–15, AW to Duke of York, 22 August 1808.
55. Dupuy, p. 228.
56. W.F.P. Napier, *War in the Peninsula*, I, p. 141.
57. *WD*, IV, pp. 164–255 (p. 203), Inquiry into the Cintra Convention.
58. Julian Rathbone, *Wellington's War: His Peninsular Dispatches* (London: Joseph, 1984), p. 30, AW to Castlereagh, 23 August 1808.
59. Esdaile, *Peninsular War*, p. 88.
60. Harriet Mary Paget, *Letters and Memorials of General Sir Edward Paget* (London: Bliss, Sands, 1898), E. Paget to Uxbridge, 28 August 1808.
61. USL, S.G.P. Ward Papers, MS 300/2/6, Hope to Mrs Hope, 3 September 1808.
62. W.F.P. Napier, *War in the Peninsula*, I, p. 171.
63. George Robert Gleig, *Personal Reminiscences of the First Duke of Wellington* (New York: Scribner, 1904), p. 3.

64. *Some Letters of the Duke of Wellington to his brother William Wellesley-Pole,* ed. Sir Charles Webster (London: Royal Historical Society, Camden 3 series, 1948), 79, pp. 9–11, AW to Wellesley-Pole, 16 September 1808.
65. Oman, *Peninsular War,* I, pp. 289–90, and UNM, Bentinck Papers, ref: Pw Jc 49/1, 14 September 1808.
66. Oman, *Peninsular War,* I, p. 295.
67. *The Times,* 22 February 1809.
68. Muir, *Wellington,* I, p. 279.
69. Charles W. Vane, 3rd Marquis of Londonderry [formerly Charles Stewart], *Correspondence, Despatches and other Papers of Viscount Castlereagh, 2nd Marquess of Londonderry,* 12 vols (London: Shoberl, 1848–53), VI, pp. 410–12.
70. *The Creevey Papers,* ed. Sir Herbert Maxwell (London: Dutton, 1903–4), Whitbread to Creevey, 25 September 1808.
71. John Gibson Lockhart, *Memoirs of the Life of Sir Walter Scott,* 10 vols (Edinburgh: Cadell, 1837–9), II, p. 226.
72. Weller, *Wellington in the Peninsula,* p. 59.
73. *Supplementary Report on the Manuscripts of Robert Graham, Esq. of Fintry,* ed. Christopher T. Atkinson (London: HMSO, 1942), p. 150, T. Graham to R. Graham, 20 September 1808.
74. *WSD,* V, pp. 66–7, AW to Castlereagh, 1 June 1807.
75. W.F.P. Napier, *War in the Peninsula,* I, p. 333.
76. *The Times,* 16 September 1808.
77. Griffith, p. 17.

Chapter Four

1. *WSD,* VI, p. 482, AW to Torrens, 29 March 1810.
2. M. Glover, *A Very Slippery Fellow: the Life of Sir Robert Wilson, 1777–1849* (Oxford: Oxford University Press, 1978).
3. Fortescue, VII, p. 136.
4. *WD,* IV, pp. 261–3, AW to Castlereagh, 7 March 1809.
5. *Wellington's Lieutenant, Napoleon's Gaoler: The Peninsula and St. Helena Diaries and Letters of Sir George Ridout Bingham, 1809–21,* ed. Gareth Glover (Barnsley: Pen & Sword, 2004), p. 18, Bingham to his mother, 29 April [1809].
6. Stanley Lane-Poole, *The Life of the Rt. Hon. Stratford Canning, Viscount Stratford de Redcliffe, from his Memoirs and Private and Official Papers* (London: Longman, 1888), p. 48, Canning to Villiers, 28 January 1809.
7. *WSD,* VII, p. 484, AW to Bathurst, 2 December 1812.
8. *The Times,* 18 April 1809.
9. E. Longford, p. 220.

10. Stanhope, p. 256.
11. M. Glover, *Wellington as Military Commander*, p. 207.
12. *WD*, VI, pp. 55–6, AW to Torrens, 7 September 1812.
13. *WD*, IV, pp. 271–3, AW to Castlereagh, 27 April 1809.
14. Oman, *Peninsular War*, II, pp. 640–2.
15. *The Dickson Manuscripts*, ed. Sir John Henry Leslie, 5 vols (Cambridge: Trotman, 1987–91), I, p. 31, Dickson to MacLeod, 28 May 1809.
16. Blond, p. 257.
17. *WD*, IV, pp. 286–7, AW to Mackenzie, 1 May 1809, and p. 368, 28 May 1809.
18. BL, General John Randoll Mackenzie Papers, Additional MS 39/201, diary 29 April 1809.
19. *WD*, IV, p. 296, AW to Beresford, 11 May 1809.
20. Londonderry, *Narrative*, I, pp. 262–3.
21. Muir, *Wellington*, I, p. 305, and Blond, p. 257.
22. *An Ensign in the Peninsular War: the Letters of John Aitchison*, ed. W.F.K. Thompson (London: Joseph, 1981), p. 42.
23. *WD*, IV, p. 325, AW to Castlereagh, 12 May 1809.
24. *An Intelligence Officer*, ed. Page, pp. 29–30.
25. *Memoirs of Combermere*, ed. Combermere, II, pp. 119–20.
26. E. Longford, p. 80 and p. 183.
27. Edwin Sidney, *The Life of Lord Hill G. C. B., late Commander of the Forces* (London: John Murray, 1845), p. 98, Hill to his sister, 22 May 1809.
28. *WD*, IV, p. 352, AW to Castlereagh, 31 May 1809.
29. Coss, *All for the King's Shilling*, pp. 133–237 (p. 143).
30. Fortescue, VIII, p. 341.
31. E. Longford, p. 178.
32. USL, Ward Papers, MS 300/8/2, G. Murray to P. Murray, 16 October 1811.
33. *Croker Papers*, ed. Jennings, I, p. 97.
34. *WSD*, VII, pp. 165–6, AW to the Duke of York, 25 June 1811.
35. *WSD*, VI, pp. 269–70, AW to Murray, 28 May 1809.
36. *WD*, III, pp. 449–54, AW to Castlereagh, 25 August 1809.
37. M. Glover, *Wellington's Army*, p. 124.
38. *Dickson Manuscripts*, ed. Leslie, III, p. 437 Dickson to Bredin, 4 August 1811.
39. *WD*, IV, p. 346, and p. 370, AW to Villiers, 19 and 30 May 1809.
40. *WSD*, VI, pp. 384–5, Beresford to AW, 2 October 1809.
41. Rathbone, p. 59, and Lipscombe, *Wellington's Guns*, pp. 92–107.
42. *WD*, IV, pp. 477–9, AW to Castlereagh, 30 June 1809.
43. Davies, p. 102.
44. Davies, p. 113.

45. Oman, *Peninsular War*, II, p. 511.
46. Lipscombe, *Wellington's Guns*, pp. 99–102, and GA, Raglan Papers, MS A/20, AW to Wellesley-Pole, 13 September 1809.
47. *Lady Bessborough and her Family Circle*, ed. Arthur Aspinall, 9th Earl of Bessborough (London: John Murray, 1940), p. 188, Ponsonby to Lady Duncannon, 3 September 1809.
48. *WD*, IV, p. 535, AW to Castlereagh, 29 July 1809.
49. Fletcher, *Galloping at Everything*, p. 107, and Fortescue, VII, p. 253.
50. Michael Glover, *The Peninsular War 1807–1814* (Newton Abbot: David & Charles, 1974), p. 111, and Lipscombe, *Wellington's Guns*, p. 99.
51. E. Longford, p. 220, and GA, Raglan Papers, MS A/93, 2 August 1809.
52. W.F.P. Napier, *War in the Peninsula*, VIII, p. 42.
53. UNM, Mellish Letters, Me 4c1/9, 30 July 1809.
54. *WD*, IV, p. 543, AW to Beresford 29 July 1809.
55. José Gómez de Arteche y Moro, *Guerra de la Independencia Historia Militar de España de 1808 a 1814*, 14 vols (Madrid: Fernández San Román, 1868–1903), VI, p. 342.
56. Gates, p. 187.
57. USL, Ward Papers, MS 300/7/1, quotes Clinton diary, 6 September 1809.
58. Fortescue, VII, p. 226.
59. David Buttery, *Wellington Against Massena: The Third Invasion of Portugal 1810–1811* (Barnsley: Pen & Sword, 2007), p. 40.
60. Fletcher, *Galloping at Everything*, p. 108.
61. *Creevey Papers*, ed. Maxwell, p. 128.
62. Griffith, p. 31.
63. Oman, *Peninsular War*, II, pp. 607–8.
64. TNA, WO 17/2464, Army Monthly Returns.
65. W.F.P. Napier, *War in the Peninsula*, I, p. 675.
66. *WD*, V, p. 148, AW to Estremadura Junta, 13 September 1809.
67. *WD*, IV, pp. 399–400, AW to Bourke, 8 June 1809.
68. Sir Charles Petrie, *Wellington: A Reassessment* (London: Barrie, 1956), p. 78.
69. Oman, *Peninsular War*, III, p. 1.
70. *WD*, V, pp. 331–2, AW to Malcolm, 3 December 1809.
71. *Croker Papers*, ed. Jennings, I, p. 347.
72. GA, Raglan Papers, MS A/34, AW to Wellesley-Pole, 5 September 1810.
73. *The Dispatches and Letters of Vice Admiral Lord Viscount Nelson*, ed. Sir Nicholas Harris Nicolas, 7 vols (London: Colburn, 1845–6), IV, pp. 379–80, Nelson to St Vincent, 22 May 1801.
74. Weller, *Wellington in the Peninsula*, p. 151, and J. Hill, p. 80.
75. E. Longford, p. 328, and M. Glover, *Wellington as Military Commander*, pp. 155–6.

76. *The Pakenham Letters, 1800 to 1815*, ed. Thomas Pakenham, 5th Earl of Longford (London: the author, 1914), p. 123, H. Pakenham to Longford, 27 August 1811.

77. Sir George T. Napier, *Passages in the Early Military Life of General Sir George T. Napier* (London: John Murray, 1884), p. 182.

78. E. Longford, p. 328.

79. *Letters of Gomm*, ed. Carr-Gomm, II, p. 189.

80. BL, Hill Paper, Additional MS 35,061 f 17-18, Hill to his sister, 10 October 1809.

81. *WD*, V, p. 235, AW to Fletcher, 20 October 1809.

82. *WD*, V, p. 373, AW to Hill, 18 December 1809.

83. *WD*, VI, p. 84, AW to Hill, 3 May 1810.

84. Oman, *Peninsular War*, II, p. 304.

85. *WSD*, VI, p. 412, Liverpool to AW, 20 October 1809, and p. 421, 1 November 1809.

86. Emperor Napoleon I, *The Confidential Correspondence of Napoleon Bonaparte with his Brother Joseph*, 2 vols (New York: Appleton, 1856), II, pp. 123–5, Napoleon to Berthier, 29 May 1810.

87. *WD*, V, p. 235, AW to Fletcher, 20 October 1809, and Gash, p. 97.

88. Lipscombe, *Wellington's Guns*, p. 126.

89. *WD*, V, p. 411, AW to Liverpool, 4 January 1810, and *Memoirs of Combermere*, ed. Combermere, p. 216, Murray to Cotton, 13 October 1811.

90. M. Glover, *Wellington as Military Commander*, p. 83.

91. Fletcher, *Galloping at Everything*, p. 124.

92. George Robert Gleig, *A Memoir of the late Major-General Robert Craufurd, reprinted from the Military Panorama of October 1812* (London: the author, 1842), p. 8.

93. William Tomkinson, *The Diary of a Cavalry Officer in the Peninsular War and Waterloo Campaign* (London: Swan, Sonnenschein, 1895), p. 34, 22 July 1810.

94. *The Times*, 21 November 1810, and Alexander H. Craufurd, *General Craufurd and his Light Division* (London: Griffith, Farran, Okeden & Welsh, 1891), p. 122, and pp. 139–46.

95. *WSD*, VI, p. 564, AW to Wellesley-Pole, 25 July 1810.

96. Oman, *Peninsular War*, III, p. 266.

97. *Memoirs of Lieutenant General Sir Thomas Picton G. C. B.*, ed. Heaton Bowstead Robinson (London: Bentley, 1835), p. 267.

98. *WD*, VI, p. 155, AW to Craufurd, 29 May 1810.

99. Peter Snow, *To War with Wellington: From the Peninsula to Waterloo* (London: John Murray, 2010), p. 116.

100. *WD*, VI, p. 429, AW to Stuart, 11 September 1810, and Fortescue, VII, p. 498.

101. *WD*, VI, p. 310, AW to Cole, 30 July 1810.
102. Lipscombe, *Wellington's Guns*, p. 133.
103. Public Record Office of Northern Ireland [PRONI], Viscount Castlereagh Papers, 1798–1822, D 3030/P/22, 4 September 1810, Stewart to Castlereagh.
104. *Memoirs of Sir Lowry Cole*, ed. Maud Lowry Cole and Stephen L. Gwynn (London: Macmillan, 1934), pp. 65–6.
105. *WD*, VI, p. 405, AW to Hill, 6 September 1810.
106. *Life of Colborne*, ed. Moore Smith, p. 140.
107. Jean-Jacques Pelet, *The French Campaign in Portugal 1810–11*, trans. Donald D. Horward (Minneapolis, MN: Minnesota University Press, 1973), pp. 175–7.
108. *WD*, VI, pp. 494–5, AW to C. Stuart, 6 October 1810.
109. TNA, Scovell's Diary, WO 37/7A, 24 November 1811.
110. Oman, *Wellington's Army*, p. 113, and Francis Duncan, *History of the Royal Regiment of Artillery*, 2 vols (London: John Murray, 1872), II, p. 277.
111. *Life of Colborne*, ed. Moore Smith, p. 140.
112. BL, Colonel J.W. Gordon Papers, Additional MS 49, 477f 101-2, Grey to Gordon, 15 October 1810.
113. *WSD*, VI, pp. 606–7, AW to Wellesley-Pole, 4 October 1810.
114. TNA, Scovell's Diary, WO 37/7A, 24 November 1811.
115. Pelet, p. 234.
116. Weller, *Wellington in the Peninsula*, pp. 144–5.
117. *WSD*, VII, pp. 1–2, AW to Wellesley-Pole, 8 December 1810.
118. *WD*, VII, p. 59, AW to Liverpool, 21 December 1810.
119. Lipscombe, *Wellington's Guns*, p. 147.
120. *Mémoires de Masséna*, ed. Jean Baptiste Frédéric Koch, 8 vols (Paris: Paulin et Lechevalier, 1848–50), VII, pp. 249–50.
121. Buttery, p. 118.
122. *WD*, VII, p. 188, AW to Stuart, 25 January 1811, and p. 315, AW to Carrera, 26 February 1811.
123. *WD*, VIII, p. 500, memo, 28 December 1811.
124. Rathbone, p. 120, AW to Leith, 21 December 1810.
125. *WD*, VII, p. 129, AW to Cotton, 11 January 1811.
126. Fortescue, VIII, p. 25, and Haythornthwaite, *Iron Duke*, p. 44.
127. *WSD*, VI, p. 582, AW to Torrens, 29 August 1810.
128. Ward, *Wellington's Headquarters*, p. 97.
129. Oman, *Peninsular War*, IV, pp. 132–4.
130. Rathbone, p. 119, AW to Wellesley-Pole, 8 December 1810.
131. *WD*, VII, p. 167, AW to Erskine, 21 January 1811, and GO, 6 February 1811. *WD*, VII, p. 359, AW to Liverpool, 14 March 1811.
132. Rathbone, p. 137.

133. Fortescue, VIII, p. 109.
134. *Dickson Manuscripts*, ed. Leslie, III, p. 363, Dickson to Macleod, 21 March 1811.
135. M. Glover, *Wellington's Army*, p. 120.
136. *WD*, VIII, p. 223, AW to Liverpool, 27 August 1811.
137. TNA, WO 17/17, and WO 17/37.
138. *WD*, VII, pp. 516–17, AW to Liverpool, 1 May 1811.
139. Dempsey, p. 46.
140. Buttery, p. 70.
141. *WD*, VII, pp. 464–6, AW to Spencer, 14 April 1811.
142. *WD*, VII, p. 475, AW to Spencer, 17 April 1811.
143. GA, Raglan Papers, MS A/34, AW to Wellesley-Pole, 5 September 1810.
144. J. Hill, p. 16.
145. *Pakenham Letters*, ed. Earl of Longford, p. 87.
146. Buttery, p. 153.
147. Larpent, p. 65.
148. Blond, p. 275.
149. *An Intelligence Officer*, ed. Page, p. 105.
150. *WD*, VIII, p. 224, AW to Liverpool, 27 August 1811.
151. Weller, *Wellington in the Peninsula*, p. 162, and E. Longford, p. 252.
152. *WD*, VII, p. 531, AW to Liverpool, 8 May 1811.
153. *WSD*, VII, pp. 176–7, AW to Wellesley-Pole, 2 July 1811.
154. Lipscombe, *Wellington's Guns*, p. 175.
155. *For King and Country: The Letters and Diaries of John Mills, Coldstream Guards, 1811–14*, ed. Ian Fletcher (Staplehurst: Spellmount, 1995), p. 46.
156. M. Glover, *Wellington as Military Commander*, p. 147.
157. *Annual Register*, 1811, p. 106.
158. *WD*, VII, p. 375, AW to Beresford, 20 March 1811.
159. Ward, *Wellington's Headquarters*, p. 139.
160. Hunter, pp. 141–9.
161. Stephen P.G. Ward, 'Brenier's Escape from Almeida', *Journal of the Society for Army Historical Research*, 35 (March 1957), 141, 23–35.
162. *Eyewitness to the Peninsular War and the Battle of Waterloo. The Letters and Journals of Lieutenant Colonel the Honourable James Stanhope, 1803 to 1825*, ed. Gareth Glover (Barnsley: Pen & Sword, 2010), p. 66.
163. Oman, *Peninsular War*, IV, p. 356.
164. Dempsey, p. 51, AW 7 May 1811 and 8 July 1811.
165. W.F.P. Napier, *War in the Peninsula*, III, p. 155.
166. M. Glover, *Wellington's Army*, p. 142.
167. *Peninsular Cavalry General: The Correspondence of Lieutenant-General Robert Ballard Long*, ed. Tom Henderson McGuffie (London: Harrap, 1951), p. 47.

168. *WD*, VII, p. 372, AW to Beresford, 18 March 1811.

169. Gerges, 'Command and Control in the Peninsula', p. 200.

170. *WD*, VII, p. 412, AW to Beresford, 30 March 1811, and Fletcher, *Galloping at Everything*, p. 137.

171. *WD*, VII, pp. 374–5, AW to Beresford, 20 March 1811.

172. *Life of Colborne*, ed. Moore Smith, pp. 152–3.

173. Fortescue, VIII, p. 132.

174. W.F.P. Napier, *War in the Peninsula*, III, p. 502.

175. *Life and Correspondence of Field Marshall Sir John Burgoyne*, ed. George Wrottesley (London: Bentley, 1873), p. 128.

176. *The Paget Brother, 1790–1840*, ed. Lord George Hylton (London: John Murray, 1918), p. 210, E. Paget to A. Paget, 12 August 1811.

177. E. Longford, p. 261, and *WD*, VII, p. 503, AW to Beresford, 24 April 1811.

178. E. Longford, pp. 217–18, and p. 256.

179. Dempsey, p. 64.

180. Londonderry, *Narrative*, I, p. 582.

181. M. Glover, *Wellington as Military Commander*, p. 91.

182. Sir Benjamin D'Urban, *Report on the Operations in the Alemtejo and Spanish Estremadura, during the Campaigns of 1811* (London: Longman, 1817), p. 17.

183. Dempsey, p. 86, and p. 248.

184. Lipscombe, *Wellington's Guns*, p. 189, records Dickson's 'missing' letter, 22 May 1811.

185. *Memoirs of Cole*, ed. Cole and Gwynn, p. 72.

186. *Memoirs of Cole*, ed. Cole and Gwynn, p. 77.

187. GA, Raglan Papers, MS B/114, Wellesley-Pole to AW, 16 June 1811.

188. *Pakenham Letters*, ed. Earl of Longford, p. 87, Pakenham to Longford, 15 April 1818.

189. Dempsey, p. 249.

190. BL, W. Windham Papers, Additional MS 37/415, letter 64, 3 September 1813.

191. Stanhope, p. 90.

192. *WSD*, VII, p. 177.

193. *WD*, VII, p. 598, AW to Liverpool, 23 May 1811.

194. Myatt, p. 45.

195. *Life of Burgoyne*, ed. Wrottesley, p. 135.

196. *WD*, IV, p. 726, AW to Major Ridewood, 6 April 1811.

197. Muir, *Wellington*, I, pp. 428–9.

198. J. Hill, p. 86.

199. University of Durham Library [UDL], Earl Grey Papers, GRE/B19/80, Gordon to Grey, 31 August 1811.

200. Arthur Griffiths, *The Wellington Memorial, Wellington, his Comrades and Contemporaries* (London: Allen, 1897), pp. 314–15.

201. Alexander M. Delavoye, Records of the 90th Regiment (London: Richardson, 1880), p. 86.
202. WD, VII, p. 599, AW to Liverpool, 23 May 1811.
203. Fletcher, *Galloping at Everything*, p. 119–20, and Fortescue, VIII, p. 260.
204. WD, VII, p. 553, AW to Howarth, 14 May 1811.
205. RAM, Jenkinson Letters, MD/212, 3 December 1811.
206. William Swabey, *Diary of Campaigns in the Peninsula for the Years 1811, '12 and '13* (London: Trotman, 1984), p. 27.
207. *WD*, IX, pp. 64–5, AW to Liverpool, 16 April 1812.
208. *WD*, IX, p. 87, AW to Liverpool, 24 April 1812.
209. *WD*, VIII, pp. 589–99, AW to Dickson, 23 February 1811.
210. Stocqueler, p. 182, AW to Liverpool, 12 March 1812.
211. *Life of Burgoyne*, ed. Wrottesley, p. 177.
212. Rathbone, p. 191, AW to Fletcher 23 February 1812.
213. Myatt, p. 108.
214. Henry N. Shore, ed., 'Letters from the Peninsula during 1812–14', *Journal of the Royal United Services Institute*, 61 (February 1916) (91–140), p. 98, Fletcher to Rice Jones, 12 August 1812.
215. Fortescue, VII, p. 539.
216. Ward, *Wellington's Headquarters*, p. 49.

Chapter Five

1. Neville Thompson, *Wellington After Waterloo* (London: Routledge, 1986), p. 174, quotes Lady Salisbury's diary, 28 July 1838.
2. *Liverpool Mercury*, 20 September 1811.
3. Fortescue, VIII, p. 415.
4. Fletcher, *Galloping at Everything*, p. 163, and Patrick. F. Stewart, *History of the XII Royal Lancers* (London: Oxford University Press, 1950), p. 71.
5. Lipscombe, *Wellington's Guns*, p. 199.
6. Griffith, p. 18.
7. TNA, WO 3/600, pp. 153–6, Torrens to AW, 24 August 1811.
8. *Pakenham Letters*, ed. Earl of Longford, p. 168.
9. *WD*, VII, p. 204, AW to Torrens, 28 January 1811.
10. *WD*, X, p. 330, AW to Vandeleur, 26 April 1813.
11. *WD*, IX, p. 183, 28 May 1812.
12. Muir, 'Wellington', 1/30, <http://www.lifeofwellington.co.uk/the-books/> [accessed 14 January 2016].
13. Larpent, p. 188–9.
14. Ward, *Wellington's Headquarters*, pp. 44–5.

15. UDL, Grey Papers, GRE/B19/118, Gordon to Grey, 25 August 1812.
16. *WD*, IX, p. 176, AW to Liverpool, 26 May 1812.
17. Bell, p. 192.
18. [A British Officer], *Letters from Portugal, Spain, and France during the Memorable Campaigns of 1811, 1812 & 1813; and from Belgium and France in the Year 1815* (Edinburgh: Anderson, 1819), p. 91, and J. Hill, p. 97.
19. Fletcher, *Galloping at Everything*, p. 7, quotes Lieutenant Colonel Hercules Pakenham.
20. McGuffie, p. 196.
21. *WD*, IX, p. 238, AW to Hill, 18 June 1812.
22. Christopher T. Atkinson, *History of the Royal Dragoons, 1661–1934* (Glasgow: Maclehose, 1934), p. 280.
23. Fletcher, *Galloping at Everything*, pp. 166–78, and Oman, *Peninsular War*, V, p. 522.
24. *The Times*, 13 July 1812.
25. USL, WP, 1/347, AW to Roche, 5 August 1812.
26. NLS, MS 3610, Graham to AW, 17 April 1812.
27. Myatt, p. 119.
28. *WD*, IX, pp. 296–7, AW to Bathurst, 21 June 1812.
29. Rathbone, p. 211.
30. *WD*, IX, p. 309, AW to Graham, 25 July 1812.
31. Tomkinson, p. 188.
32. Lawford and Young, p. 207.
33. William Grattan, *Adventures with the Connaught Rangers, 1809–1814* (London: Arnold, 1902), pp. 239–40.
34. Snow, p. 166.
35. *WD*, IX, pp. 394–5, AW to Torrens, 7 September 1812.
36. Muir, *Salamanca*, pp. 136–7.
37. *Pakenham Letters*, ed. Earl of Longford, p. 169.
38. *Memoirs of Combermere*, ed. Combermere, II, pp. 135–6.
39. Weller, *Wellington in the Peninsula*, p. 225, and E. Longford, p. 295.
40. Gates, p. 358.
41. *One-Leg*, ed. Anglesey, pp. 120–1.
42. Muir, *Inside Wellington's Peninsular Army*, p. 31.
43. Weller, *Wellington in the Peninsula*, p. 225.
44. *WD*, IX, p. 394, AW to Murray, 7 September 1812.
45. Joseph Bonaparte, *King of Spain, Mémoires et Correspondance Politique et Militaire*, 10 vols (Paris: Perrotin, 1854–5), IX, p. 64.
46. *At Wellington's Right Hand*, ed. Muir, pp. 320–3, Gordon to Aberdeen, 21 September 1812.
47. Fortescue, VIII, p. 584.

48. Ellesmere, p. 146, and *WD*, IX, pp. 562–7, AW to Liverpool 23, November 1812.
49. *Wellington at War, 1794–1815: A Selection of his Wartime Letters*, ed. Antony Brett-James (London: Macmillan, 1961), pp. 244–5.
50. Oman, *Peninsular War*, VI, p. 51.
51. Hew Dalrymple Ross, *Memoir of Field-Marshal Sir Hew Dalrymple Ross: Royal Horse Artillery* (Woolwich: RAI, 1871), p. 34, Ross to Dalrymple Ross, 18 October 1812.
52. *Dickson Manuscripts*, ed. Leslie, IV, pp. 768–9.
53. Oman, *Peninsular War*, VI, pp. 55–6.
54. M. Glover, *Wellington as Military Commander*, pp. 105–6.
55. Maurice Girod de l'Ain, *Vie Militaire du Général Foy* (Paris: Plon Nourrit, 1900), p. 189.
56. Gash, pp. 104–9, and *WSD*, VII, p. 478, AW to Cooke, 25 November 1812.
57. *WSD*, VII, pp. 482–3.
58. Rathbone, p. 247.
59. USL, WP, 1/359.
60. *WD*, IX, pp. 574–7, 28 November 1812.
61. Oman, *Peninsular War*, VI, pp. 159–61.
62. Greville, IV, pp. 141–2.
63. Oman, *Wellington's Army*, p. 43.
64. Christopher T. Atkinson, ed., 'A Peninsular Brigadier: letters of Major-General Sir F. P. Robinson, K.C.B.', *Journal of the Society for Army Historical Research*, 34 (December 1956), 153–70 (153–9).
65. *WD*, IX, pp. 611–12, AW to Vice-Admiral Martin, 10 December 1812.
66. National Army Museum [NAM], 6807-219-5, Long to Torrens, 12 August 1813.
67. USL, WP, 1/365, AW to Torrens, 22 January 1813.
68. Ian C. Robertson, *Wellington Invades France: The Final Phase of the Peninsular War, 1813–1814* (London: Greenhill, 2003), p. 41.
69. Haythornthwaite, *Iron Duke*, p. 44.
70. PRONI, D 3030/P/9, 30 May 1810, Stewart to Castlereagh.
71. Rathbone, p. 262, AW to Stewart, 1 January 1813.
72. *Croker Papers*, ed. Jennings, I, p. 346.
73. M. Glover, *Wellington's Army*, pp. 137–8.
74. Ward, *Wellington's Headquarters*, p. 160, and Larpent, p. 35.
75. M. Glover, *Wellington's Army*, p. 137.
76. Stephen Leslie, *Dictionary of National Biography* (London: Smith, Elder, 1886), pp. 350–1.
77. TNA, WO 3/598, pp. 272–3, Torrens to Campbell, 19 December 1810.
78. TNA, WO 3/598, p. 407, Torrens to AW, 6 May 1812.

79. Larpent, p. 394, 18 February 1814, and Eric Hunt, *Charging Against Napoleon: Diaries and Letters of Three Hussars* (London: Pen & Sword, 2001), p. 80.

80. Larpent, p. 96, 24 April 1813, and *Dickson Manuscripts*, ed. Leslie, V, pp. 902–6, Cairnes to Cuppage, 11 June 1813.

81. TNA, WO 55/1196, p. 42, Somerset to Waller, 17 July 1813.

82. TNA, WO 55/1196, pp. 40–1 Waller to AW, 1 July 1813.

83. Muir, *Wellington*, I, p. 514.

84. Larpent, p. 69, 6 March 1813.

85. Swabey, p. 97, 12 May 1811.

86. TNA, WO 3/604, p. 46, Torrens to Graham, 4 January 1813.

87. Parliamentary Debates, 1st series XXIV, December 1812. <http://www.hansard-archive.parliament.uk/Parliamentary_Debates_Vol_1_(1803)_to_Vol_41_ (Feb_1820) > S1V0024P0.zip [accessed 17 November 2017].

88. NLS, MS 64, pp. 148–50, Murray to Cathcart, 20 April 1813.

89. *WSD*, VII, p. 502, Liverpool to AW, 22 December 1812.

90. Rathbone, pp. 265–7.

91. *Wellington's Lieutenant*, ed. Gareth Glover, p. 186, 22 May 1813.

92. Trevor Royle, *Crimea: The Great Crimean War 1854–1856* (London: Little, Brown, 1999), p. 111.

93. Gash, p. 84.

94. *The Trial of Lieutenant General John Murray, Bart., by a General Court Martial*, ed. W.B. Gurney (London: Egerton, 1815), pp. 2–5.

95. *WD*, X, pp. 482–8, AW to Murray, 1 July 1813.

96. W.F.P. Napier, *History of the War in the Peninsula*, V, pp. 349–50.

97. *The Trial of General Murray*, ed. Gurney, p. 562.

98. *Wellington at War*, ed. Brett-James, p. 245.

99. *WD*, X, p. 393, AW to Henry Wellesley, 20 May 1813.

100. Rathbone, p. 281, AW to Henry Wellesley, 15/16 June 1813.

101. Sir George Murray, *Memoir to Accompany an Atlas* (London: Wyld, 1841), p. 93n.

102. Esdaile, *Peninsular War*, p. 428.

103. E. Longford, p. 313.

104. 'Some Unpublished Letters of Sir Thomas Picton', ed. E. Edwards, *West Wales Historical Records*, 13 (1928), 1–32 (17–19).

105. Oman, *Peninsular War*, VI, p. 449.

106. Rathbone, p. 290.

107. Esdaile, *Peninsular War*, pp. 448–9.

108. Tomkinson, pp. 247–8.

109. Rathbone, p. 290.

110. *Wellington's Lieutenant*, ed. Gareth Glover, p. 196.

111. Fletcher, *Galloping at Everything*, p. 202.

112. Oman, *Peninsular War*, VI, p. 450.
113. Fortescue, IX, p. 189.
114. Ward, *Wellington's Headquarters*, p. 151.
115. USL, WP, 1/370, AW to Bathurst, 29 June 1813, and *WD*, X, pp. 495–6, AW to Bathurst, 2 July 1813.
116. E. Longford, p. 317.
117. Tomkinson, pp. 252–3.
118. Ward, *Wellington's Headquarters*, p. 98.
119. Swabey, p. 211, 22 July 1813.
120. Lipscombe, *Wellington's Guns*, p. 288.
121. Lipscombe, *Wellington's Guns*, p. 322, Cairns to Cuppage, 25 July 1813.
122. Weller, *Wellington in the Peninsula*, p. 68.
123. Muir, *Wellington*, I, pp. 532–3.
124. *WD*, X, pp. 628–9, AW to Bathurst, 11 August 1813.
125. *WD*, XI, pp. 122–3, AW to Bathurst, 19 September 1813.
126. Charles Esdaile, *The Duke of Wellington and the Command of the Spanish Army, 1812–14* (Basingstoke: Macmillan, 1990), p. 164.
127. *WSD*, VIII, pp. 223–6, Melville to AW, 3 September 1813.
128. Mark S. Thompson, 'The Rise of the Scientific Soldier as seen through the Performance of the Corps of Royal Engineers during the early 19th Century' (doctoral thesis, University of Sunderland, 2009), pp. 184–99.
129. *WD*, X, pp. 526–7, AW to Hill, 14 July 1813.
130. USL, WP, 1/375 MS 61, WP 1/375, AW to Bathurst 23 August 1813.
131. Lipscombe, *Wellington's Guns*, p. 317.
132. Gates, p. 426.
133. *WD*, XI, p. 211.
134. Sir Herbert Maxwell, *The Life of Wellington and the Restoration of the Martial Power of Great Britain*, 2 vols (London: Low, Marston, 1893), I, p. 331.
135. John Philipparts, *The Royal Military Calendar, or Army Service and Commission Book* (London: Valpy, 1820), III, pp. 242–3.
136. WSD, VII, p. 177.
137. Oman, *Peninsular War*, VI, pp. 626–7.
138. USL, WP, 1/375, AW to Bathurst, 23 August 1813.
139. M. Glover, *Wellington as Military Commander*, p. 155.
140. *WSD*, VIII, p. 112, Murray to Cole, 23 July 1813.
141. M. Glover, *Wellington as Military Commander*, p. 161.
142. Robertson, *Wellington Invades France*, pp. 70–1.
143. M. Glover, *Wellington as Military Commander*, p. 156.
144. *WSD*, VIII, p. 121, Picton to AW, 26 July 1813.
145. *WSD*, VIII, pp. 124–5, Cole to Murray, 27 July 1813.
146. Gates, p. 413.

147. Robertson, *Wellington Invades France*, p. 82.

148. Fortescue, IX, p. 263.

149. M. Glover, *Wellington as Military Commander*, p. 159.

150. *WD*, X, p. 526, AW to Hill, 14 July 1813, and p. 563, AW to Graham, 24 July 1813.

151. Robertson, *Wellington Invades France*, p. 75.

152. *WD*, X, pp. 596–7, AW to Liverpool, 4 August 1813.

153. *Dickson Manuscripts*, ed. Leslie, V, p. 1073, Dickson to McLeod, 10 October 1813.

154. J. Hill, p. 118, Clement Hill to home, 1 July 1813.

155. *WD*, XI, pp. 116–17, AW to Graham, 17 September 1813.

156. *WD*, XI, pp. 123–4, AW to Bathurst, 19 September 1813.

157. M. Glover, *Wellington as Military Commander*, p. 113.

158. Reese, Paul P., "'The Ablest Man in the British Army." The Life and Career of General Sir John Hope' (doctoral dissertation, Florida State University, 2007), p. 351.

159. J. Hill, p. 123.

160. Ward, *Wellington's Headquarters*, p. 140.

161. *The Autobiography of Sir Harry Smith*, ed. George C. Moore Smith (London: Murray, 1910), p. 142, AW to Colborne.

162. *WD*, XI, pp. 207–8, AW to Bathurst, 18 October 1813.

163. M. Glover, ed., *A Gentleman Volunteer; The Letters of George Hennell from the Peninsular War, 1812–13* (London: Heinemann, 1979), p. 135.

164. Ross, p. 51, 12 November 1813.

165. *WD*, XI, pp. 279–85, AW to Bathurst 13 November 1813.

166. Gates, p. 441.

167. *WSD*, VIII, pp. 401–2, Bathurst to AW, 24 November 1813.

168. Robertson, *Wellington Invades France*, p. 124.

169. G.F. Nafziger, *The Armies of Spain and Portugal, 1808–1815* (privately published, 1993), p. 44, AW to Richard Wellesley, 24 August 1809.

170. Reese, pp. 275–6.

171. Joseph Vidal de la Blache, *L'Evacuation de l'Espagne et l'Invasion dans le Midi, Juin 1813 – Avril 1814* (Paris: Berger-Levrault, 1914), p. 163.

172. Oman, *Peninsular War*, VII, pp. 250–1, and Ward, 'Brenier's Escape from Almeida', p. 23.

173. *Life of Colborne*, ed. Moore Smith, p. 189.

174. *Life of Colborne*, ed. Moore Smith, p. 199.

175. NLS, Add MS 46.4.22f, pp. 26–9, Murray to Hope, 18 December 1813.

176. Robertson, *Wellington Invades France*, p. 182.

177. Sir John Cowell-Stepney, *Leaves from the Diary of an Officer in the Guards* (London: Chapman & Hall, 1854), p. 102.

178. Oman, *Peninsular War*, VII, p. 280.
179. E. Longford, p. 338.
180. W.F.P. Napier, *War in the Peninsula*, V, p. 394.
181. Haythornthwaite, *Iron Duke*, p. 68.
182. J. Hill, p. 153.
183. *WSD*, VIII, p. 654, Hope to AW, 16 March 1814.
184. *WD*, XI, p. 550, AW to Hope, 5 March 1814.
185. Reese, p. 363.
186. Finlay C. Beatson, *Wellington: The Crossing of the Gaves and the Battle of Orthez* (London: Heath, Cranton, 1925), pp. 190–1.
187. *Memoirs of Cole*, ed. Cole and Gwynn, pp. 104–5, Cole to Lady Grantham, 3 March 1814.
188. E. Longford, p. 342, and Robertson, *Wellington Invades France*, p. 211.
189. George T. Napier, pp. 248–50.
190. Mansfield, p. 53.
191. Gates, p. 461, and Robertson, *Wellington Invades France*, pp. 226–7.
192. Snow, p. 231.
193. Oman, *Peninsular War*, VII, p. 527.
194. E. Lapene, *Campaignes de 1813 et de 1814 sur L'Ebre, les Pyrénées et la Garonne* (Paris: Anselin et Pochard 1823), pp. 382–4.
195. J-C. Castex, *Combats Franco–Anglais des Guerres du Premier Empire* (Vancouver: Éditions P-O, 2013), p. 85.
196. *[New] Dispatches, Correspondence, and Memoranda of Field Marshal Arthur Duke of Wellington, K.G.*, ed. Arthur Richard Wellesley, 2nd Duke of Wellington, 8 vols (London: John Murray, 1857–80), VIII, p. 235, memorandum, 4 March 1832.
197. Ward, *Wellington's Headquarters*, p. 140.
198. J. Hill, p. 142, quotes Captain William Bragge.
199. Stanhope, p. 9.
200. Larpent, p. 306.
201. Harvey, p. 733, and p. 727.
202. Gregory Fremont-Barnes, *The Napoleonic Wars: The Peninsular War 1807–1814* (Oxford: Osprey, 2002), p. 9.
203. W.F.P. Napier, *War in the Peninsula*, VI, p. 175.
204. William Grattan, *The Duke of Wellington and the Peninsular Medal* (London: Churton, 1845), p. 340.
205. *Waterloo Archive*, ed. Gareth Glover, IV, pp. 71–91.

Chapter Six

1. *The Journal of Mrs Arbuthnot, 1820–1832*, ed. F. Bamford, 2 vols (London: Macmillan, 1950), I, p. 105, 4 July 1821.

2. *WD*, XII, pp. 267–8, AW to Castlereagh, 12 March 1815.
3. *WSD*, VIII, p. 3, AW to Burghersh, 13 March 1815.
4. Henri Houssaye, *1815, Waterloo*, trans. S.R. Willis (ebook: Pickle, 2011), p. 50.
5. *WD*, XII, pp. 288–9.
6. Adkin, p. 37.
7. Larpent, p. 88, and BL, H.E. Bunbury Papers Additional MS 37/052f, pp. 91–4, Colborne to Bunbury, 24 March 1815.
8. TNA, WO 3/609, Torrens memorandum, 4 April 1815.
9. *WD*, XII, p. 358, AW to Stewart, 8 May 1815.
10. USL, WP, 1/457, AW to Bathurst, 6 April 1815.
11. Müffling, p. 212.
12. Rees Howell Gronow, *Reminiscences of Captain R. H. Gronow, formerly of the Grenadier Guards, and M.P. for Stafford* (London: Smith, Elder, 1862), pp. 126–7, and E. Longford, p. 415.
13. John William Cole, *Memoirs of British Generals Distinguished during the Peninsular War*, 2 vols (London: Bentley, 1856), II, p. 34.
14. Fortescue, X, pp. 239–42.
15. Muir, *Wellington*, II, p. 32.
16. Fitzroy James Henry Somerset, 1st Baron Raglan, *Life of Field-Marshal Lord Raglan; with a Review of the Military Operations in the Crimea* (London: Kessinger, 2010), p. 21.
17. *WSD*, X, pp. 10–11, Torrens to AW, 1 April 1815.
18. *One-Leg*, ed. Anglesey, p. 119.
19. *Dickson Manuscripts*, ed. Leslie, V, Cairnes to Cuppage, 28 January 1813.
20. USL, WP, 1/471, AW to Bathurst 25 June 1815.
21. BL, Earl Bathurst Papers, Loan MS 57, IX, 344.
22. Duncan, II, p. 412.
23. *WSD*, VIII, pp. 38–9, AW to Bathurst, 21 April 1815.
24. *WSD*, X, pp. 41–3, Torrens to Bathurst, 8 April 1815.
25. *WSD*, X, pp. 167–8, AW to Bathurst, 28 April 1815.
26. Clayton, p. 61.
27. Sir Charles Oman, 'The Dutch-Belgians at Waterloo', *Nineteenth Century Magazine*, vol. 48, October 1900, pp. 629–38 (p. 632).
28. Weller, *Wellington at Waterloo*, p. 127.
29. Roger Parkinson, *The Hussar General* (London: Davies, 1975), p. 215.
30. *WD*, XII, p. 462, AW to Graham, 13 June 1815.
31. *WSD*, X, pp. 215–16, Bathurst to AW, 22 May 1815.
32. Weigley, p. 519.
33. *WSD*, X, pp. 31–5, Harrowby to Castlereagh, 7 April 1815.
34. *WD*, XII, p. 295, AW to Clancarty, 10 April 1815.
35. Harvey, p. 876.
36. *WD*, XII, p. 438, AW to Henry Wellesley, 2 June 1815.

37. Blond, p. 484.
38. Müffling, p. 221.
39. *Dörnberg: ein Kämpfer für Deutschlands Freiheit*, ed. Hugo, Freiherr von Dörnberg-Hausen (Marberg: Elwert, 1936), p. 176.
40. John Franklin, *Waterloo: Netherlands Correspondence* (Ulverston: 1815, 2010), p. 26.
41. Ellesmere, p. 185.
42. Weigley, p. 519.
43. *WD*, XII, pp. 478–84, AW to Bathurst, 19 June 1815.
44. Beurden, p. 18, n. 4.
45. Andrew Uffindell, *The Eagles Last Triumph: Napoleon's Victory at Ligny, June 1815* (London: Greenhill, 2006), p. 52.
46. *WD*, XII, pp. 470–2.
47. *Waterloo Archive*, ed. Gareth Glover, II, p. 148.
48. John C. Ropes, *The Campaign of Waterloo: A Military History* (London: Putnam, 1893), pp. 373–4.
49. Julius von Pflugk-Harttung, *Vorgeschichte der Schlacht bei Belle-Alliance: Wellington* (Berlin: Schröder, 1903), p. 292.
50. E. Longford, p. 424n, Lady Salisbury's diary, 18 September 1836, and Hofschröer, I, p. 228.
51. David Hamilton-Williams, *Waterloo, New Perspectives: The Great Battle Reappraised* (London: Arms and Armour, 1993).
52. Erwin Muilwijk, *1815*, 2 vols (Bleiswijk, Neth: Sovereign 2012–13), II, pp. 41–2.
53. Franklin, p. 81.
54. Karl von Ollech, *Geschichte des Feldzuges von 1815* (Berlin: Mittler, 1876), p. 125: AW letter [the Frasnes letter] of 16 June originally held in the Prussian war archives.
55. Houssaye, p. 165.
56. Muir, *Wellington*, II, p. 52.
57. Frederick William Hamilton, *The Origin and History of the First or Grenadier Guards*, 3 vols (London: John Murray, 1874), III, p. 15.
58. Fletcher, *Galloping at Everything*, p. 228, and Lipscombe, *Wellington's Guns*, p. 360.
59. Clayton, p. 205.
60. Foster, p. 53.
61. Herbert T. Siborne, *Waterloo Letters. A Selection from Original and Hitherto Unpublished Letters* (London: Cassell, 1891), p. 386, quotes Major Robert Winchester.
62. Rory Muir, *Britain and the Defeat of Napoleon, 1807–1815* (London: Yale University Press, 1996), p. 357.

63. Hans Delbrück, *Das Leben des Feldmarschalls Grafen Neithardt von Gneisenau*, 4 vols (Berlin: Reimer, 1864–80), IV, pp. 530–1, Gneisenau to Hardenberg, 22 June 1815.
64. Clayton, p. 270.
65. Weller, *Wellington at Waterloo*, p. 7.
66. Kennedy, *Notes on the Battle of Waterloo*, p. 75.
67. M. Glover, *Wellington as Military Commander*, p. 193.
68. Andrew Uffindell, *The National Army Museum Book of Wellington's Armies* (London: Sidgwick & Jackson, 2003), p. 294.
69. John Grehan, *Voices from the Past: Waterloo 1815* (Barnsley: Frontline, 2015), p. 114.
70. E. Longford, p. 437.
71. Maxwell, *Life of Wellington*, II, p. 194, and J. Moyle Sherer, *Recollections of the Peninsula* (Staplehurst: Spellmount, 1996), p. 151.
72. Reid, p. 20.
73. Hamilton-Williams, *Waterloo*, p. 332.
74. P.R. Adair, 'Coldstream Guards', *Household Brigade Magazine*, Waterloo Number (Spring 1965), 24–31 (30–1).
75. Fletcher, *Galloping at Everything*, p. 262.
76. *One-Leg*, ed. Anglesey, p. 142.
77. Müffling, p. 245.
78. *Spencer and Waterloo: the Letters of Spencer Madan, 1814–1816*, ed. Beatrice Madan (London: Literary Services, 1970), pp. 114–15, 14 July 1814, S. Madan to Dr Madan.
79. David Hamilton-Williams, *The Fall of Napoleon: The Final Betrayal* (London: Arms and Armour, 1994), p. 237.
80. *WD*, XII, pp. 478–84.
81. Hofschröer, II, p. 325.
82. *WD*, VIII, pp. 244–5, AW to Croker, 17 August 1815.
83. Edward Owen, *The Waterloo Papers, 1815 and Beyond* (Tavistock: AQ & DJ, 1997), p. 13, and Saul David, 'Wellington at Waterloo', public lecture at Windsor Castle, 14 November 2015.
84. Jean Baptiste Lemonnier-Delafosse, *Campagnes de 1810–1815 en Portugal, Espagne, France, Belgique* (Le Havre: Lemale, 1850), p. 373, quotes AQMG James Shaw and Major Andrew Hamilton.
85. *Waterloo Archive*, ed. Gareth Glover, I, p. 177, quotes Gunner Andrew Patton.
86. Sidney, p. 309.
87. Lipscombe, *Wellington's Guns*, p. 382.
88. *Waterloo Archive*, ed. Gareth Glover, V, p. 137, quotes Major General Kruse.
89. Ellesmere, p. 101.
90. E. Longford, p. 485.

91. *The Diary of Lady Frances Shelley*, ed. Richard Edgcumbe, 2 vols (New York: Scribner, 1913), I, p. 103, and Owen, pp. 33–5.

92. Hans Delbrück, 'Einiges zum Feldzug von 1815', *Zeitschrift für Preussische Geschichte und Landeskunde*, 14. Jahrgang, Berlin, 1877, p. 660.

93. USL, WP, 8/3/10, AW to Gurwood, 17 September 1842.

94. Hofschröer, II, p. 337.

95. Adkin, p. 410.

96. Alessandro Barbero, *The Battle: A New History of Waterloo*, trans. John Cullen (London: Atlantic, 2005), pp. 419–21.

97. *WSD*, XIV, pp. 618–20, AW to Mulgrave, 21 December 1815.

98. Lipscombe, *Wellington's Guns*, pp. 396–7.

99. Lipscombe, *Wellington's Guns*, pp. 389–90.

100. *WND*, VIII, p. 332, AW to Mudford, 8 June 1816.

101. *Waterloo Letters*, ed. Siborne, pp. 160–2, Vivian to Siborne, undated (19 April 1837).

102. USL, WP, 1/371, AW to Bathurst, 25 June 1815.

103. TNA, WO 3/609, pp. 302–4, Torrens to Campbell, 30 June 1815.

104. *The Life and Opinions of General Sir Charles James Napier*, ed. Sir William F.P. Napier, 4 vols (London: John Murray, 1857), IV, p. 306.

105. Beurden, p. 51.

106. *WD*, XII, p. 484.

107. Carl von Clausewitz, *On Waterloo: Clausewitz, Wellington and the Campaign of 1815*, trans. Christopher Bassford et al. (Charleston, SC: Createspace, 2010).

108. USL, WP, 2/93/17.

109. Charles C. Chesney, *Waterloo Lectures: A Study of the Campaign of 1815* (London: Longmans, 1868), p. 3.

Conclusion

1. John Kennedy, *The Business of War* (London: Hutchinson, 1957), p. 51.

2. Davies, p. xi, and Snow, p. 167.

3. *WSD*, X, p. 531.

4. Muir, *Inside Wellington's Peninsular Army*, p. 31.

5. Grattan, *Peninsular Medal*, p. 1.

6. *The Life and Memoirs of Count Molé* (1781–1855), ed. Helie G.H., Marquis de Noailles, 2 vols (London: Hutchinson, 1923), II, pp. 87–8.

7. Griffith, p. 110, and E. Longford, p. 297.

8. Frederick Sleigh Roberts, 1st Earl, *The Rise of Wellington* (London: Sampson, Low, Marston, 1895), p. 49.

9. Grattan, *Peninsular Medal*, p. 46.

10. Oman, *Peninsular War*, II, p. 307.

11. William Hill James, *Battles Round Biaritz: The Battles of the Nivelle and Nives* (Edinburgh: M'Lagan and Cumming, 1899), pp. 35–7.
12. *Life of Colborne*, ed. Moore Smith, p. 246.
13. E. Longford, p. 261.
14. Oman, *Peninsular War*, II, pp. 305–6.
15. *Memoirs of Combermere*, ed. Combermere, I, p. 134.
16. *WD*, V, pp. 424–6, AW to Villiers, 14 January 1810.
17. Julian Knight, *British Politics for Dummies* (Chichester: Wiley, 2010), p. 362.
18. USL, WP, 1/318, AW to Fane, 3 November 1810.
19. *WD*, XII, pp. 301–2, AW to Bathurst, 12 April 1815.
20. *Memoir and Literary Remains of Lieutenant-General Sir Henry Edward Bunbury*, ed. Sir Charles J.F. Bunbury (London: Spottiswoode, 1868), p. 63.
21. Haythornthwaite, *Wellington's Military Machine*, p. 24.
22. *WD*, X, pp. 495–6, AW to Bathurst, 2 July 1813.
23. Oman, *Peninsular War*, II, p. 302.
24. Grattan, *Peninsular Medal*, p. 20.
25. M. Glover, *Wellington as Military Commander*, p. 219.
26. Gash, p. 85.
27. *WSD*, X, p. 509, AW to Mudford, 8 June 1816.
28. Weigley, p. 498.
29. Dixon, p. 219.
30. Dixon, pp. 152–3.
31. Charles M. Clode, *The Military Forces of the Crown: Their Administration and Government*, 2 vols (London: John Murray, 1869), II, p. 608.
32. *Sir Harry Smith*, ed. Moore Smith, p. 38.
33. Guelzo, p. 215.
34. Oman, *Peninsular War*, II, p. 310.
35. *The Letters of Sir Walter Scott, 1787–1832*, ed. Herbert J.C. Grierson, 12 vols (London: Constable, 1932–7), IV, p. 95, Scott to Baillie, 10 August 1815.
36. John Sweetman, 'Wellington's Disciple: Lord Raglan in the Crimea', public lecture at the University of Southampton, Wellington Congress, July 2010.
37. Royle, p. 364.

Bibliography

Primary Sources

Manuscripts

Belfast, Public Record Office of Northern Ireland (PRONI)
Viscount Castlereagh Papers, 1798–1822, D 3030

Ebbw Vale, Gwent Archives (GA)
Lord Fitzroy Somerset, 1st Baron Raglan Papers, 1808–55, MS A and B

Edinburgh, National Library of Scotland (NLS)
Murray Papers, Advocates MS 36, 46, 48 and 64

Edinburgh, National Records of Scotland (NRS)
Melville Papers, Additional MS 1060

Gillingham, Royal Engineers Museum (REM)
Miscellaneous letters from R.E. Burgoyne, 4601-72

Kew, The National Archives (TNA)
War Office General Correspondence
WO 1 series, Secretary of State for War and Commander-in-Chief: In-letters and
  Miscellaneous Papers
WO 3 series, Office of the Commander-in-Chief: Out-letters
WO 17 series, Monthly Returns to the Adjutant-General
WO 37 series, Diary of George Scovell
WO 55 series, Artillery Letters: from and to Officers

London, British Library Manuscripts (BL)
General Lord Hill Papers, Additional MS 35
H.E. Bunbury Papers, Additional MS 37
W. Windham, Secretary of State for War, Papers, Additional MS 37

General John Randoll Mackenzie Papers, Additional MS 39
Colonel J.W. Gordon Papers, MS 49
Earl Bathurst Papers, Loan MS 57

London, National Army Museum (NAM)
Brigadier General Robert Ballard Long letters, NAM 6807

University of Durham Library (UDL)
Earl Grey Papers: Letters of Colonel J.W. Gordon to Lord Grey, 1807–13, GRE/B19

University of Manchester, John Rylands Library (JRL)
Sir William Henry Clinton Papers, 1769–1846, GB/133 CLI

University of Nottingham, Manuscripts and Special Collections (UNM)
Henry Francis Mellish Letters to his sister Anne from the Peninsular War 1808–1816, Me 4c1-2
Lord William H. Cavendish Bentinck Papers (1774–1839), Military Service during Peninsular War, Pw Jc

University of Southampton, Hartley Library (USL)
Wellington Papers: General correspondence 1790–1832, MS 61/WP1 and Papers of Colonel John Gurwood WP8
S.G.P. Ward, Peninsular War Papers, MS 300

Woolwich, Royal Artillery Museum (RAM)
Major George Jenkinson RA Letters, 1809–14, MD/212
Colonel Sir William Robe Papers, 1793–1818, MD/914

Published Correspondence, Memoirs and Diaries

[A British Officer], *Letters from Portugal, Spain, and France during the Memorable Campaigns of 1811, 1812 & 1813; and from Belgium and France in the Year 1815* (Edinburgh: Anderson, 1819)

Anglesey, George Paget, 7th Marquess of, ed., *One-Leg: The Life and Letters of Henry William Paget, First Marquess of Anglesey* (London: Jonathan Cape, 1961)

Atkinson, Christopher T., ed., *Supplementary Report on the Manuscripts of Robert Graham, Esq. of Fintry* (London: HMSO, 1942)

Bamford, F., ed., *The Journal of Mrs Arbuthnot, 1820–1832*, 2 vols (London: Macmillan, 1950)

Bayly, R., *Diary of Colonel Bayly, 12th Regiment, 1796–1830* (London: Naval & Military Press, 1896)

Bessborough, Arthur Aspinall, 9th Earl of, ed., *Lady Bessborough and her Family Circle* (London: John Murray, 1940)

———, *The Correspondence of Charles Arbuthnot* (London: Royal Historical Society, 1941)

Joseph Bonaparte, King of Spain, *Mémoires et Correspondance Politique et Militaire*, 10 vols (Paris: Perrotin, 1854–5)

Brett-James, Antony, ed., *Wellington at War, 1794–1815: A Selection of his Wartime Letters* (London: Macmillan, 1961)

Bunbury, Sir Charles J.F., ed., *Memoir and Literary Remains of Lieutenant-General Sir Henry Edward Bunbury* (London: Spottiswoode, 1868)

Burghersh, John Fane, Lord, *Memoir of the Early Campaigns of the Duke of Wellington in Portugal and Spain by an Officer Employed in His Army* (London: John Murray, 1820)

Carr-Gomm, Francis C., ed., *Letters and Journals of Field-Marshal Sir William Maynard Gomm from 1799 to Waterloo, 1815* (London: John Murray, 1881)

Cassels, Simon A.C., ed., *Peninsular Portrait, Letters of Captain William Bragge* (London: Oxford University Press, 1963)

Cole, Maud Lowry, and Stephen L. Gwynn, ed., *Memoirs of Sir Lowry Cole* (London: Macmillan, 1934)

Combermere, Viscountess, Mary W.G.C., ed., *Memoirs and Correspondence of Viscount Combermere* [Stapleton Cotton], 2 vols (London: Hurst and Blackett, 1866)

Compton, Herbert Eastwick, ed., *Master Mariner: Being the Life and Adventures of Captain Robert W. Eastwick* (London: Fisher Unwin, 1891)

Costello, Edward, *Adventures of a Soldier, or Memoirs of Edward Costello* (London, Colburn, 1841)

Cowell-Stepney, Sir John, *Leaves from the Diary of an Officer in the Guards* (London: Chapman & Hall, 1854)

Curling, Henry, ed., *Recollections of Rifleman Harris* (London: Hurst, 1848)

D'Abrantès, Laure Junot, Duchess de, *Memoirs of Emperor Napoleon*, trans. S.M. Hamilton, 3 vols (London: Dunne, 1901)

Dörnberg-Hausen, Hugo, Freiherr von, ed., *Dörnberg: ein Kämpfer für Deutschlands Freiheit* (Marberg: Elwert, 1936)

D'Urban, Sir Benjamin, *Report on the Operations in the Alemtejo and Spanish Estremadura, during the Campaigns of 1811* (London: Longman, 1817)

Edgcumbe, Richard, ed., *The Diary of Lady Frances Shelley*, 2 vols (New York: Scribner, 1913)

Ellesmere, Francis Egerton, 1st Earl of, *Personal Reminiscences of the Duke of Wellington* (London: John Murray, 1904)

Fletcher, Ian, ed., *For King and Country: The Letters and Diaries of John Mills, Coldstream Guards, 1811–14* (Staplehurst: Spellmount, 1995)

Foy, Count Maximilien S., *History of the War in the Peninsula under Napoleon*, 2 vols (London: Treuttel and Würtz, 1827)

Gleig, George Robert, *A Memoir of the late Major-General Robert Craufurd, reprinted from the Military Panorama of October 1812* (London: the author, 1842)

———, *Personal Reminiscences of the First Duke of Wellington* (New York: Scribner, 1904)

Glover, Gareth, ed., *Wellington's Lieutenant, Napoleon's Gaoler: The Peninsula and St. Helena Diaries and Letters of Sir George Ridout Bingham, 1809–21* (Barnsley: Pen & Sword, 2004)

———, ed., *Eyewitness to the Peninsular War and the Battle of Waterloo. The Letters and Journals of Lieutenant Colonel the Honourable James Stanhope, 1803 to 1825* (Barnsley: Pen & Sword, 2010)

———, ed., *Waterloo Archive*, 6 vols (Barnsley: Frontline, 2010–14)

Glover, Michael, ed., *A Gentleman Volunteer: The Letters of George Hennell from the Peninsular War, 1812–1813* (London: Heinemann, 1979)

Grattan, William, *Adventures with the Connaught Rangers, 1809–1814* (London: Arnold, 1902)

Greville, Charles C.F., *The Greville Memoirs*, 8 vols (London: Longman, 1874–88)

Grierson, Herbert J.C., ed., *The Letters of Sir Walter Scott, 1787–1832*, 12 vols (London: Constable, 1932–7)

Gronow, Rees Howell, *Reminiscences of Captain R. H. Gronow, formerly of the Grenadier Guards, and M.P. for Stafford* (London: Smith, Elder, 1862)

Gurney, W.B., ed., *The Trial of Lieutenant General John Murray, Bart., by a General Court Martial* (London: Egerton, 1815)

Gurwood, John, ed., *The Dispatches of Field Marshal the Duke of Wellington, during his Various Campaigns from 1799 to 1818*, 13 vols (London: John Murray, 1837–9)

Hamilton, Anthony, *Hamilton's Campaign with Moore and Wellington during the Peninsular War* (Staplehurst: Spellmount, 1998)

Henegan, Sir Richard D., *Seven Years' Campaigning in the Peninsula and the Netherlands, from 1808 to 1815*, 2 vols (London: Colburn, 1846)

Hunt, Eric, *Charging Against Napoleon: Diaries and Letters of Three Hussars* (London: Pen & Sword, 2001)

Hylton, Lord George, ed., *The Paget Brothers, 1790–1840* (London: John Murray, 1918)

Jennings, Louis J., ed., *The Croker Papers, 1808–1857*, 3 vols (London: John Murray, 1884)

Kaye, Sir John W., ed., *The Life and Correspondence of Major-General Sir John Malcolm*, 2 vols (London: Smith, Elder, 1856)

Koch, Jean Baptiste Frédéric, ed., *Mémoires de Masséna*, 8 vols (Paris: Paulin et Lechevalier, 1848–50)

Lane-Poole, Stanley, *The Life of the Rt. Hon. Stratford Canning, Viscount Stratford de Redcliffe, from his Memoirs and Private and Official Papers* (London: Longman, 1888)

Larpent, Francis Seymour, *The Private Journal of Judge Advocate Larpent attached to the Headquarters of Lord Wellington during the Peninsular War* (Staplehurst: Spellmount, 2000)

Leith Hay, Sir Andrew, *A Narrative of the Peninsular War* (London: Hearne, 1850)

Lemonnier-Delafosse, Jean Baptiste, *Campagnes de 1810–1815 en Portugal, Espagne, France, Belgique* (Le Havre: Lemale, 1850)

Leslie, Sir John Henry, ed., *The Dickson Manuscripts*, 5 vols (Cambridge: Trotman, 1987–91)

L'Estrange, Sir George B., *Recollections of Sir George B. L'Estrange: Late of the 31ˢᵗ Regiment, and afterwards in the Scots Fusilier Guards* (London: Low, Marston, 1874)

Lockhart, John Gibson, *Memoirs of the Life of Sir Walter Scott*, 10 vols (Edinburgh: Cadell, 1837–9)

Londonderry, Charles W. Vane [formerly Charles Stewart], 3rd Marquis of, *Narrative of the Peninsular War from 1808 to 1813*, 2 vols (London: Colburn, 1829)

——, ed., *Correspondence, Despatches and other Papers of Viscount Castlereagh, 2ⁿᵈ Marquess of Londonderry*, 12 vols (London: Shoberl, 1848–53)

Longford, Thomas Pakenham, 5th Earl of, ed., *The Pakenham Letters, 1800 to 1815* (London: the author, 1914)

McGuffie, Tom Henderson, ed., *Peninsular Cavalry General: The Correspondence of Lieutenant-General Robert Ballard Long* (London: Harrap, 1951)

Madan, Beatrice, ed., *Spencer and Waterloo: the Letters of Spencer Madan, 1814–1816* (London: Literary Services, 1970)

Maxwell, Sir Herbert, ed., *The Creevey Papers* (London: Dutton, 1903–4)

Moore Smith, George C., ed., *The Life of John Colborne, Field-Marshal Lord Seaton* (New York: Dutton, 1903)

——, ed., *The Autobiography of Sir Harry Smith* (London: John Murray, 1910)

Morris, Thomas, *Recollections of Military Service: Including some details of the Battles of Quatre Bras and Waterloo* (London: Madden, 1845)

Müffling, Baron Karl von, *Passages from my Life, together with Memoirs of the Campaign of 1813 and 1814*, trans. P. Yorke (London: Bentley, 1853)

Muir, Rory, ed., *At Wellington's Right Hand: The Letters of Lieutenant-Colonel Sir Alexander Gordon, 1808–1815* (Stroud: Sutton, 2003)

Munster, George Augustus Frederick Fitzclarence, 1st Earl of, *An Account of the British Campaign in 1809 under Sir A. Wellesley, in Portugal and Spain* (London: Colburn & Bentley, 1831)

Murray, Sir George, *Memoir to Accompany an Atlas* (London: Wyld, 1841)

Napier, Sir George T., *Passages in the Early Military Life of General Sir George T. Napier* (London: John Murray, 1884)

Napier, Sir William F.P., *History of the War in the Peninsula and the South of France, from the Year 1807 to the Year 1814*, 6 vols (London: Warne, 1828–40)

———, ed., *The Life and Opinions of General Sir Charles James Napier*, 4 vols (London: John Murray, 1857)

Napoleon I, Emperor, *The Confidential Correspondence of Napoleon Bonaparte with his Brother Joseph*, 2 vols (New York: Appleton, 1856)

———, *Maxims of War* (London: Kessinger, 2009)

Nicolas, Sir Nicholas Harris, ed., *The Dispatches and Letters of Vice Admiral Lord Viscount Nelson*, 7 vols (London: Colburn, 1845–6)

Noailles, Helie G.H., Marquis de, ed., *The Life and Memoirs of Count Molé (1781–1855)*, 2 vols (London: Hutchinson, 1923)

Page, Julia V., ed., *An Intelligence Officer in the Peninsula: the Letters & Diaries of Major the Hon. E. C. Cocks, 1786–1812* (Staplehurst: Spellmount, 1976)

Paget, Harriet Mary, *Letters and Memorials of General Sir Edward Paget* (London: Bliss, Sands, 1898)

Pflugk-Harttung, Julius von, *Vorgeschichte der Schlacht bei Belle-Alliance: Wellington* (Berlin: Schröder, 1903)

Robinson, Heaton Bowstead, ed., *Memoirs of Lieutenant-General Sir Thomas Picton G.C.B.* (London: Bentley, 1835)

Ross, Hew Dalrymple, *Memoir of Field-Marshal Sir Hew Dalrymple Ross: Royal Horse Artillery* (Woolwich: RAI, 1871)

Sabine, Sir Edward, ed., *The Letters of Colonel Sir Augustus Simon Frazer, K. C. B., Commanding the Royal Horse Artillery in the Army under the Duke of Wellington* (Uckfield: Naval & Military Press, 2001)

Sherer, J. Moyle, *The Military Memoirs of Field Marshal, the Duke of Wellington*, 2 vols (London: Longman, 1830–2)

———, *Recollections of the Peninsula* (Staplehurst: Spellmount, 1996)

Siborne, Herbert T., *Waterloo Letters. A Selection from Original and Hitherto Unpublished Letters* (London: Cassell, 1891)

Somerset, Fitzroy James Henry, 1st Baron Raglan, *Life of Field-Marshal Lord Raglan; with a Review of the Military Operations in the Crimea* (London: Kessinger, 2010)

Stanhope, Philip H., 5th Earl, *Notes of Conversations with the Duke of Wellington, 1831–1851* (London: John Murray, 1888)

Stewart, William, *The Cumloden Papers* (Edinburgh: the author, 1881)

Stocqueler, Joachim H., *The Wellington Manual: Being a Compilation from the Dispatches of His Grace the Duke of Wellington* (Calcutta: Rushton, 1840)

Swabey, William, *Diary of Campaigns in the Peninsula for the Years 1811, '12 and '13* (London: Trotman, 1984)

Thompson, W.F.K., ed., *An Ensign in the Peninsular War: the Letters of John Aitchison* (London: Joseph, 1981)

Tomkinson, William, *The Diary of a Cavalry Officer in the Peninsular War and Waterloo Campaign* (London: Swan, Sonnenschein, 1895)

Verner, William Willoughby Cole, ed., *A British Rifleman: The Journals and Correspondence of Major George Simmons* (Uckfield: Naval & Military Press, 2002)

Vivian, Claud Hamilton, ed., *Richard Hussey Vivian, 1ˢᵗ Baron Vivian, a Memoir* (London: Ibister, 1897)

Webster, Sir Charles, ed., *Some Letters of the Duke of Wellington to his brother William Wellesley-Pole* (London: Royal Historical Society, Camden 3 series, 1948)

Wellington, Arthur Richard Wellesley, 2nd Duke of, ed., [New] *Dispatches, Correspondence, and Memoranda of Field Marshal Arthur Duke of Wellington, K.G.*, 8 vols (London: John Murray, 1857–80)

———, ed., *Supplementary Dispatches, Correspondence, and Memoranda of Field Marshal Arthur Duke of Wellington, K.G.*, 15 vols (London: John Murray, 1858–72)

Whinyates, Francis A., ed., *Letters Written by Lieut.-General Thomas Dyneley R.A. while on Active Service between the Years 1806 and 1815* (London: Trotman, 1984)

Wrottesley, George, ed., *Life and Correspondence of Field Marshall Sir John Burgoyne* (London: Bentley, 1873)

Newspapers and Magazines

Annual Register, 1808–1814
Chartist Circular
Gentleman's Magazine
Liverpool Mercury
The Times

Secondary Sources

Books

Adkin, Mark, *The Waterloo Companion* (London: Aurum, 2001)

Arteche y Moro, José Gómez de, *Guerra de la Independencia Historia Militar de España de 1808 a 1814*, 14 vols (Madrid: Fernández San Román, 1868–1903)

Atkinson, Christopher T., *History of the Royal Dragoons, 1661–1934* (Glasgow: Maclehose, 1934)

Barbero, Alessandro, *The Battle: A New History of Waterloo*, trans. John Cullen, (London: Atlantic, 2005)

Barthorp, Michael, *Wellington's Generals* (Oxford: Osprey, 1990)

Beatson, Finlay C., *With Wellington in the Pyrenees: Operations between the Allied Army and the French from July 25 to August 2, 1813* (London: Goschen, 1914)

———, *Wellington: The Crossing of the Gaves and the Battle of Orthez* (London: Heath, Cranton, 1925)

————, *Wellington: The Bidassoa and Nivelle* (London: Arnold, 1931)

Bell, Douglas H., *Wellington's Officers* (London: Collins, 1938)

Blond, Georges, *La Grand Armée,* trans. by Marshall May (London: Arms and Armour, 1995)

British Army Doctrine Publication 2, 'Command', Code 71564 (London: MOD, 1995)

Buckley, Roger N., *The British Army in the West Indies, Society and the Military in the Revolutionary Age* (Tallahassee, FL: Florida University Press, 1998)

Bunbury, Sir Henry Edward, *Narrative of Some Passages in the Great War with France, 1799–1810* (London: Davies, 1927)

Butler, Lewis, *Wellington's Operations in the Peninsula 1808–1814* (London: Unwin, 1904)

Buttery, David, *Wellington Against Massena: The Third Invasion of Portugal 1810–1811* (Barnsley: Pen & Sword, 2007)

Castex, J-C., *Combats Franco-Anglais des Guerres du Premier Empire* (Vancouver: Éditions P-O, 2013)

Chandler, David G., *The Campaigns of Napoleon* (London: Weidenfeld & Nicolson, 1966)

————, *Dictionary of the Napoleonic Wars* (London: Arms and Armour, 1979)

————, *Atlas of Military Strategy: The Art, Theory and Practice of War, 1618–1878* (London: Arms and Armour, 1980)

————, *On the Napoleonic Wars* (London: Greenhill, 1994)

————, *The Oxford Illustrated History of the British Army* (Oxford: Oxford University Press, 1994)

Chesney, Charles C., *Waterloo Lectures: A Study of the Campaign of 1815* (London: Longmans, 1868)

Clarke, Francis L., ed., *The Royal Military Chronicle* (London: Davis, 1810)

Clausewitz, Carl von, *On War,* trans. J.J. Graham (London: Trübner, 1873)

————, *On Waterloo: Clausewitz, Wellington and the Campaign of 1815,* trans. by Christopher Bassford et al. (Charleston, SC: Createspace, 2010)

Clayton, Tim, *Waterloo: Four Days that Changed Europe's Destiny* (London: Little, Brown, 2014)

Clode, Charles M., *The Military Forces of the Crown: Their Administration and Government,* 2 vols (London: John Murray, 1869)

Cole, John William, *Memoirs of British Generals Distinguished during the Peninsular War,* 2 vols (London: Bentley, 1856)

Connolly, T.W.J., *History of the Corps of Royal Sappers and Miners,* 2 vols (London: Longman, 1855)

Coss, Edward J., *All for the King's Shilling: An Analysis of the Campaign and Combat Experiences of the British Soldier in the Peninsular War, 1808–1814* (doctoral dissertation, Ohio State University, 2005; pub. Norman, OK: University of Oklahoma Press, 2010)

Craufurd, Alexander H., *General Craufurd and his Light Division* (London: Griffith, Farran, Okeden & Welsh, 1891)

David, Saul, *All the King's Men: The British Soldier from the Restoration to Waterloo* (London: Viking, 2012)

Davies, Huw J., *Wellington's Wars: The Making of a Military Genius* (London: Yale University Press, 2012)

Delavoye, Alexander M., *Records of the 90th Regiment* (London: Richardson, 1880)

Delbrück, Hans, *Das Leben des Feldmarschalls Grafen Neithardt von Gneisenau,* 4 vols (Berlin: Reimer, 1864–80)

Dempsey, Guy C., *Albuera 1811: The Bloodiest Battle of the Peninsular War* (Barnsley: Frontline, 2011)

Dixon, Norman, *On the Psychology of Military Incompetence* (London: Jonathan Cape, 1976)

Duncan, Francis, *History of the Royal Regiment of Artillery,* 2 vols (London: John Murray, 1872)

Dupuy, Trevor N., *Numbers, Predictions & War: Using History to Evaluate Combat Factors and Predict the Outcome of Battles* (London: Macdonald and Jane, 1979)

Esdaile, Charles J., *The Duke of Wellington and the Command of the Spanish Army, 1812–14* (Basingstoke: Macmillan, 1990)

——, *The Peninsular War* (London: Lane, 2002)

——, *Peninsular Eyewitnesses: The Experience of War in Spain and Portugal 1808–1813* (Barnsley: Pen & Sword, 2008)

Fletcher, Ian, *Galloping at Everything: The British Cavalry in the Peninsular War and Waterloo, 1808–15: A Reappraisal* (Staplehurst: Spellmount, 1999)

Fortescue, Sir John, *A History of the British Army,* 10 vols (London: Macmillan, 1899–1930)

Foster, Ruscombe E., *Wellington and Waterloo: The Duke, the Battle and Posterity* (Stroud: Spellmount, 2014)

Franklin, John, *Waterloo: Netherlands Correspondence* (Ulverston: 1815, 2010)

Fremont-Barnes, Gregory, *The Napoleonic Wars: The Peninsular War 1807–1814* (Oxford: Osprey, 2002)

——, ed., *Armies of the Napoleonic Wars* (Barnsley: Pen & Sword, 2011)

——, *Waterloo 1815: The British Army's Day of Destiny* (Stroud: Spellmount, 2014)

Fuller, John F.C., *The Decisive Battles of the Western World,* 2 vols (London: Granada, 1970)

Gash, Norman et al., *Wellington: Studies in the Military and Political Career of the First Duke of Wellington* (Manchester: Manchester University Press, 1990)

Gates, David, *The Spanish Ulcer* (London: Allen & Unwin, 1986)

Girod de l'Ain, Maurice, *Vie Militaire du Général Foy* (Paris: Plon Nourrit, 1900)

Glover, Gareth, *Waterloo: Myth and Reality* (Barnsley: Pen & Sword, 2014)

Glover, Michael, *Wellington as Military Commander* (London: Batsford, 1968)

——, *Britannia Sickens: Sir Arthur Wellesley and the Convention of Cintra* (London: Leo Cooper, 1970)

——, *The Peninsular War 1807–1814* (Newton Abbot: David & Charles, 1974)

——, *Wellington's Army in the Peninsula 1808–1814* (Newton Abbot: David & Charles, 1977)

——, *A Very Slippery Fellow: the Life of Sir Robert Wilson, 1777–1849* (Oxford: Oxford University Press, 1978)

Glover, Richard, *Peninsular Preparation: The Reform of the British Army 1795–1809* (Cambridge: Cambridge University Press, 1963)

——, *Britain at Bay: Defence against Bonaparte, 1803–14* (London: Allen & Unwin, 1973)

Grattan, William, *The Duke of Wellington and the Peninsular Medal* (London: Churton, 1845)

Grehan, John, *Voices from the Past: Waterloo 1815* (Barnsley: Frontline, 2015)

Griffith, Paddy et al., *Wellington Commander: The Iron Duke's Generalship* (Chichester: Bird, 1983)

Griffiths, Arthur, *The Wellington Memorial, Wellington, his Comrades and Contemporaries* (London: Allen, 1897)

Grose, Francis, *Advice to the Officers of the British Army* (London: Kearsly, 1782)

Gudmundsson, Bruce I., *On Artillery* (Westport, CT: Praeger, 1993)

Guelzo, Allen C., *Gettysburg: The Last Invasion* (New York: Vintage, 2013)

Hamilton, Frederick William, *The Origin and History of the First or Grenadier Guards*, 3 vols (London: John Murray, 1874)

Hamilton-Williams, David, *Waterloo, New Perspectives: The Great Battle Reappraised* (London: Arms and Armour, 1993)

——, *The Fall of Napoleon: The Final Betrayal* (London: Arms and Armour, 1994)

Harvey, Robert, *The War of Wars: The Epic Struggle between Britain and France 1789–1815* (London: Constable, 2006)

Haythornthwaite, Philip, *Napoleon's Military Machine* (Tunbridge Wells: Spellmount, 1988)

——, *Wellington's Military Machine* (Tunbridge Wells: Spellmount, 1989)

——, *Wellington: The Iron Duke* (Dulles, VA: Potomac, 2007)

Heathcote, T.A., *The British Field Marshals, 1736–1997: A Biographical Dictionary* (Barnsley: Leo Cooper, 1999)

——, *Wellington's Peninsular War Generals and their Battles* (Barnsley: Pen & Sword, 2010)

Heinzen, Jasper, *Making Prussians, Raising Germans, A Cultural History of Prussian State Building after Civil War, 1866–1935* (Cambridge: Cambridge University Press, 2017)

Henderson, George F.R., *The Science of War: A Collection of Essays and Lectures, 1892–1903* (London: Longmans, Green, 1905)

Hendrick, J. Kevin, *A Campaign Of Ropes: An Analysis Of The Duke Of Wellington's Practice of Military Art During The Peninsular War, 1808 to 1814* (Fort Leavenworth, KS: US Army General Staff College, 1998)

Hibbert, Christopher, *Wellington: A Personal History* (London: HarperCollins, 1997)

Hill, Joanna, *Wellington's Right Hand: Rowland Viscount Hill* (Stroud: Spellmount, 2011)

Hofschröer, Peter, *1815: The Waterloo Campaign*, 2 vols (London: Greenhill, 1998–9)

Holmes, Richard, *Acts of War: the Behaviour of Men in Battle* (London: Jonathan Cape, 1985)

————, *Redcoat* (London: HarperCollins, 2001)

————, *Wellington: The Iron Duke* (London: HarperCollins, 2002)

Horne, Alistair, *How far from Austerlitz? Napoleon 1805–1815* (London: Macmillan, 1996)

Houssaye, Henri, *1815, Waterloo*, trans. S.R. Willis (ebook: Pickle, 2011)

Hunter, Archie, *Wellington's Scapegoat: The Tragedy of Lieutenant-Colonel Charles Bevan* (Barnsley: Leo Cooper, 2003)

James, Charles, *A New & Enlarged Military Dictionary in French and English*, 2 vols (London: Egerton, 1802)

James, William Hill, *Battles Round Biaritz: The Battles of the Nivelle and Nives* (Edinburgh: M'Lagan and Cumming, 1899)

Johnston, Alex Keith, *Atlas to Alison's History of Europe* (Edinburgh: Blackwood, 1875)

Joint Chief-of-Staff, US Department of Defense, *Dictionary of Military & Associated Terms*, JP1-02 (Honolulu, HI: University Press of the Pacific, 2002)

Keegan, John, *The Face of Battle* (London: Jonathan Cape, 1976)

Kennedy, Sir James Shaw, *Notes on the Battle of Waterloo* (London: John Murray, 1865)

Kennedy, John, *The Business of War* (London: Hutchinson, 1957)

Knight, Julian, *British Politics for Dummies* (Chichester: Wiley, 2010)

Konstam, Angus, *Historical Atlas of the Napoleonic Era* (London: Mercury, 2003)

Lapene, E., *Campaignes de 1813 et de 1814 sur L'Ebre, les Pyrénées et la Garonne* (Paris: Anselin et Pochard, 1823)

Lawford, James P. and Peter Young, *Wellington's Masterpiece: The Battle and Campaign of Salamanca* (London: Allen & Unwin, 1972)

Leslie, Stephen, *Dictionary of National Biography* (London: Smith, Elder, 1886)

Lipscombe, Nick, *Wellington's Guns: The Untold Story of Wellington and his Artillery in the Peninsula and at Waterloo* (Oxford: Osprey, 2013)

Longford, Elizabeth, *Wellington: The Years of the Sword* (London: Weidenfeld & Nicolson, 1969)

Mansfield, Nick, *Soldiers as Workers: Class, Employment, Conflict and the Nineteenth-Century Military* (Liverpool: Liverpool University Press, 2016)

Marshall, S.L.A., *Men Against Fire: The Problem of Battle Command* (New York: Morrow, 1947)

Maxwell, Sir Herbert, *The Life of Wellington and the Restoration of the Martial Power of Great Britain*, 2 vols (London: Low, Marston, 1893)

Mitchell, John, *Thoughts on Tactics and Military Organization* (London: Longman, 1838)

Moorsom, William Scarth, *History of the Fifty-Second Regiment, 1755–1816* (Felling, Tyne and Wear: Worley, 1996)

Muilwijk, Erwin, *1815*, 2 vols (Bleiswijk, Neth: Sovereign 2012–13)

Muir, Rory, *Britain and the Defeat of Napoleon, 1807–1815* (London: Yale University Press, 1996)

———, *Salamanca, 1812* (London: Yale University Press, 2001)

———, *Wellington*, 2 vols (London: Yale University Press, 2013–15)

——— et al., *Inside Wellington's Peninsular Army 1808–1814* (Barnsley: Pen & Sword, 2006)

Myatt, Frederick, *British Sieges of the Peninsular War* (Stroud: Spellmount, 1995)

Nafziger, George F., *Napoleon's Invasion of Russia* (Novato, CA: Presidio, 1988)

———, *The Armies of Spain and Portugal, 1808–1815* (privately published, 1993)

Ollech, Karl von, *Geschichte des Feldzuges von 1815* (Berlin: Mittler, 1876)

Oman, Sir Charles, *History of the Peninsular War*, 7 vols (London: Clarendon, 1902–30)

———, *Wellington's Army 1809–1814* (London: Arnold, 1913)

Owen, Edward, *The Waterloo Papers, 1815 and Beyond* (Tavistock: AQ & DJ, 1997)

Parkinson, Roger, *The Hussar General* (London: Davies, 1975)

Partridge, Richard and Michael Oliver, *Battle Studies in the Peninsula, May 1808 – January 1809* (London: Constable, 1998)

Pelet, Jean-Jacques, *The French Campaign in Portugal 1810–11*, trans. Donald D. Horward (Minneapolis, MN: Minnesota University Press, 1973)

Petrie, Sir Charles, *Wellington: A Reassessment* (London: Barrie, 1956)

Philipparts, John, *The Royal Military Calendar, or Army Service and Commission Book* (London: Valpy, 1820)

Rathbone, Julian, *Wellington's War: His Peninsular Dispatches* (London: Joseph, 1984)

Reid, Stuart, *Wellington's Army in the Peninsula 1809–14* (Oxford: Osprey, 2004)

Reiss, Tom, *The Black Count, Napoleon's Rival and the Real Count of Monte Cristo – General Alexandre Dumas* (London: Vintage, 2013)

Roberts, Andrew, *Napoleon and Wellington* (London: Weidenfeld & Nicolson, 2001)

———, *Napoleon the Great* (London: Lane, 2014)

Roberts, Frederick Sleigh, 1st Earl, *The Rise of Wellington* (London: Sampson, Low, Marston, 1895)

Robertson, Ian C., *Wellington at War in the Peninsula 1808–1814* (Barnsley: Leo Cooper, 2000)

———, *Wellington Invades France: The Final Phase of the Peninsular War, 1813–1814* (London: Greenhill, 2003)

———, *An Atlas of the Peninsular War* (London: Yale University Press, 2010)

Robinson, Mike, *The Battle of Quatre Bras 1815* (Stroud: History Press, 2009)

Ropes, John C., *The Campaign of Waterloo: A Military History* (London: Putnam, 1893)

Royal Artillery Institution, *Minutes of Proceedings of the Royal Artillery Institution V* (Woolwich: RAI, 1870)

Royle, Trevor, *Crimea: The Great Crimean War 1854–1856* (London: Little, Brown, 1999)

Seymour, William, *Great Sieges of History* (London: Brassey's, 1991)

Sidney, Edwin, *The Life of Lord Hill G. C. B., late Commander of the Forces* (London: John Murray, 1845)

Smith, Digby, *The Napoleonic Wars Data Book: Actions and Losses in Personnel, Colours, Standards and Artillery, 1792–1815* (London: Greenhill, 1997)

Snow, Peter, *To War with Wellington: From the Peninsula to Waterloo* (London: John Murray, 2010)

Stewart, Patrick F., *History of the XII Royal Lancers* (London: Oxford University Press, 1950)

Thompson, Neville, *Wellington after Waterloo* (London: Routledge, 1986)

Trimble, W. Copeland, *The Historical Record of the 27th Inniskilling Regiment* (London: Clowes, 1876)

Uffindell, Andrew, *The National Army Museum Book of Wellington's Armies* (London: Sidgwick & Jackson, 2003)

———, *The Eagles Last Triumph: Napoleon's Victory at Ligny, June 1815* (London: Greenhill, 2006)

Urban, Mark, *Generals: Ten British Commanders Who Shaped the World* (London: Faber, 2005)

Vibart, H.M., *History of the Madras Engineers*, 2 vols (London: W.H. Allen, 1881)

Vidal de la Blache, Joseph, *L'Evacuation de l'Espagne et l'Invasion dans le Midi, Juin 1813 – Avril 1814* (Paris: Berger-Levrault, 1914)

Walter, J., ed., *Rules and Regulations for the Formations, Field Exercises and Movements of H.M. Forces* (London: [War Office], 1798)

Ward, Stephen G.P., *Wellington's Headquarters: A Study of the Administrative Problems in the Peninsula, 1809–1814* (London: Oxford University Press, 1957)

Weigley, Russell F., *The Age of Battles: The Quest for Decisive Warfare from Breitenfeld to Waterloo* (London: Pimlico, 1993)

Weller, Jac, *Wellington in the Peninsula, 1808–1814* (London: Vane, 1962)

———, *Wellington at Waterloo* (London: Longmans, 1967)

———, *On Wellington: The Duke and His Art of War* (London: Greenhill, 1998)

Wood, Sir Evelyn, *Cavalry in the Waterloo Campaign* (London: Low, Marston, 1895)

Internet

British Army Guide, 'Developing Leaders' <http://www.army.mod.uk/documents/general/rmas_developing_leaders.pdf> [accessed 21 September 2015]

Gerges, Mark T., 'Wellington, the Odium of Relief and the Cavalry Generals, 1812–1813' <http://www.napoleonicsociety.com/english/pdf/j2011gerges.pdf> [accessed 23 August 2015]

Howieson, W.B. and H. Kahn, 'Leadership, Management and Command: The Officer's Trinity' <http://www.raf.mod.uk/pmdair/rafcms/mediafiles/225f3a4a_5056_a318_a8f33369f4c3b15f> [accessed 10 June 2016]

Inquiry into the Convention of Cintra, 1808 < http://www.napoleon-series.org/research/government/diplomatic/c_inquiry.html> [accessed 16 November 2015]

McGuigan, Ron, 'British Generals of the Napoleonic Wars 1793–1815' <http://www.napoleon-series.org/research/biographies/BritishGenerals/c_Britishgenerals1.html> [accessed 14 August 2015]

Military History Encylopedia, 'Peninsular War Campaigns' <http://www.historyofwar.org/> [accessed 25 November 2015]

Muir, Rory, 'Wellington', commentary <http://www.lifeofwellington.co.uk/the-books/> [accessed 14 January 2016]

Parliamentary Papers, 'Proceedings upon the Inquiry Relative to the Armistice and Convention, etc., made and Concluded in Portugal, 1809' <http://babel.hathitrust.org/cgi/pt?id=hvd.32044106489826;view=1up;seq=202> [accessed 18 November 2015]

UK Parliament <http://www.hansard-archive.parliament.uk/Parliamentary_Debates_Vol_1_(1803)_to_Vol_41_(Feb_1820) > S1V0024P0.zip [accessed 17 November 2017]

University of Leeds, 'The Charge of the Cavalry', A study of the British Cavalry in the Peninsula <https://wiki.leeds.ac.uk/index.php/The_Charge_of_the_Cavalry._A_study_of_the_British_Cavalry_in_the_Peninsula.#The_Cavalry:_Officers_and_Generals> [accessed 12 October 2015]

University of Leeds, 'The Manichean General', Robert Craufurd's Peninsular Reputation <https://wiki.leeds.ac.uk/index.php/The_Manichean_General:_Robert_Craufurd%27s_Peninsular_Reputation> [accessed 16 March 2016]

Yardley, Ivan, 'The British Army's Command approach explained', Business Command <http://businesscommand.co.uk/blog/06/12/2010/british-army-mission-command-approach/> [accessed 9 June 2016]

Unpublished Theses
Bartlett, Keith J., 'The Development of the British Army during the Wars with France, 1793–1815' (doctoral thesis, University of Durham, 1998)
Buerden, Kyle van, '"No Troops but the British": British National Identity and the Battle of Waterloo' (masters thesis, University of Queensland, 2015)
Gerges, Mark T., 'Command and Control in the Peninsula: The Role of the British Cavalry 1808–1814' (doctoral dissertation, Florida State University, 2005)
Moon, Joshua Lee, 'Wellington's Two-Front War: The Peninsular Campaigns, 1808–1814' (doctoral dissertation, Florida State University, 2005)
Reese, Paul P., '"The Ablest Man in the British Army." The Life and Career of General Sir John Hope' (doctoral dissertation, Florida State University, 2007)
Thompson, Mark, 'The Rise of the Scientific Soldier as seen through the Performance of the Corps of Royal Engineers during the early 19th Century' (doctoral thesis, University of Sunderland, 2009)

Articles and Periodicals
Adair, P.R., 'Coldstream Guards', *Household Brigade Magazine*, Waterloo Number (Spring 1965), 24–31
[An Officer of Dragoons] 'The British Cavalry in the Peninsula', *United Services Journal and Naval and Military Magazine*, I (1883), 33–40, and II (1883), 63–70
Arnold, James R., 'A Reappraisal of Column versus Line in the Napoleonic Wars', *Journal of the Society for Army Historical Research*, LX, 244 (Winter 1982), 196–208
Atkinson, Christopher T., 'The Composition and Organisation of the British Forces in the Peninsula, 1808–14', *English Historical Review*, LXVII (1902), 110–33
———, ed., 'A Peninsular Brigadier: letters of Major-General Sir F. P. Robinson, K.C.B.', *Journal of the Society for Army Historical Research*, 34 (December 1956), 153–70
Coss, Edward J., 'The Misadventures of Wellington's Cavalry from the Peninsula to Waterloo', *Journal of the Waterloo Committee*, X (April 1988), 18–28; presented at the University of Southampton, Wellington Congress, 1987
Delbrück, Hans, 'Einiges zum Feldzug von 1815', *Zeitschrift für Preussische Geschichte und Landeskunde*, 14. Jahrgang, Berlin (1877)
Edwards, E., ed., 'Some Unpublished Letters of Sir Thomas Picton', *West Wales Historical Records*, 12 (1927), 133–66 and 13 (1928), 1–32
Lipscombe, Nick, 'The Peninsular War – An Allied Victory or a French Failure', *British Army Review*, 148 (Winter 2009/10), 82–9

————, 'Shrapnel's Shell, A Force Multiplier', *British Army Review*, 161 (Autumn 2014), 100–7 and 162 (Autumn 2014/15), 112–19

Oman, Sir Charles, 'The Dutch-Belgians at Waterloo', *Nineteenth Century Magazine*, vol. 48, October 1900, 629–38

Pflugk-Harttung, Julius von, 'Die Vorgeschichte der Schlacht bei Quatre-Bras', *Neue Militärische Blätter* [Berlin], 60 (1902), 176–83

Shore, Henry N., ed., 'Letters from the Peninsula during 1812–14', *Journal of the Royal United Services Institute*, 61 (February 1916), 91–140

Ward, Stephen P.G., 'Brenier's Escape from Almeida', *Journal of the Society for Army Historical Research*, 35 (March 1957), 141, 23–35

————, ed., and J.M. Wynyard, 'Vimeiro to Corunna: An Eyewitness Account', *Journal of the Royal United Services Institute*, 114 (December 1969), 33–42

Woolgar, Chris, 'Wellington's Dispatches and their Editor, Colonel Gurwood', *Wellington Studies I* (Southampton: Southampton University Press, 1996), 189–210

Zucker, Kevin, 'Napoleon's Last Gamble: Study Folder', Operational Study Group (Havre de Grace, MD, 2015), 12–22

————, 'Fleurus 1794: Study Folder', Operational Study Group (Havre de Grace, MD, 2016), 9–11

Public Lectures

David, Saul, 'Wellington at Waterloo', Windsor Castle, 14 November 2015

Esdaile, Charles, '"Hard pounding Gentlemen": The Tactics of Waterloo', public lecture at University of Nottingham, 8 July 2015

Sweetman, John, 'Wellington's Disciple: Lord Raglan in the Crimea', University of Southampton, Wellington Congress, 11 July 2010

Index